David Matthews was born in London in 1967. After pursuing a variety of careers and academic studies, he worked as a crime reporter before becoming a freelance journalist, writing for the *Observer*, *Sunday Telegraph* and the *Caribbean Times* among others, as well as being a part-time lecturer.

Praise for *Looking for a Fight:*

'Matthews' pens pulls no punches . . . a hell of a tale' *Daily Telegraph*

'[*Looking for a Fight*] has huge vitality, beguiling characterisation, authentic dialogue and a fine evocation of time and place' *Sunday Times*

'Riveting' *Guardian*

'Compelling . . . it's like a detective novel: you urgently want to know whether the fight will take place and how it will go' *Observer*

'An epic journey of discovery . . . painfully honest.' *Independent*

'A great effort, the book and the punch-up both' *The Times*

Looking For a Fight

How a writer took on the
boxing world – from the inside

David Matthews

headline

First published in 2001
by HEADLINE BOOK PUBLISHING

First published in paperback in 2002
by HEADLINE BOOK PUBLISHING

10 9 8 7 6 5 4 3 2 1

ISBN 0 7472 6235 7

Typeset by Avon Dataset Ltd, Bidford-on-Avon, Warks

Printed and bound in Great Britain by
Mackays of Chatham plc, Chatham, Kent

HEADLINE BOOK PUBLISHING
A division of Hodder Headline
338 Euston Road
London NW1 3BH

www.headline.co.uk
www.hodderheadline.com

For Luca

Man will not merely endure: he will prevail because he has a soul, a spirit capable of compassion and sacrifice and endurance. The writer's duty is to write about these things.

William Faulkner

Boxing is the sport to which all other sports aspire.

George Foreman

acknowledgements

In the two and a half years that it took me to research and write this book, I met some remarkable characters, both inside and outside the ring. Through their experiences and sacrifices, wisdom and insight, I was privileged to gain an understanding of the fight game that not only changed my perception of boxing and boxers, but also prompted a fundamental psychological and physical change within myself. I may not be a better person for what boxing has taught me, but I am certainly a different one. For this altered state of awareness, I would especially like to thank the following for their time, help and encouragement:

Isola Akay and the All Stars Boxing Club, Ian Allcock, John Ashton, the Bowers family, Michael Bentt, Brian, Mark Brooks, Carlie Carew, Richard Clayton, Jane Couch, Ben Coward, Craig, Danny Daley, Dave from Swinton, Dougie, Terry Dunstan, Justin Fleming, Tyrone Forbes, Herol 'Bomber' Graham, 'Cool' Carl Greaves, Dennis Hobson Jr, Dennis Hobson Snr, 'Big' Dave Howe, Waj Khan, 'Knocker', Mark 'The Butcher' Krence, Scott Lansdowne, Dave Lewis, Colin McMillan, Andy Marlowe, Bill Mitchell, Naz, John Naylor, Kelly Oliver, Jon 'Pit Bull' Penn, Mark Prince, 'Big' Ned Rawlins, Bruce Reynolds, 'Tall' Richard, Spencer and Tim Rowland, Matt Scriven, Shaun Stokes, Daniel Teasdale, Takaloo, Arthur Urry, Victor 'The Pain

Inflicter', Dean Walker, Jamie Warters, Scott Welch, Paul Wellings, Clinton Woods, Young John and anyone with the stomach to train at the Henry Cooper.

Confucius said, 'Even the longest journey starts with one small step.' I thank my friend Michael Bale for inspiring me to take the small step that led me to boxing, and for producing some superb pictures. Phil Fisk also deserves praise for his exceptional skill with a camera.

Julian Alexander was unstinting in his support of this book and in me as a writer, long before either proved to be of any merit, as was Ian Marshall at Headline who gave me some invaluable editorial advice. Copy editors are the unsung heroes of publishing, so I'd like to say a big thank you to Marion Paull for doing a great job on the draft manuscript.

To Sparrow: your love, compassion and support were rock solid when it mattered most. Ditto, ditto, ditto!

Lorna, what can I say? You are truly one in a million. Your hospitality and generosity in no small way redeemed my faith in humanity. How you withstood my mood swings, mania, whining, depression, tantrums and dirty washing for 14 months I'll never know.

I did some amazing and invaluable 'work' with Paul Dorking, which gave me the mental strength and determination to deal with some tough situations.

Finally, I reserve my greatest thanks and appreciation for Howard Rainey, a man to whom I owe a debt I can never repay. Howard is supremely modest and uncomfortable with flattery, so in place of an embarrassing, long-winded eulogy, I will simply say this: to have worked with him and to have walked in his shadow was an honour. But, having endured the best and worst of times together, to consider him a friend is a greater honour still. Thanks for everything, Captain.

prologue

The partisans in the crowded arena brought the fight to a bloody climax with raucous chants of 'TAK-A-LOO! TAK-A-LOO! TAK-A-LOO!' Six hundred or so neutrals added a chorus of jeers, screams, applause, laughter and abusive commentary in keeping with the bacchanalian spirit of the evening. Everyone was drunk. In the ring, two half-naked bodies whirled violently across the canvas, painting each other black and blue with their fists. 'TAK-A-LOO! TAK-A-LOO! TAK-A-LOO!' The chanting reached a crescendo, then a husky voice cried 'Knock his fucking head off' and the chorus collapsed in a stinking heap of expletives and rapid-fire insults.

It was Friday night at the Grundy Park Leisure Centre in Cheshunt, Hertfordshire, 7 February 1998. This was no Caesar's Palace or Madison Square Garden. This was your common or garden municipal shithole, the armpit of the fight game. This was boxing, small-hall style.

Takaloo was the ring name of Mehrdud Takalobighashi, a twenty-two-year-old light-middleweight prospect hailing from Tehran via Margate. He was coasting towards a fifth consecutive win when, with less than one minute of the fourth and final round remaining, his opponent, Jawaid Khaliq, caught him with a bone-crunching left hook – BOOM – right on the button. Visibly shaken by the blow, Takaloo careered straight into Khaliq's line of fire as he grappled for something to support his legs, which were wobbling like a jellyfish on amyl nitrite.

Bloodied and bruised, his face distorted with fear, he looked helplessly for some respite as Khaliq, a sinewy Pakistani with the physique of a skinned rabbit, wrenched his arms to shake him off and bully him into the ropes. He tried desperately to stay composed and box his way out of trouble but relentless pressure from Khaliq, a former ABA champion, forced him into holding and grappling.

Takaloo held on to Khaliq certainly not to seek solace in his tormentor's arms but to try to ride out the last moments of the contest, preferably on his feet. In the dying seconds of the fight, a non-title bout worth no more than £700 or £800 to either man, Takaloo's years of training as an amateur and then a pro gave way to just one thing – heart.

Boxers may have varying physiques, styles, techniques and what have you but there is no underestimating the potent mix of guts, determination, desire, ambition and mental strength that fighting men refer to collectively as heart. In the brutal endgame of a fight where the sweet science of boxing yields to a primordial need for survival, heart is the stock-in-trade of the professional boxer and is the definition of his bravery.

Too much bravery however can be a fighter's undoing. In the real world, courage is unquestionably a treasured quality, a strength, an asset; but in the twilight zone of the prize ring, it can become a weakness, even your nemesis.

Halfway into the fourth round, twenty-seven-year-old Khaliq, a mini-cab driver by day and gladiator of the squared circle by night, went into overdrive, releasing a reserve of energy that had lain dormant for most of the fight. In the second round he had suffered the mild indignity of a flash knockdown and was now trailing on points by at least two rounds. He needed a knockout to win. Sensing Takaloo was on his last legs, he stepped up another gear and nailed him with a double left jab and then a right cross.

Takaloo tried to bear hug his way to the end of the fight but Khaliq caught him again – POW– with a tight right hook to the chin that sent him reeling backwards and on to an appointment with the canvas. The startled Iranian gamely got to his feet, helped by ever desperate cries of 'TAK-A-LOO! TAK-A-LOO! TAK-A-LOO!' from the seething crowd inside the makeshift arena. No sooner had the referee started reeling off 'one . . . two . . . three . . .' than Takaloo's trainer Jimmy Tibbs gestured frantically for him to stay down and take full advantage of the count.

The knockdown boosted Khaliq as if he had just had a shot of neat adrenaline pumped into his heart. He continued to stalk his prey, doubling up a few more punches with force and pinpoint accuracy, culminating in a left hook that rocked Takaloo again. Khaliq grabbed Takaloo and tossed him to one side like a broken plaything, pushing him against the ropes to line him up for the inevitable knockout. As he hit his opponent with another barrage of shots and pressed him into the corner of the ring, the colour drained from Takaloo's olive-skinned face.

Staring into his dark eyes from the comfort of my ringside seat, I tried to get some sense of what he was going through. All I could see was anxiety and fear written across his ashen face. He seemed wretched, like a mangy dog huddled in a corner licking his wounds. Sensing his desperation, Khaliq grinned maniacally, poked his tongue out at Takaloo and floored him with a blistering left hook. The crestfallen Iranian dragged himself limply off the canvas but within seconds Khaliq delivered the *coup de grâce* – a swift right–left combination that sent Takaloo tumbling on to his backside for the third and final time.

Referee Dave Parris had no choice but to end the fight and save Takaloo from further punishment and embarrassment. The announcement from the MC, a fat guy in a cheap tuxedo, was a final humiliating footnote to Takaloo's less than brilliant performance: 'After two minutes forty-four seconds of the fourth round, referee Dave Parris has stopped the fight. The winner by technical knockout is Jawaid Khaliq.'

The hapless Takaloo may have ended the fight prone but as the MC continued with the post-fight formalities, the raging members of his fan club who had travelled a hundred-odd miles from the south-east coast to see him box, weren't going to take his defeat lying down.

'You Paki bastard, you Paki cunt . . . you're a fucking cheat, you bastard.' Two rows behind the thin blue line of reporters, photographers, boxing officials and security guards a skinny young blonde had leapt out of her seat and up on to her strapped white stilettos (or 'fuck me sling-backs' as they are commonly known) and fired a tirade of abuse at Khaliq.

Relishing his third professional win in as many fights, Khaliq paraded around the ring with his arms aloft, oblivious of the heckler. She was a piece of trailer-park trash dressed in all-white, fake designer clothes and dripping with less than solid nine-carat gold jewellery – the archetypal female fight fan.

The crowd of mainly Reebok-clad drunken white boys was becoming increasingly antagonistic and threatened to erupt at any moment. A hardcore had already pelted the ring with assorted projectiles as a show of disgust after an eastern European journeyman knocked out the 'IBF Intercontinental' middleweight champion, Jason Matthews (no relation) during the eleventh round of the main event. The rising level of intimidation and anger in the arena made me question my presence in such a bear pit of hostility. It also got me thinking about the concept of boxing as a public spectacle in a so-called civilised society. Boxing was supposed to be a sport but this chest-beating exercise was more like preparation for war.

I looked round at the faces in the crowd for something conveniently to explain away or at least rationalise my own reasons for being party to such an event. All I discovered was a strange, perverse tableau. Hysterical laughter belied grimaces of intense hate. Faces reddened by too much shouting and booze created a waxwork effect of hideous caricatures. The genuine neutrals read their programmes or hid their faces in copies of the *Sun* while all around them grown men stood on plastic chairs yelling at no one in particular, 'You're gonna get your fucking head kicked in.' Why did I choose to be in such a volatile atmosphere? To make sarcastic notes and jaded observations?

In my role as a reporter, I had witnessed men and women at ringside behave like animals, and thought little of it. Yet in any other context, as Joe Public, I would have had zero tolerance for the same conduct. In the cauldron of emotions that is the boxing arena, I somehow accepted that racism, bigotry, intimidation and violence came with the territory. Professional objectivity screws with your personality. I felt mildly ashamed that I could be so hypocritical about my feelings. I also felt disturbed by the pleasure I derived from watching men fight and my inability to reconcile this pleasure with whatever principles I held as a human being. Was it civilised to be an observer at a boxing match? Should I have been there in the first place? Was I guilty by association?

I concluded that if I was not part of the solution, I was part of the problem. Whether inside or outside the prize ring, boxing exploited people like me – working-class blacks, white trash, the red necks, the browned-off. I owed neither boxing nor its knuckle-headed supporters any favours. I should have turned round to the stiletto woman and told her what an arsehole she was for being a racist mutt. Alternatively, I could have explained to her, politely, that Pakistan was not a million miles away from Iran either geographically or culturally. But I didn't. I sat still and wondered if she was aware of the irony in her words. She supported an Iranian from the home counties who was beaten by a Pakistani . . . from the home counties. Both of these young men were Muslims; both were born to submit to Allah, not prejudice. Her behaviour typified the very personal relationship a bigot has with his or her bigotry. Racism, it seems, is never just a black and white issue.

In the end, I was another mute bystander. I said nothing, I did nothing. Was it fear, lack of civility or just plain apathy? Or maybe it was simply that at that moment the hatred and vitriol wasn't directed at me. Perhaps I had fallen into the trap of witnessing someone else's misfortune, feeling safe and thankful that I wasn't the victim. Maybe there was even a touch of schadenfreude in there.

Then it occurred to me, how would I feel if I were Khaliq, a winner without applause? Would I register the hatred directed at me or would the glory, the sense of personal triumph and my fifteen minutes of fame, anaesthetise me from such considerations? Or what if I was in Takaloo's shoes? What if one day I stepped into that ring in some shabby hall, under harsh lighting, feeling all the fear, pain and resignation that I'd just seen him experience. What if?

Part One

So you wanna be a boxer

chapter 1

Jimmy Tibbs was the first boxing trainer I ever met. He was anything but cordial. Surly and uptight, he treated me with the kind of hospitality you might reserve for a burglar or a gatecrasher at your mother's funeral. His expression, as I approached him in the foyer of the Peacock gym was stamped with frustration and watermarked by tiny beads of sweat that bubbled on his meaty face like a hot spring. I got the impression instantly that my arrival was in some way less than welcome.

'We've had 'em down 'ere before, people from the media. You get what you want and then fuck off. But what about the fighters? What do they get? I'll tell you what they get. Nuffin!'

Jimmy Tibbs – a legend in his own Lonsdale trunks. He punctuated his invective with sharp, jabbing finger movements which he used, in the local vernacular, to 'boy me off'. In between discourtesies (most of which featured 'fuck' rather prominently) he hollered instructions and asides to the motley crew of fighters displaced around the gym. 'Nice work, son, nice work,' barked Tibbs in a twangy cockney accent as the gym whistled with the rhythmic rat-tat-tat-tat of skipping ropes crashing on wooden floorboards and the repetitive thud of gloved fists on heavy leather bags. 'That's it, boy. Jab and move, jab and move . . . nice work my saaaaaaan.'

I followed Tibbs gingerly through the gym past an array of dumb-bells, barbells, shiny weight machines and beat-up boxing equipment. I was the tsetse fly to his baboon's arse. Every time I tried crawling up his backside to explain the purpose of my visit, he swatted me with his cursed tail. 'Fuck this' and 'fuck that' he'd say, sneering with just enough menace to make me feel uncomfortable while at the same time not appearing too confrontational.

'So Jimmy, could I possibly have a couple minutes of your precious time . . .'

'Fuck that . . .'

Tibbs treated me like something he had just scraped off his shoe but I couldn't help but lukewarm to the man. He had the middle-aged swagger and cockney charisma of a villain from *EastEnders*, a sort of Costa del Cool complete with suntan and chunky jewellery. He was in good shape too, compact and muscular with swarthy Romany features, barrel chest and firm stocky legs that were fit enough to put a Ukrainian weightlifter half his age to shame. What with his physique and his sweaty grey 'No Fear' T-shirt and Nike apparel, for a guy in his mid-fifties he looked the part, the epitome of the gracefully ageing fighter.

Despite his foul-mouthed rhetoric, Jimmy Tibbs was not only an accomplished trainer, but also a man of God. Somewhere in the late 1980s Jimmy had seen the light and begun preaching the gospel in his own inimitable way, successfully spreading the good word to a number of other figures in the fight game. However, as born-again Christians go, he seemed to approach his faith with less than evangelical zeal. For one thing, his language and demeanour weren't quite what you would associate with the Christian canon – you know, goodwill to all men, turn the other cheek and all that. But fighting men make – and break – their own rules. The fraternity of the squared circle is catholic, with a very small 'c'. After all, where else but a boxing ring can a guy profess brotherly love for his fellow man while simultaneously bashing the shit out of him?

Perhaps old bad habits die hard. From what I knew of East End folklore, Jimmy had once had something of a reputation in this part of the world. Throughout the 1970s and early eighties, the name Tibbs was synonymous not so much with boxing but with other less sporting and God-fearing exploits.

Tibbs was an irascible ex-scrap metal dealer, erstwhile bad guy, former middleweight and now a trainer. He had coached the likes of Nigel Benn, the former WBC world super-middleweight champion whose brute force and visceral punching power had put Gerald McClellan in a coma after an explosive battle at the London Arena in February 1995. Benn is now a nightclub DJ. McClellan is blind, paralysed and permanently confined to a wheelchair.

Jimmy Tibbs, like so many men I would come to meet in boxing, was a man of few, well-chosen and usually colourful words. He trained, he swore, he trained some more. He didn't need to roll out the red carpet for me, or anyone for that matter. But he was a one-man welcoming committee of sorts, a harbinger, and the gatekeeper of a portal that led me into the strange and violent world of professional boxing.

I had gone to the Peacock in Canning Town, far east London, that freezing January morning in 1998 to find out what it meant to fight for a living, to be a professional boxer. I had set out with an old friend, a photographer named Michael Bale whose father knew the owners of the gym. We – well Michael specifically – had a fanciful idea that a glossy men's magazine such as *GQ* or *Esquire* might go for a feature on boxing, something with big pictures of big geezers with big broken noses.

It was meant to be a fairly run-of-the-mill task, just another one of those workaday projects that a struggling young hack hopes will help pay the rent, alimony, bailiffs and anything else pressing. I had recently fallen into the freewheeling world of freelance journalism, having previously worked as a wage slave for a regional newspaper group writing mainly crime stories on gangland shootings, deaths-in-custody, child murders and the like. The job, frankly, had become mildly depressing. My New Year's resolution was to focus on more lighthearted and inspirational subjects. What better place to start than the murky world of professional boxing . . .

With hindsight, I realise that I was on the cusp of a pre-midlife crisis. As a staff reporter I had become a thirty-year-old robot, an automated desk jockey, a media rat dedicated to scurrying along the skirting board of society. My despatches were from the 'frontline' of Brixton and spoke lazily of communities that were 'engulfed in an endless spiral of violence'. I made cardboard cut-out references to murder as 'senseless killing'. I wrote endless stories about drug dealers who were 'gunned down in a hail of bullets' which I recycled from old stories I'd written about other drug dealers who, conveniently, had also been 'gunned down in a hail of bullets'. A bonfire of mediocrity was torching my life. I worked sixty to seventy hours a week for monkey food. My salary was lower than a rattlesnake's gonads. I hated my job. I hated my life. I needed a change of linguistic scenery away from the landscape of clichés and hyperbole I had become accustomed to as a chronicler of the ghetto. I needed job satisfaction. Jesus, I needed to work less and earn more. For the sake of professional integrity, sanity and my bank manager, I therefore quit my poorly paid staff job to become a poorly paid freelancer.

Originally, the boxing project was photo-led. My mandate was to ride shotgun, so to speak, and provide the necessary written word to

Michael's grainy coffee-table photography. In the beginning, I thought it would be a simple enough task. I'd talk to a few fighters, hang around the gym a bit, look and listen, and Michael would take a few snaps – the usual journalistic exercise. The intention was to do a sort of stylised pictorial essay about the kind of men who lived, breathed and ate boxing in modern-day Britain, something informative, insightful and aesthetically appealing – a piece of cake really.

To penetrate the tightly knit world of boxing I needed to overcome not just the kind of cynicism Jimmy Tibbs displayed, but also a few cultural barriers and even risks. Beyond the smoke-filled municipal venues and the theatrics of small-hall boxing, the unseen world of the fight game is one of shadowy figures, intimidating gyms and backroom offices where men's lives are traded like cattle. I had heard various tales of odd goings-on in the fight game, ranging from innocuous rule bending such as cheating on a few pounds at a weigh-in, to what one might call match fixing. And of course over the years, both inside and outside of the ring, there has been the occasional 'accident' involving some of the sport's more unsavoury characters.

Like any business, boxing has its tricks of the trade, dark secrets and black arts. For a journalist to gain an insight into boxing beneath its surface level would be a challenge without the right connections to ensure a smooth passage. Michael's familial ties to the Peacock meant that from the outset I had contacts who could give me an entrée into a potentially closed-shop environment, without having my street credentials or motives brought into too much question.

Apart from an armchair fan's appreciation – and I had long been a fan – I knew nothing about boxing. I knew no one in boxing. In fact, the most I had ever written on any sport was a matchday report on a women's darts team for some local rag. What little boxing knowledge I had came from the fantasy of film and television. I had little understanding of the mechanics of the boxing subculture, so when I arrived at the Peacock, apart from Michael, ignorance, cynicism and a mild sense of anxiety were my only companions. As usual, I was out of my depth.

We strode up to the double doors of the gym and I hesitated for a moment. I took a deep breath and exhaled. The puff of condensation hit the cold morning air in a billowing, thick cloud of mist. I marvelled at the steamy shape lingering in front of me. A short blonde woman in a ski jacket two sizes too big for her stepped out of the gym and stared at me as if I was wearing a straitjacket and had 'axe wielding maniac' tattooed across my forehead. What the hell are you looking at, I thought. You're the one who's trying to hide a bubblegum-coloured Lycra leotard and leggings under that ridiculous jacket, not me. Besides, what was someone like her doing in a boxing gym?

I thought that boxing gyms were located behind rusting, steel-reinforced doors that led up steep or winding staircases to dimly lit speakeasies that sold violence on tap. Alternatively, they were in basement hellholes, dark, dank infernos of sweat, with no natural light and no clocks so that the fighters lost all sense of time. I imagined fighters using sides of beef as punch bags and every trainer looking like a cigar-chewing Burgess Meredith. Men, real men with cauliflower ears and six-inch facial scars would just keep punching and punching until they dropped. Those who could crawl up the slimy walls back on to their feet earned a brief reprieve – a mouthful of water, by convention spat out at a scrawny three-legged mongrel dying in a corner. The deadbeats and runts who couldn't cut it were simply shovelled up and dumped in the street to make way for more fighting flesh. Yeah, that was a proper boxing gym. Of course, the Peacock wasn't anything like that.

'It's like a factory, this place,' said Jackie Bowers, fidgeting for a cigarette. 'Boxing's as popular now as it ever was, but the gym can't survive on boxing alone.' Jackie was a grey-haired old geezer who crunched his words out through gritted teeth, his lips quivering like a bad ventriloquist. He'd been in the fight game for thirty years and for over half that time his family had been involved in some form of boxing gym. Jackie said that to be financially viable the Peacock ran every conceivable sporting activity on the premises, bar horse racing. They had tae kwon do classes, five-a-side football teams, circuit training, and even organised an annual strong-man contest in Docklands.

I suppose the Peacock wasn't that bad. It did have old leather punch bags strapped with gaffer tape to stop the giblets of stuffing from being ripped out by repeated blows. There was a pictorial hall of fame with dog-eared photos of long-forgotten fighters, the Cooper twins flexing their muscles, Ali, Tyson *et al*. Then there was the ubiquitous three-minute timer. A feature of boxing gyms from Brooklyn to Bangkok, its sole purpose is to mark hurting time. Ceaselessly it clangs the end of one round, rests for a minute, clangs again, signalling the start of another, pauses for three minutes as if taking a long, deep breath and then gringgggggggg – over and over again, gringgggggggg, shattering any hope of silence, gringgggggggg, butting into every conversation like a pesky schoolkid. Grrrrrrrinnnngggggggggggggg . . .

Tucked away at the back of the gym as if engaged in some secret ritual were the fighters – anonymous figures dripping with sweat in ripped-up T-shirts and ragged shorts. They skipped, shadow boxed and paraded round the two rings, occasionally posing in front of huge mirrors fit for any narcissist, their gnarled faces staring intently at corporeal reflections. This apparent fascination with self-imagery intrigued me.

Sure, the Peacock had it all but it didn't fit my image of a proper boxing gym. It was not evocative of, say, Martin Scorsese's *Raging Bull* or Stanley Kramer's 1949 classic *Champion*, you know, the one in which Kirk Douglas actually trained with pros for the role. The Peacock didn't conjure up images of spit and sawdust dives like the defunct Times Square gym or Stillman's in New York, places I'd read about in books or seen in the movies. Referring to the grubby nature of his gym, Lou Stillman once said, 'The way these guys like it, the filthier it is the better. Maybe it makes them feel more at home.' For years, I had harboured a notion of boxing gyms as dirty, raw, seedy places where muscle-bound, tattooed warriors slaved away with their fists in the half-light of a one-ring circus. I imagined the interiors of these places to look like rat-infested galleys. I thought dirt and deprivation came with the territory. Didn't a hard, tough gym equal hard, tough fighters?

The Peacock was bright and airy. It had whitewashed walls and MTV. There were rowing machines and apparatus for toning inner thighs and buttocks. On some nights of the week, they had step classes and aerobics upstairs. And of course, there were women – gym queens, female kick boxers, bull-dyke body builders and pretty city slickers who ventured bravely from the safety of their Canary Wharf dealing rooms to the Dodge City of Canning Town, dressed in bubblegum-coloured leotards and leggings. Jesus! What kind of gym was this? What had I come to? Surely women were prohibited from such places? Weren't boxing gyms supposed to be sacrosanct, male-only fleapits, too grimy and decrepit for the hygienic pedantry of the fairer sex? Shouldn't professional boxers be separated from women, focused and clear of libidinous distractions?

My fantasy had been shattered. The mythology of boxing as a hard, macho sport, where women existed only as pin-ups in gym lockers or card girls on fight night, had been exploded. Fighters trained in the same environment as women and neither seemed bothered by the other. I was beginning to realise that the reality of professional boxing in the late 1990s was far from the reference points of my celluloid imagination.

'Listen, these lads are very busy mate,' grunted Tibbs. 'You can't go getting in their way. Besides, what about the money?' Money? What money? All I wanted to do was hang out with the fighters and talk to them, find out what made them tick. Tibbs ignored me as best he could as I continued to follow him dutifully round the gym like a clumsy apprentice the first day on the job. The occasional hostile stare from some of the fighters did not help either as I tried to explain that I was not like the rest of the media.

'I'm not going to do a tabloid number on anybody, Jimmy,' I said meekly as he took off into the backroom office. Screw you and all this cloak and dagger bullshit, I thought. Was this a boxing gym or a kindergarten?

The deal was you had to go through the trainers or managers or one of their flunkies to talk to the fighters. Even if you tried to ask someone their name some busybody would step in with, 'Has this been cleared with Frank?' This seemed a rather juvenile way of doing business, like these grown men who were hard enough to get their faces busted wide open were not man enough to speak for themselves without someone else's permission. But as Jimmy was responsible for many of the up-and-coming prospects at the Peacock, some of whom I'd been assured I could talk to, I needed his cooperation, at least for the time being. As for the question of money . . .

'Well, Jimmy, I don't exactly have a budget for this. I mean, there's no money in it for anybody in the short term and . . .'

It was apparent that Tibbs didn't have the time or the inclination for dealing with a young hack and certainly wasn't interested in anything that didn't involve money. Money made the world of boxing go round.

'I told you already,' said Jimmy irritably, 'we always get you people from the media coming down 'ere wanting to do something on boxers. Trouble is, what do they get out of it? You always end up walking away with what you want, but what's in it for the fighters? How much are they gonna get paid?'

'Well at the moment I'm not in a position to pay anybody anything,' I reiterated. 'It's early days but I'm sure we can work something out. Now getting back to the fighters . . .'

I was full of bullshit. I was never going to pay anybody for anything. Chequebook journalism wasn't my style. Besides, I didn't have a brass farthing.

'I know a lot of people don't like talking about it,' said Jimmy, easing slightly as we sat down in the café of the gym. 'But I had to ask about the money. These fellas don't make a lot of dough. D'you know what I mean?' Did I know what he meant!

When I first crossed the threshold of the Peacock gym that afternoon, I passed a bronze statue of a boxer in a fighting stance. Below it was a plaque with an inscription. It read:

> *In Loving Memory of Bradley Stone*
> *Little Gem*
> *1970–1994*
> *A Brave Young Man*
> *Who Died*
> *In Pursuit of His Dream*

Money – in boxing, as in life, men died for it but was it only money that drew men to the sport? Injury and occasionally death were by-products of this exploitative and largely low-paid profession. Were men born to be fighters or did society engineer them? What else inspired the fighter – love, hate, religion? Did boxing offer perhaps some form of catharsis, an opportunity to exorcise the demons of a nightmarish upbringing through the rigours of the gym and the ring? What were the motivating forces that led men to fight for a living in such a tough, unforgiving business?

'These kids in 'ere, they're not going to be doctors or lawyers, are they?' said Jackie, lugging hard on another cigarette as we stood outside in the winter gloom. 'It's the same now as it was in the thirties and forties. It's money . . . earning a pound note. They start on maybe four hundred quid a fight and then, OK, so they get up to say fifteen hundred a fight. But what's that if you only fight four or five times a year? I prefer them to have a day job. It takes their minds off boxing.'

Jackie gave me a vacant look as if to say, 'Well, what more do you want?' Maybe I was naïve to think I could find profundity in a boxing gym.

'You know when they do that, before they go in the ring?' he said, crossing himself like the Latino dishwashers Prince Naz regularly smashed for a fistful of dollars. 'That helps . . . but only if you know how to fight. Remember, you've got to *want* to fight.' Jackie stubbed out his cigarette, gave me a nod and returned to the production line of his factory.

I could quite easily have left it at that. I could have written the shortest story on boxing ever, two hundred pages with just one word on each: money. Jimmy said it was about the money, so did Jackie. Boxing was rooted in a mythology that revolved around money. But that was too simple a definition. What motivated someone, as an individual, to become a professional fighter? The money was an obvious reason, as obvious for boxers as it was for accountants, street sweepers or Premier League footballers. The central point of any job, of any profession, is money; we take that as given. But very few fighters make serious money out of boxing. There had to be more to it than that.

After years of blind consumption as an armchair fan of boxing, I never really gave fighters much credit for what they did or thought about why they did it. I found it inconceivable that anyone in his right mind should want to take up boxing as a career, regardless of the potentially big money to be earned. Prize fighting was a business for bums and losers. To become a boxer, I thought, showed a lack of imagination, a commitment to a life of mental and physical torture, and penury. Boxing was Russian roulette played with fists. The stakes were high and the gamble promised what? Passing recognition? Fleeting glory? If you were lucky, maybe you got a plastic belt and a slap on the back.

Colin McMillan, the former WBO world featherweight champion and secretary of the Professional Boxers Association, once told me that a leading London promoter used to brag, 'Fighters are like whores – the more you fuck 'em, the more they like it.' Such a sentiment confirmed my suspicions that boxing was the red-light district of sport, fighters were prostitutes and promoters were like so many pimps feeding off their backs. Boxing was a 'fuck business'. Men in suits were out to shaft men in shorts. Any man who became a professional fighter was deluded if he thought his chosen sport offered salvation from poverty or a way out the ghetto. The odds on succeeding in boxing, on earning enough wealth to transform your lifestyle radically were stacked against you the moment you stepped into the ring. The Evander Holyfields and Mike Tysons of this world, the 0.1 per cent with the sponsorship deals, Ferraris and penthouse suites, may indeed earn up to 10, 20, even 30 million dollars a fight. But at the grassroots, the average struggling up-and-coming pro earned £400 or £500 a fight, lived in a council flat, used public transport and drew the dole or worked in a dead-end job.

As Jackie said, after a few fights a boxer progressed to a grand, maybe £1,500. Given that the average professional boxer fights only three or four times a year, their meagre purses amount to nothing.

Managers, promoters and trainers all take their cut. Then there are medical expenses, fees, licences, income tax, and what about training equipment, vitamins, supplements and sundries?

World champions aside, only journeymen fight frequently enough to earn anything near a regular wage from boxing. And what a life that is! Human punch bags who take a beating week in week out, fighting anyone anywhere, often with only a couple of days' notice. And when they retire what do they get? A gold watch and a pension? No, brain damage. A fighter's pay translated into a basic hourly rate would make the £3.60 minimum wage look like a small fortune. Professional boxing is not the career for men who want to earn a decent living.

It was getting dark outside the Peacock now. The remaining daylight cast a shadow across the small bronze statue of Bradley Stone. I wondered how many of the fighters who passed it each day ever considered the risk they were taking when they stepped into the ring. How many of them secretly wondered if one day fate would call on them to make the ultimate sacrifice? I thought about Little Gem, and what his dream had been before he fell into a coma and silently slipped away. More questions and still no answers. Maybe this wouldn't be a piece of cake after all.

chapter 2

The referee's decision was barely audible over the white noise echoing round the arena. 'Eight ... nine ... ten ...' He gave a melancholic shake of his fat head and, with arms waving like an umpire signalling four runs, he indicated that the fight was over. Takaloo was beaten. He looked confused.

'That's it, son. Sorry.' The referee, as is customary in these situations, tried to offer some conciliatory words to the young fighter, and then embraced him with the kind of overenthusiastic bear hug your granny grabs you with at Christmas. Gravity fought bravely to keep the pair upright as they teetered their way to the centre of the ring like a couple of drunks swaying on the dance floor of a cross-channel ferry.

I sighed deeply, sucking in the stale air of the arena, a bittersweet mixture of booze, cigarette smoke, body odour and cheap aftershave that stuck in the throat with fishbone determination. Not for the first time that evening I thought about failure and what drove the Takaloos of this world to take up the often brutal and humiliating trade of prize fighting.

I had only ever been to a fight once before, in 1993. It was at the York Hall, Bethnal Green. An old friend, a light-middleweight called Kevin Adamson, battered an ageing journeyman senseless in a one-sided, one-round fight. Kevin had left the East End to train with Brendan Ingle in Sheffield and had become pally with Naseem Hamed when the future Prince was still a pauper. For a few seasons, he was a prospect, then a contender. Then he became another statistic in the *Boxing Yearbook* after he lost badly to Lloyd Honeyghan in a Common-wealth title fight. As far as the boxing world was concerned, Kevin had his chance and blew it. In this business, it was often a case of one strike and you're out. Kevin had long since retired and so had my interest in small-hall shows until Takaloo invited me to the Grundy Park Leisure Centre to watch him box.

I'd been hanging out at the gym for about four weeks. I'd kissed so much ass my breath stank of shit but I was still on the outside looking in. What did I expect? Fight people were not the easiest in the world to get on with. It seemed I had overestimated my powers of ingratiation. It also didn't help that my snooping around and Michael's furtive picture-taking had aroused suspicions that our *GQ/Esquire* angle was just a cover story and we were in fact a couple of snitches from the DSS.

Takaloo was more easygoing than most of the patrons at the Peacock. Maybe this was down to his culture. He had come to Britain as a four-year-old after his family had fled the Islamic revolution in Iran. 'I want to do for my country what Naz has done for the Yemen,' he told me. He had won a couple of titles as a junior before turning pro in 1997 under the tutelage of Jimmy Tibbs. In the time that I had seen him working on the heavy bags, skipping, doing groundwork and pad work he seemed an impressive prospect. He was quick with both hands, stylish and carried himself with self-assurance but not arrogance.

He was no oil painting but he wasn't a bad looking guy, for a fighter. The Grundy fight, however, had taken its toll on his chiselled middle-eastern features. His eyes were badly swollen, he had a fat lip and a nose that had migrated across his face. He was a mess. His upper body was laminated with a coagulant of blood and sweat that trickled down his abdomen, dripping steadily on to his white satin shorts as he stood dejected in the centre of the ring.

For a sport that owes its origins to the amphitheatres of Rome, the Grundy, a seventies-built concrete carbuncle, was a cruel place for a gladiator of the ring to fall on his sword. The evening's seven bouts took place in the main sports hall. With its basketball-court lines and hastily concealed climbing frames and ropes it was a carbon copy of a thousand monolithic leisure centres, school or university gymnasiums throughout the country. In such an Identikit arena, any sense of history, space and location was irrelevant.

Nothing in boxing is permanent. Unlike football, cricket, rugby or athletics stadiums, boxing venues are not purpose-built; they are here one day, gone the next. Small-hall promotions are transient. They roll into cities and provincial towns in Britain like travelling circuses and rely on a dwindling number of largely unknown fighters to keep the sport alive at the grassroots. It is in these arenas that the Takaloos of the fight game ply their trade having served their apprenticeships as amateurs in working-men's clubs, hotel banqueting suites and other cheesy venues.

Takaloo had gone down three times. He later said he was 'weakened by a flu bug that was going round the Peacock'. Fighters are full of excuses.

'He looked great in the gym,' said Michael as we got up to leave. We are both Spurs supporters. We congratulated ourselves for backing another loser.

Humiliation is a consequence of boxing. To taste the sweetness of victory you have to be prepared for the bitterness of defeat. There are no good losers in boxing. How can you suffer a beating, a busted nose, a broken jaw or a detached retina and say, 'It's not the winning or losing, it's the taking part that counts.' If I had learnt one thing in the short time I had spent around the fight game, it was that boxing was exempt from all that idealistic Olympian bullshit. Boxing was about winning; unless, of course, you were paid to lose.

I stepped out into the darkness of the Grundy car park. It was wet and miserable. My copy of *Boxing News*, which had doubled up as an umbrella, was soaked and falling apart but at least I had my pride and dignity intact, unlike some of the fighters I'd seen that evening. People were milling around and I could hear shrieks of laughter, friendly banter, yelling, singing, a medley of post-fight sounds.

Takaloo was nowhere to be found. I waited for him but he had gone. I wanted to offer my commiseration but he had disappeared into the night to console himself, to think about his first taste of defeat and consider his future. I had similar ideas on my mind, about the future at least. I leant against a pillar outside the Grundy to collect my thoughts and make some more notes. Light rain trickled down my face and after the heat of the arena, it was vaguely comforting. Droplets of water smudged some of the words I had just written, so I closed my notebook and stood a while longer, thinking.

It was easy to be critical, to mock someone like Takaloo from the sidelines. Defeat in boxing could be mortifying, but these men put their pride, their health, everything on the line. They were stripped practically naked in the ring, literally and metaphorically; they bared themselves physically and mentally in public so that people like me, who had no concept of what it was really like to be a fighter, could ridicule their efforts. This may be a mug's game, but Jesus you had to have balls of steel to be a professional fighter. Did I have the bollocks to do something like that? Could I, a smug, pot-bellied journalist, hack it as a fighter?

21

My contemplative expression must have betrayed me. A peroxide blonde in her forties with a tinker's smile and the worse for drink came out of an exit, kicking her heels up. She stopped in front of me, grinning, her reddened, glazed eyes rolling. She had her arms around the blubbery necks of two skinheads whom she yanked round to bring square with herself. They rocked back and forth and stank of booze. I got the impression a ménage à trois in the back of a transit van was on the cards.

'Cheer up, love, it might never happen,' said the woman, cocking her head back and breaking into a drunken guffaw as her lecherous companions dragged her off into the night. Very original. '. . .it might never happen.' Maybe it just did.

chapter 3

The idea hit me like a rabbit punch to the kidneys. Forget the *GQ/Esquire* coffee-table thing. That was for girls. *Real* men took on *real* challenges. Perhaps it was a cruel twist of fate that Takaloo's misery should be my inspiration. For his defeat drew me to this conclusion: if I really wanted to understand what it meant to be a professional fighter, *I should become one myself.*

There is a Native American philosophy that goes something like 'you must walk in a man's moccasins for ten days before you can talk about him.' With this in mind, I reasoned that if I wanted to talk the talk, I had to walk the walk. Well, why not? I was young enough to get away with it – just. I had everything to gain and nothing to lose . . . except my life maybe. Moreover, at thirty years of age this was, realistically, my last chance of ever becoming a professional athlete, in the truly physical sense. Aside from golf, snooker and darts (activities in which you break wind more than you break sweat), professional sport was the preserve of youth. If I was to take up a physical challenge like boxing, and get paid for it, now was the time – now was the only time. At the rate I was going, soon I would be so overweight and irreversibly unfit it would be an achievement to walk let alone box. This was my swan song. I would see out my youth with a bang.

I realised that to become a fighter I would have to go the whole hog. I would have to give up the merry-go-round of parties, booze, recreational drugs, munchies, fast food, late-night TV. I would need to lose at least two stone to reach a decent fighting weight. At 15½ stone, I was technically a heavyweight. However, in terms of fitness, I was nothing short of a lightweight. I would have to train five days a week, run four or five miles a day for months on end, and how many broken noses or cracked ribs would I sustain in this time? I'd have to walk into the maddening atmosphere of the arena, enter a ring and fight a man –

theoretically to the death – having previously never boxed either as a professional or as an amateur. The contest would be no exhibition, no play act, no exercise. It would be the real McCoy. A fight to the finish!

I felt like Luke Rhinehart's *Dice Man*, like somehow I had just spun the dice and my number had come up. 'Double six: got to fight!' Leaving my fate to chance, so I thought, would transform my life from one that had wound its way down to a tedious crawl of everyday predictability to one of endless possibilities.

I was under no illusions about my limited abilities as an athlete, or as a writer for that matter. But like many wannabe tough guys who fancy themselves, whenever I saw a boxing match I often thought, with a touch of hubris, 'Yeah, I could do that. I could do better than that.' My conceit belied the reality of the day-to-day training regime of the pros I had seen at the Peacock with the endless sadistic rounds of skipping, shadow boxing, sparring, bags, pads, sit-ups, press-ups, weight-training, 6.00 a.m. five-milers and monastic diets. With a mixture of envy and disbelief I guess I had a grudging admiration for professional fighters, not because of that noble art crap but because they had something I didn't have. Trouble was, I didn't know what that something was – but I wanted to find out. I had to scratch the itch. As Oscar Wilde said, 'The only way to get rid of a temptation is to yield to it.'

So I decided to become a professional boxer. When I told my girlfriend Lara the great news of my epiphany, she thought I had lost my mind. 'You're mad. What if you get hurt? What if you get killed?' she said with touching concern for my wellbeing. She soon dismissed my ambitious idea as some pie-in-the-sky pipe dream.

Lara is the mother of my child. We had been together, on and off, for five years. Sometimes she shone a light so bright into my life that I thought I would go blind with love. But at other times . . . She was a former fashion model – tall, pallid, ectomorphic, a waif. She had a fondness for expensive clothes and cheap remarks and lived in a fantasy world of aromatherapy oils, I Ching, feng shui, rune stones, bean pulses and assorted New Age crap. She had no comprehension or interest in what I did for a living. To her, journalists were deadbeats, freeloaders who ambled through life (as I did) on drunken junkets, free trips to Zanzibar, boozy book launches and nights out at the Groucho Club. She thought everything I did was a joke. Maybe she had a point.

As I was already hanging out at the Peacock, I thought that it would be the ideal place for me to start training. I paid the £10 membership fee, bought some new sweats and for the next few days pumped some iron and bandied my bright idea around the guys at the gym. The response was nothing short of sheer hysteria. When I asked Jackie Bowers if he would consider training me, he thought I was nuts and gave me some spiel about boxing being for idiots, not smart guys like me. 'What d'you wanna get in the ring for, get yourself busted up?' he said. 'Smart lad like you . . . what d'you wanna do something stupid like boxing for?'

While I admired Jackie's concern, his attitude smacked of double standards. The fight game hated the negative view outsiders had of it, yet Jackie was happy to reinforce the stereotype that all boxers were thick, that somehow stupidity was a prerequisite to climbing into the ring. Admittedly, I had bought into this idea once upon a time. But my attitude was slowly changing and I thought by casting myself as a guinea pig I could shed some light on the dark world of boxing, maybe even dispel a few myths.

'I was just telling Jackie that I want to have a fight,' I said to Martin Bowers as I strained to lift a pair of dumbbells. Martin was Jackie's nephew, an ex-pro who also trained fighters at the gym. 'I think it'll give me a new perspective on the fight game,' I added.

'That'll give you a new perspective all right,' he replied, sniggering his way to the inevitable punch line. 'From the fucking canvas, mate!'

'No, seriously, I want to fight. I want to experience what it's like.'

'What weight you gonna fight at, then?'

'Probably cruiser.'

'Phwoar, those cruisers . . . They're still big fucking lumps, Dave. They pack a punch.' Martin strode off, shaking his head and frowning in mock disapproval.

Jackie had advised me to 'go to an amateur gym, like Repton'. He said at thirty, as a rank novice, I was too long in the tooth and wet behind the ears to turn professional. He also said my age would be a problem when it came to obtaining a licence from the British Boxing Board of Control. This presented a very practical problem. Jackie's professional opinion cut like a knife. My fragile ego would not accept that I was too old and too inexperienced to make it as a fighter. I scanned the *British Boxing Board of Control Yearbook 1998* for evidence of men who had turned pro late in life. The results were not reassuring. The fighters with the worst records were all in their thirties: Dean Bramhald, 36, light welterweight, 148 contests, 36 wins, 14 draws, 98 losses; Peter Buckley, 30, featherweight, 100 fights, 22 wins, 6 draws, 72 losses; Shamus Casey, 39, middleweight, a staggering 153 fights, 28 wins, 5 draws and an unenviable 120 defeats; Des Gargano, 39, super-bantamweight, 117 contests, 32 wins, 3 draws, 82 losses (one of the oldest pros in the business); Miguel Matthews (no relation), 34, super-featherweight, 103 fights, 12 wins, 11 draws, 80 losses.

Jackie Bowers and Lara were not the only people who thought I would never make it as a pro. Most of my friends and family felt I would find the task insurmountable. People who knew me based their disbelief on my lifestyle, and my beer gut. When I told my father he just said, 'You're going to do what?' belched over his chicken curry, took a swig from his can of Guinness and laughed. The thought of him having to eat crow, seeing me box with youthful vigour and power, was a great motivating force. After years of his boring tough guy tales and of him constantly undermining me as weak and spineless, here was my chance to get one up on the old fart.

Then there was my mother. She heaped scorn on anything and everything I did. I anticipated a barrage of sermons and lectures from her on the perils of boxing and all that 'bad company' I would be keeping. Mothers have a right to know what their naughty little boys are up to, but letting her know the full extent of my plans early on was not a good idea. Any anxiety my mother felt about me boxing would be immediately transferred in my direction and in the long run that could have serious consequences on my sanity. She was also capable of maximum embarrassment. I foresaw her pulling a stunt like Minna Wilson, the mother who jumped into the ring and battered her son's opponent with a high-heeled shoe to save him from a third-round pasting. To avoid such a situation in the future, I thought it prudent to keep her in the dark for a while. I therefore waited a year or so before I told her what I was up to.

Whenever I told friends and acquaintances of my intention to box, they would usually break into fits of laughter or smile sympathetically as if to say, 'You poor stupid sod'. Most of them hated boxing and would get all holier than thou and counsel me against going the whole way. When they asked me if I was scared at the prospect of becoming a fighter, I'd say, 'No' glibly and deliver a well-rehearsed line on boxing being statistically safer than rugby, motor racing, show jumping or even football. They would counter with horror stories of brain damage, blindness, heart attacks and comas. Some would attempt to dissuade me from boxing by ridiculing me, in the hope that I would succumb to the humiliation and give up. One friend who was a staunch opponent of boxing said that she would only come to the fight if I entered the ring to 'Eye of the Tiger', the theme tune to *Rocky*, while wearing an Afro wig. Another suggested that I get a professional fighter to pose as me and take a fight on my behalf!

One guy asked me, when I told him of my intention to become a fighter, if I was 'too intelligent to box'. He wondered whether my intellect (whatever that is) would cause unnecessary philosophising and get in the way of the simple task of being, well, violent. His inference was that 'unintelligent' people were too dumb to think of the consequences of boxing so they carried on regardless, whereas us eggheads knew that it was a stupid thing to do and thus abstained from it. But could someone possibly be too intelligent to box? Jackie Bowers had thought so, as had many people I had met both inside and outside the fight game. Some even went so far as saying you had to be clinically insane to be a fighter. Part of my mission was to beg to differ.

Norman Mailer once wrote: 'They [sports writers] do not try to comprehend fighters. They prefer to treat them in tried and true ways, as rather heroic but silly fellows, or as clowns with a penchant for off-beat or gnomic remarks.' He theorised that this hackneyed attitude appeased the man in the street because for Joe Public to believe (the possible truth) that a boxer was capable of outfighting and out-thinking him at the same time was a most despicable concept. The stereotype of the fighter as an imbecile was thus a prophylactic for Joe Public's mental and physical insecurities. I was to discover, however, that a professional fighter possesses a level of wit and guile that in many ways is far superior to that of Joe Public. Fighters commonly lacked education but they did not lack nous.

Screw the critics, the doubters and the piss takers anyway. So what if they thought I was thick, mad, sad, pathetic or all of those things. Opportunities for characters like me were thin on the ground. I needed to get my arse in gear and do something with my life. The telephone wasn't exactly overheating with offers of work and I had mouths to feed. If I had had a cushy number writing restaurant reviews for the *Observer* or wrote celebrity interviews for the *Sunday Times*, would I have embarked on such a hazardous career? Probably not. Journalists like an easy life. Like my peers, I wanted to be successful and have the creature comforts I thought I deserved, but I also had to be realistic about the means at my disposal for achieving them. I was a black, working-class male with a second-rate education operating in a white, middle-class, Oxbridge-dominated industry. I had to ride my luck. Maybe boxing could be a way out for me, albeit tangentially.

I was determined to become a pro boxer for that one fight, that once-in-a-lifetime experience. In spite of the opposition, the lack of support and the overwhelming odds against success, there was no stopping me. By left hook or by crook, I was going to get in that ring and I was going to fight, even if it bloody killed me.

chapter 4

I was living on borrowed time anyway. When I was eight years old, I almost drowned while on holiday in Devon. I had badgered my father for days to buy me a rubber dinghy and one afternoon his will finally broke. I couldn't go out in it straightaway, though. An old duffer walking along the beach with a metal detector said something like, 'I wouldn't go out on that if I were you. It's a bit choppy today.' The gods had granted me a temporary reprieve.

The following morning I was out on that dinghy splashing around and having a whale of a time. I'd drifted about fifty or sixty metres out from the shore before I remembered I couldn't swim. I tried to paddle back to shore but simply drifted further out to sea. So I foolishly stepped out of the dinghy, hoping I would find the seabed beneath my feet – no such luck.

I have heard it said that when you are drowning you see your life flash in front of you. As an eight-year-old, I had not had much of a life, so I did not see much apart from scummy water and seaweed. My memory of the episode, however, is vivid. The thought of that day still makes me feel claustrophobic, as if an invisible hand is slowly choking me. Drowning puts you in a state of absolute helplessness. Death stares you in the face and you smell it, you taste it.

As I wrestled frantically with the tide I could make out my sister screaming on the beach and my father fighting to rip off his jeans, and then diving in still wearing them. The experience lasted about thirty seconds. It felt like thirty minutes ... thirty hours ... thirty years. An old man who looked like Santa Claus without a beard eventually saved me.

Santa disappeared. I lay on the beach coughing and spluttering. My father lost it completely and didn't speak to me for the next three days. I remember him giving me dirty looks as he hung his money out to dry in our chalet. My mother, who was estranged from my father and living in Canada at the time, held the old boy personally responsible for my near death and even went so far as to accuse him of engineering the whole incident. My father may have been capable of some unforgivable acts in his time but infanticide was not one of them.

Before the dinghy incident, from as young as five years old, I can remember having nightmares about death. I'd wake up crying and screaming, 'I don't want to die, I don't want to die.' I can't ever remember having my fears allayed. I had my whole life ahead of me then and yet the three score and a bit years owed to me seemed like precious little time. I wonder now whether other children feel as I did then, that it was a sin not to be able to live forever.

I do not come from the sun-dried tomatoes and Chianti school of soft touches, but I wouldn't say I'm from the school of hard knocks either. My upbringing was not particularly impoverished; just a normal, dysfunctional, working-class one. My folks always grafted. I never saw either of them draw the dole. I always had three squares a day and a roof over my head and my clothes didn't have too many holes in them. My parents separated a number of times and eventually got divorced just before I left school. Then they got back together again. And then they split. And so on and so forth.

My mother had to cope with four children who perhaps did not have the best start in life. I was the baby, but I always felt the pressure to succeed where perhaps my siblings, through no fault of their own, had failed. My eldest sister, Yvette, became pregnant at seventeen thanks to some Lothario she met while growing up in Guyana. He did the 'right thing' and married her. Trouble was he forgot to mention one minor detail – he was already married. Within a matter of weeks the marriage was dissolved. (The footnote to that is that she is now happily married with four children.)

My brother Michael was a genius in waiting. He was a real geek, obsessed with maths and sciences. He had an intellect way beyond his age. Somewhere in his late teens, though, drugs got a hold of him and a bright, intelligent young man rapidly turned into a confused and brainless freak. I'll never forget him flipping out in Prospect Park, Brooklyn, running around in just his underpants hollering, screaming and laughing maniacally. The last time I saw him he was babbling incoherently about aliens or some shit and smoking cigarette after cigarette. That was ten years ago.

My sister Jackie was born mentally and physically handicapped, the victim of undiagnosed German measles. She never had a chance. She didn't have the opportunity to accept failure as an option. My mother tried as best she could to care for her when we were young but Jackie was too much to handle. She required constant professional care, the kind that the wages of a sewing machinist and a welder don't run to. Jackie wound up in a home. The last time I saw her was when I was a small boy. My mother took me to the home in Colchester, Essex. The sight and sound of all those children crying, screaming, rocking back and forth overwhelmed me. They were lost souls. I ran out of the place in tears. My mother thought I would be traumatised if I went there again and never took me back. I haven't seen Jackie since.

Mike Tyson once said that a middle-class man could make a good boxer, 'but to be the champ you have to know struggle'. On paper, I suppose I was middle-class by virtue of having a degree and being a writer – but that's on paper. In reality, as a young black man growing up in Britain, I was all too familiar with struggle. I knew what it was like on the street. I'd seen glue-sniffing buddies come to a sticky end; taken my fair share of pastings from local thugs, the cops and a variety of other knobheads. I had lived through an environment of torment and hatred that occasionally ground my father down to a point where he'd beat me until I pissed my pants because the system was beating the shit out of him. I came from a world where 'sorry, the job/flat/golden opportunity has already gone' had an insidious meaning.

When I was a boy, I lived in an East End terraced house that had an outside toilet, tragic carpets and peeling woodchip wallpaper. There was no polished pine floor, no picket fence, no gravelled driveway, and no power shower. Between 1979 and 1980, I lived in a rat and cockroach infested apartment in a crumbling tenement block in one of New York's shittiest neighbourhoods – Flatbush, Brooklyn. I went to a school that had bars on the windows and security guards patrolling the corridors. I was mugged on several occasions and constantly bullied. Once, three thugs hung me by my feet from a fourth-floor lavatory window, just for the hell of it. They thought it was a riot! Oh, how they laughed! My twelve-month stretch in the Big Apple was a nightmare. It was the closest I have ever come to living in what you could loosely call the ghetto. Life in New York left an indelible mark on me. I returned to Britain a stranger to myself.

My struggle, for what it is worth, was not so much material for there are far worse places on earth than Flatbush and certainly the East End. No, my struggle was psychological. Poverty has a way of eating into your self-respect, your psyche, like a tumour. Being broke makes you feel literally worthless. But you have to rise above it, or else you fail. As much as Mike Tyson, I was a product of my environment and my experiences.

I grew up in a world that destroyed many of my contemporaries through drug abuse, crime and various avenues of death. I escaped that world. Maybe I was lucky. Despite my apparent cynicism, I do believe I am serendipitous. But as an armchair existentialist, I have always considered myself to be fundamentally the architect of my destiny. I succeeded where others failed because I was unwilling to succumb to a life of desperation. Growing up in the endless boredom and stagnation of London's crummier suburbs was a challenge, not a life sentence. Times were tough. However, if you had the brass nuts and the wherewithal there was always a way out, somehow. And it didn't have to be through boxing.

I must admit I occasionally find the notion of free will uncomfortably Thatcherite in its simplicity, as if all you need to get on in life is chutzpah, a Protestant work ethic, or the ability to work like a nigger (depending on your cultural persuasion).

This was the 1990s, baby. Let's be real. I understood that drugs, teenage sex, violence, crime, police brutality – all the classic inner-city deprivation stuff – were the kind of obstacles that young fighters faced. After all, I had faced the same pressures myself as a youth, which wasn't that long ago. But there was nothing cast in stone, no rule, written or otherwise, that said a working-class boy like me had to fight for a living. Plenty of people have come from far worse backgrounds than me, or Mike Tyson for that matter, and have made an honest go of it without soaking their hands in the blood of others. The idea that boxing is the *de facto* sport of the ghetto is rubbish. Muhammad Ali, Sugar Ray Leonard and scores of top fighters have come from very modest but not poverty-stricken circumstances. It is not essential that you come from the ghetto to become a fighter.

For as long as I can remember I have had an interest in boxing. As a child, I dreamed of seeing – of being – Muhammad Ali. It was a dream I shared with millions. I have often heard people say that their initiation into boxing as an observer or participant came from seeing 'The Greatest' in action. But for a long time I have also had a rather pendulous relationship with boxing. My feelings towards the sport have swung from my boyhood adulation of Ali to revulsion at the tragedies I witnessed as an adult. I had seen fighters like Michael

Watson and Gerald McClellan, men of my generation with backgrounds similar to my own, reduced to shadows of their former selves. And I had heard and read of others who had paid the ultimate price in pursuit of ephemeral fame and mythical paydays.

Nevertheless, some of my fondest memories as a boy are rooted in boxing. I remember listening to the legendary Rumble in the Jungle on a beat-up old radio – 30 October 1974. My dad and I huddled round the old gas fire while the radio crackled away with commentary of the Ali v. Foreman fight in Kinshasa, Zaire. Such memories are a comfort for as a child I had a difficult relationship with my father. Occasionally I even had Oedipal fantasies about bashing his brains in (although my mother reneged on her side of the deal when I was seven years old and ran away 'to find herself', conveniently leaving me behind). Once, when I was about four or five years old, I did, quite by accident (or perhaps, subconsciously, not by accident) hit my father over the head with a claw hammer as we played rough and tumble under the kitchen table. He wound up with a nasty lump on the head. He has never forgiven me for it and would often recall the incident at any opportune moment, as a means of proving I had it in for him.

My mother didn't return to the family home until I was fourteen, so my father brought me up single-handedly for most of my adolescent years. It was a difficult task for him and it wasn't easy for me either. When I was very young, we had very little in common. He was a gregarious, blue-collar, macho guy, obsessed with John Wayne, horse racing, boozing and hard graft. I was an effete pretty-boy who played with Lego and enjoyed solitude. I found it difficult to fit in at school. I always felt under pressure to live up to some macho fantasy my father had created. He would say things like, 'I'd rather have a prostitute for a daughter than a poof for a son,' and give me the stare as if his words were some sort of warning. He regaled me constantly with his sexploits as a young man. As a quiet, introspective boy, I was fair game for his taunts. I always felt he was subtly trying to undermine my masculinity by comparing his cavalier attitude to sex with my naïve sensitivity. Consequently, I grew up sexually repressed and shy of girls until I lost my virginity at sixteen to a twenty-five-year-old single mum. I was nothing like my father. I never wanted to be like him. I never liked getting my hands dirty or doing anything remotely practical, arduous or painful. I hated his working-class hero crap and his gambling, hard-drinking ways.

My mother used to joke with me, 'You always know who your

mother is, but you can never be quite sure about your father,' just to add her tuppence worth of mind gaming. I sometimes wondered if she knew something I didn't, as my father and I were so different. The one thing we did have in common, however, apart from a grudging affinity towards each other, was a love of boxing, which helped to maintain our fragile father–son ego-system.

When I think about it, I could so easily have been packed off to a boxing gym by my father when I was a boy. I met the criteria. If anyone needed to learn how to look after himself as a youngster it was me. But he never encouraged me to take such a rite of passage. I honestly think he thought I was too weak, too soft for boxing. Later in life, as I filled out, he would joke that he could have made a fortune out of me if he had got me into the squared circle from an early age.

At school, none of my friends boxed, apart from one skinny kid called Ricky Wiseman. I remember him showing off his little blue medical card (effectively a form of amateur boxing licence) in the playground at Ruckholt Manor junior school.

'This means I can't get into a fight with anyone on the street,' he said. He was now a 'proper boxer' and had to abide by a strict code of honour that forbade him from using his still developing fists of fury outside the ring. The card looked like one of those rent books that you get in WH Smith and had rows and columns into which details of each bout that was fought were to be entered. It was mostly blank apart from one or two scribbled entries but I was impressed nonetheless.

Strange as it seems now, back in those halcyon days of the 1970s and early 1980s, amateur boxing was screened regularly on ITV and BBC1 and most major world championship fights were broadcast free on terrestrial television. The mind boggles to think what Sky could charge today on a pay-per-view channel for Ali v. Frazier live from Manila or Sugar Ray Leonard v. Tommy Hearns at Caesar's Palace, Las Vegas.

The first TV set I remember in the family home was a black and white DER rental. Ali, of course, was the first fighter I ever saw on that goggle box. As we moved up in the world to Bush and Grundig colour sets, the likes of Hagler, Hearns, Leonard, Larry Holmes, Ken 'Mandingo' Norton, George Foreman and Smokin' Joe Frazier, all in their prime, were beamed into our living room.

In 1980, boxing introduced me to the concept of sport as a forum for racism, long before I experienced it on England's football terraces. The Marvin Hagler–Alan Minter world middleweight title fight at Wembley Arena was the first time I had supported a fighter, or any athlete for that matter, because of colour. Before the fight Minter had said, rather discourteously, 'No black fella is going to take my title.' Minter's snide remark infuriated me, so I felt vindicated as a black youth when Hagler made Minter eat his words and demolished him in three rounds to become the new world champion. Minter's fans pelted the ring with bottles and coins and the rioting led to Hagler's speedy exit under police escort.

Six years later, the enigma that was, and still is, 'Iron' Mike Tyson, at the tender age of twenty years four months and twenty-two days, became the youngest man in history to win a world heavyweight championship belt. Tyson rocked my world with his awesome power and hyper-aggressive fighting style. Like many boxing fans, I thought he was unstoppable and would go on to smash every heavyweight record there was. He was like a black Hulk, a laboratory experiment gone wrong. I never read comic books so in a way characters like Tyson and Ali were my superheroes, my Masters of the Universe.

As I got older my tastes changed and I began to develop something of a love–hate relationship with boxing. By the early 1990s, cracks began to appear in my affection for the sport. Part of me, the new liberal, bohemian me, the one that had spurned the mayhem and violence of the East End streets of my adolescence, viewed boxing as a morally and ethically bankrupt business. This was due partly to what had happened to Michael Watson at the hands of Chris Eubank. But the other me, the old working-class, neo-conservative me, saw boxing as a gung-ho expression of muscular artistry, the ultimate challenge and a celebration of a self-indulgent, dog-eat-dog world. Something inside me felt that boxing wasn't right, it wasn't fair, it wasn't just. But as if in the grip of some kind of addiction I couldn't turn my back on it, no matter how bad I thought it might be for the system.

When I was a boy, I squandered every opportunity I ever had to be an athlete. My sports career to date had been less than illustrious. In those plimsoll days of liniment and regulation sports kit, when PE teachers (repressed homosexuals to a man) administered the slipper for insubordination, because of my height, size and colour I was press-ganged into every lousy team at school. Only the fleabags and weeds with their little notes from mum escaped the humiliation of PE. The remaining lumps, blacks (of any description), degenerates, time wasters and arse-licking glory boys with an unnatural amount of natural talent, were corralled into hours of mindless games. Why? So the school trophy cabinet could collapse under the weight of assorted tin pots and toe-punting plastic figures on ersatz marble.

I always made the sports teams. Getting into them was easy. But my appearances were about as useful as Rock Hudson giving blood. I was kicked off the school tennis team for a McEnroe-type tantrum and dropped from the football squad after my first match for scoring an own goal. I was bowled for a duck in my maiden cricket match and removed from the field of play during a rugby try-out for fighting. As a team player, I was an unmitigated disaster.

Academically, I was no better. I left school with a pocketful of third-rate CSEs and a couple of low-grade O levels in English language and literature and at fifteen blew education out of the window to become an apprentice electrician with Hackney council. My mother got me the job having chanced across an advertisement in a local paper. She applied on my behalf and then sat through the interview with me, occasionally breaking into tears for good measure. My mum at a job interview with me – tsch! I was asked a few rudimentary technical questions such as 'how do you wire a three-pin plug?' I responded by saying something idiotic about the brown being earth (well, it looks like it), green/yellow was neutral and blue was live. What a mess! I didn't even know how to wire a plug and I still got the job. It was in the days of political correctness gone mad. I had to have the job because out of all the dumbass niggers who applied for the post, I was the smartest one they interviewed. And I couldn't wire a plug!

I was too much of a white-bread eating pussy to stay with manual labour for long. Due to my dislike of anything physical, manual, tortuous, boring, repetitive, poorly paid and dirty, I decided to get out of blue-collar work and escape to the pampered world of Vax coffee machines, air conditioning and soft toilet paper. Office work, however, proved as stimulating as a blow job from a piranha, so I hatched a grand plan to become an actor and screw my way to Hollywood where I'd reach superstar status. I'd have homes in Aspen, Monte Carlo and Martinique and at least one Aga, 2.2 kids, a wife, a mistress and a bank balance that read like a New York City telephone number. Alas, my life went more in the direction of Holloway than Hollywood. I made it to second lead with a fringe theatre company in Kentish Town, lived in a bedsit in Kilburn, had a Baby Belling but no kids, a frigid girlfriend, and a bank balance that read like the directory inquiries number.

My first performance on stage was in a play called *Planet Suicide* about a group of wacky street thugs who hung around an amusement arcade in Kings Cross beating each other up. It was no Oscar winner. No agents called, no casting directors tried to rugby tackle me on to the proverbial casting couch. So I was left to finance my fledgling acting career doing menial jobs as a cycle courier and van driver which, because they were physical, manual, tortuous, boring, repetitive, poorly paid and dirty, led me on to the dole.

After a while the novelty of poverty began to wear thin. My private income (as I euphemistically called unemployment benefit) did not go very far. The hours I spent on a daily basis as a resting actor, smoking weed and watching daytime TV, gave me time to reflect on how unproductive my life had become. I returned to the construction industry until I made enough money to leave the country for a year with my new bride, whom I married after a whirlwind romance and courtship which took all of six weeks.

Suffice to say the marriage did not last. The wife dumped me in India. I returned to Britain for another round of menial, dead-end jobs in telesales, fundraising for charities, more courier work, electrical engineering, promoting raves and working as an infrequently paid assistant film producer. I had lost all sense of career direction. I had no idea what I wanted to do with my life. At a loss, I went back to college and university and learnt how to draw squiggly lines on flip charts and write parish-pump news stories about pussies stuck in trees. Four years later, I resurfaced in the big bad world with a degree in something to do with money and a couple of diplomas in journalism. For what seemed like an eternity, I worked for a crummy newspaper struggling to raise my young family on a derisory salary. Then one day I took a good look at my payslip and saw a figure not too dissimilar to what I once would've blown on a good night out. At this point I realised I was not earning what I was worth, so I quit. The cost of resignation, financial or otherwise, was negligible. There is no value in mediocrity. Success, however, regardless of how you choose to measure it, always comes at a premium.

chapter 5

The guys at the Peacock thought I was a joke. Firstly, they derided my lack of experience. Professional boxers primarily learned their craft during lengthy amateur careers; those who didn't were usually converts from other martial arts such as kick boxing. Many pros started out as young as ten or eleven and spent a decade or so honing their skills in the rings of working-men's clubs, hotel ballrooms and civic centres. By the time they turned pro (usually in their early twenties) most fighters would have had anywhere between thirty and seventy amateur bouts under their belts.

Lack of experience also put me at a psychological disadvantage. Jackie Bowers had told me that without the benefit of an amateur career I would be unable to cope with a crowd of hundreds of screaming, jeering people. Others said I would fall to pieces in the dressing room before the fight, if I even had the balls to get that far. And of course my age meant I was past it.

It was my physical condition, however, that engendered the most pessimism. Admittedly, I had something of a weight problem. I wasn't 'Jerry Springer Show' material or on the verge of a sponsorship deal with Weightwatchers, but I was a fat bastard nonetheless. That football chant, 'Who ate all the pies?', was conceived with people like me in mind. I had a gargantuan appetite. I loved food. I could easily eat my own bodyweight in fried chicken, pizzas and cream cakes in a single sitting.

I thought I could make cruiserweight, but this was an arbitrary decision. The blubbery 215 or so pounds I was carrying around was way over my natural bodyweight, whatever that was. I figured getting down to cruiserweight, with an upper limit of 13 stone 8lb, was a realistic target for me. Anything above 13–8 was the heavyweight division, and decidedly heavier-handed opposition.

My first realistic goal was to lose a few pounds so that the guys at the Peacock would notice a physical change in me and thus start taking me more seriously. Having one chin to protect was enough; I was not getting into the ring with two. I also had to admit to myself that I was too unfit to just dive in at the deep end so I set about an initial phase of training which I called, euphemistically, pre-conditioning.

In addition to joining the Peacock, I took out a membership at a sports centre near my home in Ladbroke Grove. For the time being, staying local was more convenient than traipsing across London to Canning Town every day; and in the less competitive environment of my neighbourhood gym I could train in peace with a bunch of other fatties without embarrassing myself as I did at the Peacock. To avoid bulking-up and gaining more weight, I stopped doing heavy weight training and concentrated on cardiovascular exercises such as step classes, circuit training, cycling and light jogging. I gradually added isometric exercises – press-ups, pull-ups and the dreaded sit-ups – to my regimen. It was also in the comfort of my local gym (and the privacy of my own home) that I began to learn the art of skipping. Initially, I skipped like a pansy. My legs and arms would flail wildly, I'd get about half-a-dozen strokes together, whip myself and trip over. During a three-minute round of skipping, I'd fall apart every fifteen seconds. It took months to be able to jump rope like a pro.

For all my effort, somewhere in the midst of all the sweaty socks, jogger's nipple and saddle soreness, I was doing something wrong. I had lost a negligible amount of weight. In fact, the more I trained, the more I ate. I was under the impression that exercise acted as an appetite suppresser, but I was finding it increasingly difficult to control my food intake. Having given up alcohol, the occasional joint and anything else that was doing the rounds, food had become my only vice; and boy was I sinning. Around six weeks into my training, I went to weigh myself on the scales at the Peacock. It was one of those six-foot, old-style glass and chrome jobs, very impressive. Just as I was about to pop twenty pence into the machine, Martin Bowers walked past. 'Oi, don't break that, Dave,' he quipped. 'It cost us a lot of money you know.' I had made zero impression on the Peacock. It was the first and last time I nearly used the Peacock's scales.

On my way home from the gym, I stopped off at Boots for a sandwich – OK, and a packet of crisps, a bar of chocolate and a Danish pastry. I noticed one of those electronic scales by the exit and decided to weigh myself. I slipped the coin into the machine and a slip of paper emerged accusing me of being 97.8kg (approximately 15 stone 5lb in old money). Even allowing for my bulky winter clothes, it confirmed what I had learnt earlier at the Peacock – I was still at least 15 stone. The machine claimed my ideal weight was 13 stone 5lb or 85.2kg.

Between eleven and twelve years old, I had turned from a short tub of lard into a beanpole. But what goes around eventually comes around. Right up until my mid-twenties I was still distressingly thin, so I got into pumping iron in order to fill out my bony frame. This attempt at creating comic-book biceps and pecs to die for was in vain; with the passage of time, I settled down, bought cable TV, discovered Ben and Jerry's and became a less frequent visitor to the gym. My metabolism eventually went into stasis; aided by a now overenthusiastic diet of recreational eating, previously taut muscle metamorphosed into flab. For all that working out, all I wound up with were stretch marks and a belly more reminiscent of a Party Seven than a six-pack. In short, I had become a slob.

Disadvantages aside, I convinced myself the glass was half full, not half empty. Although I lacked stamina and fitness, was overweight and had no boxing experience whatsoever, on the positive side I hadn't spent a lifetime getting my brains bashed in, so I was still relatively physically and mentally fresh. My lack of experience could be overcome with the right trainer and training methods. I took the view of Ralph Bellamy in *Trading Places* – someone with strong enough genes (i.e. not a total imbecile) could adapt to any environment or situation given the right education or training. Thus, I cast myself as the Eddie Murphy of the boxing world. I knew I had the willpower to run the gauntlet. I just needed to find the right person to help me do it. I needed an exceptional trainer, one who would not just put me through the motions but could, against all the odds, train me to fight and beat a seasoned professional boxer.

I was up against it. I had nothing going for me apart from desire. I was starting at an age when most fighters were about to hang up their gloves. I was about to do something that overweight journalists just did not do. Part of my agenda was to prove that not all writers are wankers and demonstrate that you don't have to be a candidate for a lobotomy to box. Once I had convinced myself I was going to, as they say in boxing, 'live the life', I began to indulge myself in a fanfaronade of wild statements, claims and predictions. 'Yeah, I'm going to become a professional boxer and write a book about the experience,' I would tell anyone who'd listen. This was usually followed by a pompous proclamation along the lines of '. . . and I'll probably get killed in the process and go down in history as one of the literary greats of my generation.' Yeah, right.

Whenever I turned up at the Peacock I'd badger Jackie and Martin about training me but I soon realised they were too cynical to see any sense in what I was trying to achieve. As for Jimmy Tibbs, he still treated me like a wart, so I didn't even bother broaching the subject with him. Rather than waste any more time taking up space and being the butt of crude jokes, I decided to go in search of pastures new. The Peacock wasn't the only gym in the world. Besides, what did they know about boxing anyway?

As late winter became spring and spring turned to summer, I worked hard to find a way to finance what would be a rather costly affair. I could not afford the expense of training full time without financial support; and convincing a professional trainer to take me on as a charitable cause was proving unsuccessful. I needed to work and unless I could broker a publishing deal, my bright idea was doomed. Money was getting tight. This invariably led to conflict with Lara.

'Why don't you get a proper job?' Lara would say, dismissing my occupation as some sort of dilettantish exercise. 'I want to be normal. I want us to be a normal, happy family.'

Lara thought I was spending too much time at the gym. Although working from home gave me the luxury of extra time with my daughter (unlike the daily twelve-hour shifts I did as a staff reporter), Lara made me feel as though I was a neglectful father. 'You're not spending enough quality time with Luca,' she'd say. I wanted the best for my family and this involved taking a few risks. If I continued plodding along as just another struggling hack I'd never get anywhere. Given the choice, I would rather sit on my arse all day getting loaded than buy into the Protestant work ethic. My parents worked like dogs all their lives and all they had to show for it was heart disease. Ambition is an unfaithful whore.

I appreciated that the constant needs of a one-year-old child made it difficult for Lara to see beyond her own disenfranchisement. As far as she was concerned, I had too much time on my hands while she was stuck indoors looking after baby. If I were not in a dead-end nine-to-five, surely I ought to be at home minding her and Luca?

Naturally, the bills still needed paying, so I concentrated on free-lancing and accepted a part-time post lecturing in journalism at my old college in south London. My former tutor, who was the course director, had offered me the post during the summer, even though I was suitably unqualified for the job. What did I know about teaching? Or even journalism! I knew many other journalists with years of teaching experience who could have filled that post, but political correctness and tokenism dictated that my face fitted. Ironically, not for the first time in my life, I managed to get a job because of my skin colour, not in spite of it.

But a few hours a week wearing sandals, a cardigan and corduroy pants was not enough. My earnings from lecturing and freelancing were barely enough to support three people; in order to finance my career as a professional fighter, I needed serious money. Without some form of financial backing, the incentive to continue gradually waned. My training dwindled down to occasional runs around Wormwood Scrubs and the odd visit to my local gym. I was on the brink of quitting when, after months of pounding the streets hawking my idea for a book, I finally convinced a publisher that a few grand was a small price to pay for the cachet of having a journalist kill himself for his art. What a book! What publicity! What sales!

Before securing a publishing deal my approach to boxing had been, well, rather amateur. Although I believed that there was more to boxing than money, economics dictated that I could only become a professional fighter, and write about it, if someone paid me to do it. Now call me cynical, but as a professional journalist seeking to become a professional fighter, money had to come into the equation at some point. Writing was my job. Fighting would become my job. To do either for no financial reward would have been, well, unprofessional.

With cash in pocket, I thought I could employ a trainer. But despite the lure of filthy lucre, this still proved to be more difficult than I had imagined. Many trainers I met liked my idea, but when it came to the pitch, they just weren't prepared to give me a shot. The reaction was always the same: without at least one amateur fight under my belt, I could never become a pro. To a trainer I was a liability, an albatross. I was surprised at how conservative people in boxing could be, given the risks and unconventional nature of the sport. Selling the crazy idea of a writer becoming a prizefighter to a publisher was one thing; selling it around London's boxing gyms was like finding a Jehovah's Witness with an organ donor card.

chapter 6

Most of the boxing gyms I visited I had heard of by reputation, although I did find one or two by chance. One afternoon while on a wild goose chase in south London looking for the British heavyweight contender, Danny 'the Brixton Bomber' Williams, I stumbled across a gym called Oxygeem in Herne Hill. A Nigerian bodybuilder and ex-amateur boxer named Pedro had recently opened the place inside a couple of renovated railway arches. Since the opening, things hadn't gone too smoothly.

'See this 'ere,' said Pedro, pointing to a scabby two-inch gash over his left eye. 'Last week two brothers wielding a gun and a baseball bat came by looking for some guy. They didn't find what they were looking for so they decided to take their frustration out on me. What's wrong with black people? Why are we always preying on each other? They wouldn't have done that shit if I was a white guy.'

I felt for Pedro. His heart was in the right place. He wanted to 'give something back to the community' and what had he got for his troubles? A good hiding.

'I see so much talent, so much potential on these streets,' he went on, 'but most of it goes untapped. If I can just get through to, say, five per cent of these guys I'll be on to something.'

I gave Pedro the spiel about wanting to be a fighter. He was impressed with my gumption and said he'd willingly give me a shot as an amateur. But I insisted my one and only fight would be as a pro. Typically, he thought I was pushing my luck.

'To be a professional fighter, you've got to want it more than anything else in the world,' he warned. 'It comes before everything – your wife, children, everything. That's how much sacrifice and dedication it takes.' I thanked Pedro for his time and consideration and hit the road, still searching for that elusive break.

My next port of call was the Henry Cooper on the Old Kent Road.

The gym had a familiar air – a speedball drumming rhythmically; the syncopated rat-tat-tat-tat of two men skipping, their ropes slicing the air like bullwhips; the cracking and smacking of fists and pads and bags colliding. Frank Warren's right-hand man Dave Lewis, whom I knew through Michael my photographer friend, had arranged for me to interview a twenty-eight-year-old fighter from Tottenham named Mark Prince at the gym. Mark was the undefeated WBO Intercontinental light-heavyweight champion and number one contender to fight the Polish-born WBO world light-heavyweight champion, Darius Michalczewski. More importantly for me, he was a born-again Christian and as such I thought he might be able to shed some light on the curious connection between boxing and religion.

When I spoke to Mark earlier that day to confirm our meeting, he answered the telephone as though he were in a trance. I thought that perhaps I had stirred him from a mid-morning nap. 'No, you didn't wake me,' he said languidly. 'I was just reading my bible.' Mark punctuated our brief conversation with words such as 'peace' and 'love' – I had seen little of either in the prize ring.

I waited for an hour in the claustrophobic gloom of the gym, but there was no sign of Mark. The Henry Cooper stank of boxing: BO, stale sweat, saliva from spittoons, and the aroma of piss from the lavatory without a door. Frankly, the place was a shithole. Nevertheless, despite the stench, stepping into the Henry Cooper was a breath of fresh air compared with the sterility of the Peacock. After all, fighters didn't come here to admire the decor. It was a grotty little place with one ring and barely enough room to swing a cat let alone a right hook. A small floor area and a little alcove were crammed with mainly black fighters, shadow boxing, skipping and doing groundwork. Bags bore the scars of a million punches from a thousand fighters. Layers of dust and grime gave the pictures and posters on the wall a faux patina of age. Boxers bobbed and weaved their way around the tight space in balletic fashion, their movements synchronised to avoid collision with one another. The rawness of the gym seemed to complement the fighters' hardness. The equation was simple: tough gym did equal tough fighters.

I was about to leave when I noticed a lean, light-skinned black guy in his late thirties arrive. Within seconds he was collared by a battered-looking character with dark, leathery skin who looked like a lizard coated in creosote. The lizard man was complaining about something. He was so punch-drunk he seemed to hum rather than speak. As he resonated, I made out patches of conversation, but it was mainly a hum, like an electricity sub-station on a wet day. I heard the lizard man mumble something and then say, 'Hmmm . . . yeah, Carlie . . . um . . . you know'm sayin' . . . um.' I recognised the name Carlie [Carew] from newspaper reports as Mark's trainer, so I introduced myself.

'If he ain't here by three o'clock you've probably missed him,' said Carlie breaking away from the lizard man. 'It's a long way and a lotta traffic from Tottenham to here.'

Carlie was one of only a handful of black trainers in the country. He had taken a familiar route into boxing but had also studied a number of martial arts. He was cynical and self-opinionated, but also knowledgeable, clever, witty and refreshingly candid about the fight game. 'I don't give a fuck about the politics of boxing,' he said, voicing his contempt for boxing's mandarins. As I continued to wait for Mark Prince, Carlie and I chewed the fat. I was impressed by his knowledge of philosophy, art and science, subjects more attuned to the salons of west London than a flesh factory on the Old Kent Road. I asked Carlie whether someone off the street, someone with no talent, someone like me, could become a pro fighter.

'If you've got heart and you're dedicated, sure, why not?' he said. 'There are plenty of guys out there who can do the most press-ups, sit-ups, burpees, miles of running and all that shit. But if you haven't got the attitude, the will to win, all that training don't mean nothin'.' Maybe I was on to something here. 'Listen, brother,' he added. 'It's the trainers who win or lose a fight for a fighter. If you've got some idiot in your corner, you're finished.'

Carlie excused himself and stepped into the ring to take a middleweight, Maurice Forbes, on the pads. 'No one wants to fight Maurice,' said Carlie, slipping through the ropes. 'He's too rough.' As the pair worked together, Forbes struck me as mean, unforgiving and so hungry his punches groaned like a starving child when they connected with his target. I had seen him fight two weeks earlier in Brighton; he had destroyed a guy called Danny Quacoe inside the distance.

Carlie called the Henry Cooper authentic. He was right. The gym oozed with soul; not the music kind, but a kind of spirituality, devotion, love, worship that comes from tortured men with hearts of steel. It also had the blues. Desperation was written on many of the charred faces of Cooper's fighters. The place was as depressing as it was inspirational. Hard was as good as it got.

I waited a little while longer but Mark Prince never showed up for the interview. It was typical of many fighters to do that. They occasionally became moody, aloof or just plain forgetful for no apparent reason. Mark was not the first or the last fighter to stand me up for a meeting. I had come to realise that fighters were flaky when it came to appointments. Time was relative, contextual. The attention to detail most fighters displayed through the discipline of daily training, anal preoccupation with weight, physical aesthetics and vanity did not stretch to timekeeping, unless money, sex or some form of instant self-gratification were involved. To a fighter, anything that was not immediately important was unimportant and thus forgettable.

The following week I returned to the Henry Cooper to track down the elusive Mark Prince and persuade Carlie Carew to take me on as a novice fighter. I thought as Carlie had shown some interest in my idea that I could work with him. But Des, one of the regulars, told me he had gone walkabout in the Gambia or some place. He just upped and left. Nobody at the gym knew why or for how long, or if they did, they weren't telling.

'You can't fight . . . you're not a fighter,' said a guy shadow boxing in the ring as I told Des about my project and explained that I desperately needed a trainer.

'Don't listen to him, he's nuts,' said Des. The shadow boxer kissed his teeth and continued to bob and weave round the ring. He came over to the ropes, spitting distance from where we were standing.

'What makes you think you can fight, eh?' he said, panting and trying to look menacing. 'You look too soft. What . . . do you want to be one of those manufactured fighters, like Bruno?'

'No. But what makes you such a great judge of character?' I said and he kissed his teeth again and danced off muttering something about fighters being born not made.

'Don't worry about that idiot,' said Des. 'He's just bitter 'cos he's not making any money out of the game. What part of London you from?'

'Ladbroke Grove, Shepherd's Bush,' I said.

'Why don't you try the All Stars club on Harrow Road,' said Des. 'It's a good amateur club and it's near where you live. I'd go and do some training at an amateur club first if I were you.'

Des explained that he had trained as an amateur at All Stars and said they had a good track record in regional and national competitions. He suggested it might help me to learn a few basic skills at an amateur club first so that a professional trainer would not have to spend aeons going through the rudiments of boxing with me.

I left the Henry Cooper and hit the road again. Des's advice seemed like a useful strategy but I didn't have time for amateur boxing on a competitive level. That would defeat the whole object of the exercise. I just wanted one professional fight. Nevertheless, time was passing me by. I had nothing to lose, except a few brain cells maybe, by going to All Stars.

chapter 7

All Stars was located in a schizophrenic part of London. It lay on the
split personality of Harrow Road, an area where the stucco façades and
BMWs of 'swinging' Notting Hill sat uncomfortably close to the
tenement buildings and burnt-out Ford Fiestas of North Kensington's
housing estates. It was a place where the chattering classes lived in the
lap of luxury with their Palm Pilots™ and Agnes B outfits while petty
crooks and crack-addicts prowled the streets at night in search of rich
pickings. The neighbourhood had a decadent, ghetto chic about it.
Minor celebrities and record company execs rubbed shoulders with
prostitutes and drug dealers. Yardies and gay barristers shared a Red
Stripe and a spliff in the local shebeen. And for two days of the year
when the Notting Hill carnival came to town, everyone got to play the
nigger for a weekend, even the cops.

A faded sign nailed to one side of a pair of heavy double doors gave
the game away. From the outside, All Stars looked like just another
rundown Victorian Presbyterian church. At the bottom of the stairwell
was a poster of a forthcoming boxing show featuring the British
heavyweight champion Julius Francis and my old mate Takaloo. What
had happened to him, I thought? I climbed a flight of concrete steps,
went through another set of double doors and was in the gym. The
interior was bigger than I imagined and it reminded me of the crummy
under-funded youth clubs I went to as a boy. A stocky guy was
pummelling at a bag just behind the door as I entered.

'Who's in charge of this place?' I asked with unconvincing cockiness.
Without ceasing his medley of speedy body shots to the bag, he glanced
over his shoulder and nodded in the direction of a highly animated
Buddha-like figure across the other side of the gym.

I introduced myself to the Buddha. He was cracking jokes with some
trendy looking characters who didn't seem like the usual boxing meat.

He gave me a firm but gentle handshake and smiled as I went into a monologue about my book.

'Aha! So you wannabe a boxer,' said the Buddha in a soft west African accent, still holding my hand. 'You better lose some weight then. Ha, ha, ha . . .' He dug his fingers into my podgy stomach.

The Buddha was Isola Akay or Mr Akay or just Akay as many people in boxing knew him. Apart from the onset of middle-age spread, Akay was an extremely fit and vibrant sixty-two-year-old. How did he keep in such good shape?

'Daily exercise,' he said, 'and I've never drunk alcohol or smoked.' This simple rule made him look genuinely ten years younger. A testament to his youthful vigour was his second wife Terri, who was little more than half his age. They had two sons aged five and thirteen. Akay also had four children from his first marriage, one of whom, TJ, fought Evander Holyfield in the 1984 Olympics.

Akay was a former oil engineer with Texaco. He came from what he described as a 'respectable middle-class family' in Ghana and started the gym in 1974 on a shoestring as a diversion for the local youths. Having piled his own time and money into the club for many years he eventually went to the Sports Council in search of £100,000 needed to renovate the building. They told him he could have 'matching funding', i.e. they would give him £50,000 if he could come up with the equivalent amount. 'I went home smiling thinking I'd had a result until my wife said, "But where are you going to get £50,000 from?" I thought oh yeah, well . . . Anyway, I didn't sleep for four months. I sent begging letters to individuals, organisations, anyone, to raise the money.' Thanks to Akay's dogged determination, money came in from a variety of sources, mainly wealthy private individuals who were impressed with his chutzpah. All Stars managed to survive on these handouts, grants and subs from the amateurs. But the regular money spinner was the KO circuit – a two-hour regime especially tailored toward local yuppies who wanted a professional fighter's workout without the jaw-breaking physical contact of regular boxing training.

I wandered around the gym on a self-guided tour of the scores of dog-eared posters from boxing magazines, drawings and faded photos of club shows that lined the walls. Apart from providing that touch of nostalgia that is incumbent in old boxing gyms, the ephemera covered the peeling paint and flaking plaster. The windows were blacked out with sheets of canvas not only to prevent the fighters from gazing out into the urban sprawl outside, but also to stop the prying eyes of travellers on the passing double-decker buses from peeking in.

'You're a bit late for this evening's class,' said Akay. 'Why don't you come back tomorrow and do the KO circuit. You can learn the basics in KO – how to throw punches, move, etc – so you don't make an idiot of yourself when you start working with the fighters. Hahahahahaha . . .' Me, make an idiot of myself? Come on . . .

The combination was two left jabs, followed by two right hooks. The moment I went to swing the right, Colin took a quarter of a step back and raised his arms.

'Shit,' I said. I knew instantly I had screwed up by leading with the right.

'Again,' shouted Colin. 'Four straight punches . . . six straight punches . . . eight straight punches . . .' My arms were flailing wildly. The black dots on Colin's pads, centred inside the white target area, grinned at me, egging me on to hit them harder, faster. 'One left jab, one straight right. Four straight punches.'

'Shiiiit!' I screamed.

'I'm gonna slap you in a minute,' barked Colin raising his right paw up momentarily which drew me into an embarrassing loss of balance as I leaned forward and missed the target. Once again, tiredness had affected my concentration.

'Get it right, you prick. Left right, left right. Military fashion,' I said to myself. Colin went through another drill.

'One left jab, one right hook. One left jab, one right hook. Four straight punches, six straight punches. Eight straight punches.'

I didn't have a clue how to throw a punch, not a proper one anyway. The street corner scraps and bar-room brawls I had encountered in my youth were an inadequate preparation for boxing. Until now I had had no appreciation of the finesse required to execute accurate, clean punches.

Boxing, it can be argued, is a question of style. And of course, I had none. It also has a lot to do with balance, footwork, distance and the distribution of maximum punching power with minimum physical effort. I didn't have any of these skills either. When a regular Joe throws a punch he remains stationary, extends his arm and makes a motion similar to pulling the handle of a slot machine or a beer pump in a country pub. This sort of arm punch is little more effective than a good backhand slap. But when a boxer throws a punch, the energy of the punch begins in the tips of his toes and moves through the legs, hips and shoulders as he twists his entire bodyweight into the blow. The punch is given greater efficacy by turning the arm (anti-clockwise for the right and clockwise for the left) and twisting the fist some four inches before contact is made with the target (in most cases an opponent's face). By twisting the arm it locks it into position creating a stiffer, harder blow with greater resistance than if the arm is bent.

There are around eight basic types of punch a fighter can throw, and learning each one is deceptively difficult. Harder still is moulding them into combinations of punches while also maintaining correct form and balance, using effective footwork and coordinated movement, and also blocking, slipping, dipping, ducking, bobbing and weaving and countering an opponent's punches for a full three minutes per round.

After two hours of what seemed like sheer hell, I was drained of all energy. The KO circuit was designed to be an authentic example of a fighter's workout for wasters like me. 'Hit and not be hit!' proclaimed the KO flyer. On average around twenty people took part in the sessions which Colin, a thirty-nine-year-old ex-amateur with fifty-one fights to his name, and two or three other trainers ran from 7.30 p.m. to 9.30 p.m. on Monday to Thursday evenings and Saturday mornings. The amateurs and a couple of pros trained from 5.30 p.m. to 7.30 p.m. on Monday to Friday evenings.

Apart from overseeing the KO class, Akay handled two professional fighters – an Egyptian and a Syrian. Since becoming a professional coach, Akay was prohibited by the rules of amateur boxing from coaching amateur fighters. My game plan was to fast track my way through a few KO sessions, train with the amateurs for a couple of months, convince Akay I was good enough to turn pro, and then bingo, have the fight. Theory is always easier than practice.

The KO circuit was my induction into boxing training. The sessions consisted of a 20-minute warm-up and stretch; 4 x 3 minute rounds of skipping; 4 x 3 minutes of hammering the punch bags; one round on the pads with a trainer; 5 x 3 minutes shadow boxing (with and without a partner); 15 minutes' weights exercises; 15 minutes of groundwork (press-ups, sit-ups, squat thrusts, etc.); 15 minutes warming down and stretching.

During my first session, after the warm-up and stretch I was called into the ring along with four other novices. For about fifteen minutes Akay went through the rudiments of boxing: maintaining a correct stance, holding a guard, throwing a jab and a straight right, pivoting, slipping, bobbing, weaving and rolling under punches. Part of the warm-up routine at All Stars was going through these moves, which were then worked on in greater detail throughout the sessions on a variety of bags, on the pads and while shadow boxing.

The clientele of the KO circuit was a ragbag of social misfits and social climbers. You had Rastafarian dykes; fat teenagers sent by their parents to shape up or ship out; bored housewives; local bad boys; the odd film producer or TV presenter; businessmen; a *Sunday Times* journalist; even a doctor from the A&E department.

All Stars was a victim of the modern era. The number of registered amateur boxers in England had crashed from over 100,000 in its glorious heyday in the 1960s to just under 9,000 in the latter part of the 1990s. Boxing, on the Harrow Road at least, was more popular with the liberals and trendies than the street kids who used to flock to the club for some sanctuary from the inner city mayhem outside. The previously passive middle-classes, ever fearful of street attacks, muggings and the well-publicised if phantom menace of 'Rolex robbers' who targeted the local rich and famous from St John's Wood to Notting Hill, were now arming themselves with self-defence techniques, martial arts and of course boxing skills. Perhaps if legislation allowed, these same people would carry Saturday Night Specials and mace spray.

'The black kids don't want to come in here and train any more like they used to,' said Akay. For nearly two decades All Stars had a reputation for being predominantly black. Boxing once served as a lifeline for a certain kind of black male, for a black male who is very brittle, for a black masculinity that is very fragile. But times were a-changing. 'Years ago, when I first started the gym, I used to get a lot of black guys in. But now, as you can see, most are white and not just guys. The black guys, they hang around on the street.' His expression darkened as he added, 'Now that they've got guns, what do they want boxing for?' While there was still a decent representation of African and African-Caribbean boxers in the club, Akay was noticing greater interest from local Arabs and Asians than from the surrounding black community.

'I think Naz has probably been a role model, an influence on these guys, which is why so many of them are getting into boxing. But young blacks have plenty of role models in boxing and still they don't come in the numbers you'd expect in an area like this.' Akay had a thing about role models. 'Lennox [Lewis] drives by here, he gets his hair cut just up the road, but will he come in and say hi to the youths here? No! He knows there's a gym here but he doesn't come. "Why is that?" I ask myself. The likes of him and Bruno, all these guys, why don't they go back to their roots?'

Lewis, the WBC heavyweight champion, had opened a college for disadvantaged youngsters in Hackney in the early 1990s. He had reputedly set it up with £1 million of his own money and maintained its running costs with 10 per cent of his purse winnings. But despite Lennox's apparent goodwill, the college had foundered and run into debt. Attempts by Lewis's people and two local authorities to save it failed. Now it's a training camp for fighters.

I had completed my first two-hour circuit, just. Colin said it was harder than the workout the amateurs did earlier in the evening. I just wanted to get home, eat and soak my aching body in a bath of salts. I exchanged a few pleasantries with Akay and promised to return in a few days' time.

'Hey, strong man. You can't get enough?' he said, feigning some body shots to my ribs. Trudging down the concrete stairs to the street below, I noticed Colin was shadowing me, like a security guard escorting an unwanted guest out of a private members' club.

'So how was that for your book, then?' he said, sarcastically.

'I want to go all the way,' I replied. 'I want to fight.' The matter-of-factness of my reply had not registered.

'Oh, you wanna do some sparring do you?' said Colin, assuming the depth of my research was as thin as the paper the book would be written on.

'Oh no,' I said. 'I want to fight . . . for real.'

'Hmmm,' said Colin, still unimpressed and feigning indifference. With that I was out on the street and he was halfway back up the stairs.

'See you on Saturday,' I called up, like an eager Boy Scout trying his best to show enthusiasm for his new troop. He was already gone, lost in the darkness of the staircase. Echoing from the top of the stairs, I thought I could hear Colin 'hmmming' in response to me.

That evening's training session was the toughest I had encountered since the masochistic cross-country runs of my schooldays. I began to doubt my capability of going the distance. I thought I was tough, but Colin and the guys at All Stars made me feel as if I'd walked into the gym in a mini skirt, fishnet stockings and high heels. I crawled home and called Mark Prince on his mobile.

'Hi Mark. It's David Matthews. Remember me? The journalist.'

'Oh yeah. You're the guy doing the book. Dave [Lewis] told me about it. Yeah, right.'

I reminded Mark that we had spoken three times already on the same subject and asked him, politely, why he had stood me up several times. Suffice it to say he offered some feeble excuses and changed the subject. I didn't discount the possibility that maybe he was simply displaying early signs of *pugilistica nervosa*.

'I'm leaving tomorrow to train with Carlie in LA,' he said abruptly. 'But look, when I get back from Germany with the world title, we'll sit down and talk.'

'Maybe I'll come out there and help you bring it back,' I said, sounding like an ingratiating creep.

'Yeah, yeah, whatever,' he replied and the line went dead.

The Michalczewski fight was on. For the next couple of weeks, Mark would complete his pre-fight preparation at Freddie Roach's Hollywood gym in California. He was then bound to head straight to Germany and spend a few days there before his showdown with the thirty-year-old champion at the Oberhausen Arena. If I were to get to Mark before the fight, I'd have to get on a plane and fly somewhere. He had given me the slip so many times that I had become mildly obsessed with meeting him, if only to satisfy my own sense of dogged determination.

For the first time in living memory I had cash at my disposal so the following day I arranged a press pass for the fight and booked a return plane ticket to Dusseldorf.

chapter 8

Dusseldorf airport, 18 September 1998. I managed to clear customs and immigration without the indignity of a strip-search or having my bag dissected for cannabis, forged travel documents, weapons-grade plutonium or whatever it was the control freaks of fortress Europe were currently paranoid about. The last time I was in Germany, back in '91, I had had a particularly humiliating experience at Munich airport with a sniffer dog, a customs officer and a pair of rubber gloves. I was keen not to repeat the episode.

I caught the 14:05 train from the airport, which was due to arrive in Oberhausen at 14:41. My ticket seemed to indicate that the train was leaving from platform 1a but as my German only extended to 'ein Big Mac und regular fries s'il vous plaît' I had to take a chance on which rattler to catch. I eventually caught the 14:05 with seconds to spare. That old cliché about German trains running like clockwork is for real. In fact, the rail network is so punctual, when you call the speaking clock in Germany, a rail announcer instead of a recorded message gives you the time.

The cloud cover hung heavy over Oberhausen, enveloping the town in a steady, irritating drizzle as the train pulled in. Like its people, Oberhausen was pallid and grey. It had the zest and vigour of a drunk tramp lying in a shop doorway. Twenty miles south of Dusseldorf, Oberhausen was the subdued home of Europe's largest shopping mall, the Centro. It seemed a remorseless venue for a world championship fight.

I caught another train on an elevated light railway and four stops later reached the Oberhausen Arena. The arena and the adjacent mall rose out of the mist like a new Atlantis. I headed through the blanket of rain for the arena, which wasn't due to open for another three hours, and tried to sneak in and get a view of it in all its 12,000-seater glory.

Every entrance was locked, so I made for the mall.

Inside the mall was a glittering array of retail outlets. Five storeys of stores stretching as far as the eye could see. Now I realised why the streets of Oberhausen were deserted. The townsfolk were all in the shopping mall for the day. Outside it was pissing down with rain. Inside it was pissing down with people – thousands of them meandering through miles and miles of thoroughfares lined by hundreds of stores crammed with even more shoppers. The sheer volume of people and the titanic scale of the place was sickening. I wanted to throw up on the excess of consumer greed.

After walking aimlessly around killing time until the big fight, I took a breather at one of the many fountains-cum-marbled-squares in the mall. Just as I was wondering whether to indulge myself in another bratwurst I noticed a young trendy black couple walk past the fountain. Apart from the odd Turk, I hadn't seen any outlanders since I'd left the airport. I started following the couple and within seconds, Carlie Carew joined them. He caught sight of me and did a double take. 'What the . . .' He was genuinely surprised to see me and I was pleased to make contact with a familiar face; especially as I didn't have a hotel room for the night. We exchanged salutations and carried on cruising through the crowds.

'We're going to get some lunch. Some Chinese food and shit,' said Carlie. 'Why don't you come and hang with us for a while?'

'Sure, why not? By the way, where's Mark?' I inquired.

'Over there.'

Carlie pointed to a tall lean figure about twenty feet away wearing dark sportswear and striding towards the exit of the mall. As Mark bounded through the crowds, he parted a Red Sea of wallets and shopping bags for his posse of supporters to follow. I entertained myself with the idea that here was the boxer as Moses, leading his people to the Promised Land of the WBO championship belt. I ran ahead of the group to catch up to him.

'Hey Mark, so we finally meet,' I said.

'Uh?' Mark grunted as he unplugged himself from his Walkman.

'Sorry,' I said, extending my arm. 'I'm David Matthews, the journalist, the guy writing the book, remember?'

'Oh yeah, right. What ya sayin'?'

Mark gave me a nonchalant handshake and carried on bounding along like a man on a high-speed mission. He was accompanied by an all-black posse which included his best friend and fellow fighter Cham

Joof; Carlie; a brick public convenience called Colin who had biceps like legs of lamb – his muscles were so pronounced that when he flexed them he looked like Popeye on steroids; a mean-looking bald-headed dude; KC, who was one of his three seconds; and his sister Natalie.

'What do you think of Germany, Mark?' Clever interviewers always ask a few dumb questions first to relax the interviewee.

'Germany sucks,' he said scornfully, plugging himself back into the Walkman.

'Germans are lame, man,' he added.

'Are you looking forward to the fight?' I asked as we continued to speed through the shopping centre like a group of steamers on a Network Southeast train.

'How can I not be looking forward to becoming world champion?' said Mark abruptly. Ask a silly question I suppose . . .

We eventually reached the Chinese restaurant, a gauche pagoda-style affair just outside the mall. There was an uncomfortable silence as we sat at the table and pored over the menu. Everyone opted for the all-you-can-eat buffet. Apparently the others had had it the previous day and it had not resulted in salmonella poisoning.

It was typical all-you-can-eat fare, no better than the high-street junk you find in most Chinese takeaways in Britain. The prawn balls spewed grease with each bite. Glutinous concoctions of meat resembled chicken but tasted unconvincing. Everything was mixed with cashew nuts, green peppers, bean sprouts, egg fried rice and noodles. It was cheap and cheerful, lousy food laced with MSG and that all too familiar flavour of salty sludge that's best consumed after eight or nine pints of vodka and half an ounce of skunk weed. It was the kind of food eaten by students, bedsit neurotics, self-haters and people who believe that eating is a form of substance abuse. Surely second-rate Chinese food was the last thing a first-rate contender should eat hours before a big fight? Strange food, strange country – it didn't fit.

Mark took a bite from a mountain of food piled up on his plate from the buffet. He checked himself for a moment, realising he had made something of a *faux pas*, said a quick grace under his breath and resumed eating.

'I hear Roy Jones is running scared from him,' said the bald guy referring to Darius Michalczewski.

'Hmm. Roy Jones?' I said.

'What's his record?' asked Baldy. I quickly flicked through my copy of *Boxing News*. Second paragraph down it read '12 defences'. Further down it said '37–0'.

'Thirty-seven and zero?' gasped Baldy. 'Shit.'

More uncomfortable silence gripped the table for thirty seconds or so. Thirty-seven and zero. That's thirty-seven wins and no defeats – a very impressive record. Mark's in comparison was eighteen zero.

'The guy's got experience,' said Baldy. 'And he can fight, too.' The bald one was the only person doing the talking and the conversation had taken a downward turn. Considering his man was hours away from the most important fight of his career to date, the pessimistic tone of the conversation needed a little uplifting. I thought now might be a good time to broach one of Mark's pet subjects, religion.

'How do you reconcile your religious beliefs with the violence of boxing?' I asked as Mark feasted on microwave prawn toasts, preheated noodles and chicken wings. Now you throw in the smart questions, see.

'That's easy,' said Mark. 'I've thought that one through a lot. It used to be hard for me to give an answer but now I know. God has put us here for different reasons and I know that God has chosen me to do my work through boxing. That's why I don't feel no way about doing what I do.

'I really don't know if God would say it's fitting to hit someone in the ring,' he added, 'but it's my job and I do not fight outside the ring.'

I had heard other fighters speak in this vein about religion and boxing. Danny 'the Brixton Bomber' Williams, an up-and-coming heavyweight I had eventually met at the Peacock, told me he saw himself not so much as a Christian but as a 'man of God'. He had an ambition to learn the bible in Hebrew and 'become a more spiritual person' – and British champion. He too felt that boxing was a vocation chosen for him by a higher being.

Muhammad Ali popularised the link between religion and boxing with his conversion to Islam back in the late 1960s. Since then a cavalcade of well-known current and ex-fighters, including George Foreman (the 'Punching Preacher'), Mike Tyson and Chris Eubank (both converts to Islam), Ernie Shavers (another puncher-turned-preacher who ministers in the north of England) and British heavyweight champion Julius Francis, all publicly profess their belief in and allegiance to God.

Religion and boxing – what a strange mix. Writers, commentators, critics, aficionados, me, we have all dismissed this pervasive aspect of the fight game as trite and banal. Fighters were apt to say at the end of a fight '. . . and I'd like to thank God for getting me through this fight. Praise the Lord . . .' or some such standard religious acknowledgement. Had we become so cynical about religion that we just accepted these protestations as the ramblings of men we already thought were crazy for being fighters in the first place?

Still it was safe to say that boxing was riddled with more religious rhetoric than genuine divinity. Proselytes and heathens alike were apt to sermonise at an opportune moment in order to sell themselves or a fight. Don King watchers will recall how the shock-haired one, the undisputed Mephistopheles of boxing, waxed spiritual before the first epic Tyson v. Holyfield encounter. 'I have touched the hem of his garment,' said King referring to Holyfield. 'Evander Holyfield said to me, "Believe in me and I will set you free." And he did set me free. I was a Tyson believer. But Evander has converted me. I was blind and now I can see.' Evander, as you may or may not know, is a devout Christian . . . albeit one with eight children from four different partners.

My own feelings toward religion are agnostic. Deep down I want to believe in God, an omnipotent force, call it what you will, but I could never get beyond the absurdity of the rambling contradictions and hallucinatory fantasies that permeate religious folklore. It is no coincidence that all the major religions (monotheistic or otherwise) originate from countries where opiates, cannabis, marijuana, magic mushrooms and various as yet undocumented narcotics are found in abundance.

Without getting on a Freudian trip, a lot of my religious scepticism stems from the teaching of my parents. Never were two people more diametrically opposed than my mother and father when it came to religion (or anything else for that matter. How they tolerated each other's absurd behaviour for nearly forty years beats me.)

My father, the product of a myopic Guyanese-Catholic upbringing (he is half Portuguese, half black) became an atheist when he was about twelve years old. It was at this age that he was once ordered to 'kiss the bishop's ring' as a sign of submission to his holiness. He promptly ran from the frocked one right on cue and received a severe caning for his troubles.

My mother's upbringing was that of the archetypal Negro Anglican – conservative, rigid, anally retentive. She had bought into all that colonial religious claptrap and while far from being a Sunday morning doorstepper, she was apt to try to instil in me as a young man the best spiritual hypocrisy the King James bible had to offer.

The less wholesome strains of Caribbean religion in those dark days of British imperialism were a mumbo-jumbo hotch-potch of bible scriptures, obeah, ignorance and sadistic cruelty. Religion then, much as it is now, was a means of control. Spirituality I can understand. I can appreciate and respect someone's beliefs when they say they have a 'personal relationship with God', even if it does sound a little wacky in the twenty-first century. But religion, the organised manipulation and control of one's spiritual and moral self, I don't know about that one.

I have a couple of close friends who are 'born again' and a buddy who has flirted with Buddhism. They have all at times tried the conversion number on me with zero effect. The closest I've ever come to buying into a religion was during my travels through North Africa and the Middle East. I met many very kind and genuine Muslims and on their advice bought myself a Koran to consolidate my growing interest in Islamic philosophy. I even ran into a perfume seller in Cairo who took me back to his shop and showed me pictures of himself with Muhammad Ali taken just after he had converted to Islam. Wearing a skullcap, growing a long beard and being pious seemed like a great idea . . . until I remembered I had a serious interest in sex, drugs and rock'n'roll which conflicted with the central tenets of most religions.

I wanted to believe, but I couldn't. Dependent on your point of view, I was either too weak or too strong to believe. Over the years, having borne witness to racism, social injustice and violence – and that was just in school – I took the hackneyed view that if there was a God he had a bloody good sense of humour because the world as I knew it was one big rotten onion. I was rational, reasonably intelligent, modestly educated and someone with left-leaning pretensions. I refused to accept tales of burning bushes, walking on water and reincarnation as anything other than allegory or metaphor. The world was a mess for Chrissake! OK, so Adam bit the apple and screwed it for the rest of us. But wasn't God supposed to be compassionate? Eight thousand years is a long time to hold a grudge.

'If I cut a man with a right hook, that's nothing,' continued Mark. 'The truth is people shouldn't be criticising what goes on in the ring. They should be criticising what goes on outside it. It's the promoters and managers. They're the ones responsible for bringing boxing down. To the promoters, fighters are just meat, pieces of meat.' Mark shook his head clearly revelling in his solemnity, as if he'd just given a sermon from the pulpit. His sister Natalie chipped in, 'Yeah, boxing's a meat market.' Hallelujah!

I could see Mark's angle. To him boxing was a form of muscular Christianity, a good, wholesome means of keeping fit, abstaining from vices (he used to smoke before he found the Lord) and earning a few bob. It had the whole Catholic guilt trip and Protestant work ethic rolled into one. Amen!

'We're a fucking side-show to these guys,' said Carlie, somewhat against the flow of conversation, '. . . a fucking joke.' He scanned the restaurant eyeballing the pasty faces of the German diners who made furtive glances in our direction. I could see what Carlie was driving at. The last time these people had seen so many blacks was when the Harlem Globetrotters were in town.

The after-dinner conversation continued its downward spiral after a brief squabble over how the bill should be split. In the end we all agreed to equal shares. It soon became apparent that there were more important unresolved financial problems in the Prince camp. Oh, and another thing, Mark hadn't signed a contract for the fight.

'What would you do if you were in my position, Cham?' asked Mark. Cham leant back in his chair and put his hands behind his head. He paused, rubbed his chin and rocked forward. Everyone around the table was looking at him in anticipation and you could see he felt pressured.

'You've got to weigh up the situation, Mark,' he finally said, trying to sound noncommittal.

'I know what you're saying,' said Mark, 'but I need to know what *you* think. What would *you* do?' As number one confidant, Cham was in a tight corner. With hours to go before the fight and Mark in a state of indecision, he had to be sensitive. In the end, his honesty saw him through.

'If it were me, Mark, I wouldn't go ahead with the fight without a contract.'

Mark leant back in his chair, clasped his hands together and nodded approvingly muttering, 'OK, OK.' He closed his eyes. 'Carlie, you with me on this? You know what I'm saying don't you?' said Mark abruptly.

I hit the buffet (for the third time) for my 18 Deutsch marks' worth of food. When a restaurant offers 'all you can eat', I eat all I damn well can. When I returned to the table a clandestine conversation was in progress. I soon made out that Mark was considering pulling out of the fight.

'You know I'm with you,' said Carlie. 'I'm with you all the way on this, brother. Whatever you wanna do, I'm behind you.'

With less than three hours to go before showtime, Mark had no contract. This was supposed to be the biggest fight of his career yet he had no idea what he was earning for it.

Frank Warren emerged from a doorway in the hotel foyer. He was casually dressed in a light brown, soft suede blouson, black slacks and an open-necked shirt. He looked almost human when not dressed in his usual garb of penguin suit, camel hair coat and snakeskin shoes, familiar from his big fight promotions.

Warren, followed by Dave Lewis, led Mark and Cham Joof into a secluded alcove near the reception desk. As the group disappeared, Warren twitched uneasily. He always did during moments of high anxiety. He had a peculiar way of nervously cocking his neck to one side like Jimmy Cagney in *White Heat*. He had strange mannerisms. His infamous handshake was a cross between a Masonic grip and being stroked with a wet fish.

Not everyone liked the way Warren did business. Someone had taken a pot shot at him outside a show at Barking Town Hall in 1989. Terry Marsh, the former fireman who became IBF light-welterweight world champion, was arrested in connection with the shooting but was eventually acquitted of the promoter's attempted murder. Ironically, the shooting revealed a tumour in Warren's neck of which he was previously unaware. Had he not have been shot, he may well have died of cancer.

Warren's luck, however, was being tested. His ongoing courtroom battles with Don King (which eventually cost him £7.2 million) had sapped his finances and were threatening his position as Britain's kingpin of boxing. Despite his problems, he still had the sense of humour to have the song 'Always Look on the Bright Side of Life' from Monty Python's *Life of Brian* playing on his telephone call waiting system.

The small group that had wandered over from the Chinese restaurant dispersed in the foyer.

'Why don't you come and chill with us for a while,' said Carlie, subtly directing me away from the lift as Mark and a couple of his entourage headed up to his room. I took the hint that my presence around the challenger would be less than appreciated as he prepared for the fight of his life and so I followed Carlie and KC up to their room. The wait seemed endless.

'The suspense is killing me,' I said fidgeting in the cramped Formica and chipboard twin room. 'All this waiting.'

KC lay sprawled out on the bed watching mindless images flash by on the cable TV. Carlie pottered around collecting bits and pieces and made a final check of all the equipment needed for the big fight. It all went into an oversized kitbag – shorts, gloves, hand wraps, boots, gumshields, socks, pads and sweats. Now his pre-fight preparation was done. He'd watched the videos of Michalczewski, packed the bags and gone through the game plan in his mind. Now all he had to do was wait.

My thoughts wandered to the man who'd soon be saying his prayers on the other side of the flimsy partition wall. What was going through Mark's head right now? Was it a mental dress rehearsal of him lifting the gaudy green and gold WBO belt while the announcer proclaims (in German of course): 'And the new light-heavyweight champion of the world is . . .' Or was he considering the possibility of defeat and all its implications?

As tempting as it was to knock on the door of room 116b and satisfy my curiosity about whether Mark was quaking in his boots or arrogantly punching holes in the walls mumbling 'die, Darius, die', I thought it better not to gatecrash his pre-fight ritual. Being nosy, intrusive and often uninvited was the stock in trade of the journalist, but so was living by your wits. Tension was mounting in the Prince camp and as I was without a hotel room for the night, I didn't fancy getting on the wrong side of Mark, Carlie and the gang, so I erred on the side of caution. Spending the night on a park bench in the pouring rain was not my idea of fun.

The fighters on the undercard were wheeled out into the arena with, to use a cliché, typical German efficiency. One by one they stepped into the ring concealing their nerves by bobbing, weaving and shadow boxing. They seemed to come and go on a conveyor belt of hope. Some went the distance, others didn't. A few hit the canvas, even fewer got back up. At a world title fight only the die-hard fans – the relatives, the drunken mates, the girlfriends and wives – gave a monkey's about the journeymen and the hopefuls. The undercard is the underbelly of boxing.

Minutes before the main event I collared Dave Lewis as he walked through the crowd. I liked Dave. He was young and ambitious but he wasn't a scumbag like so many of his contemporaries. He was always very accommodating with press passes, contacts etc. I figured if he could see some mileage in what I was trying to do, he could maybe sell the idea to Frank Warren. Now wasn't the best time to talk business but I made the pitch anyway.

'. . . so that's what I plan to do. What d'you reckon? D'you think you could fix me up with a fight?' Dave looked dumbfounded.

'Er, right. Yeah, er . . . we'll talk.' He smiled, shook my hand and took off into the sea of bodies at ringside before I could sell him the benefits of having a scholarly puncher like myself on Big Frank's books.

I settled back into my seat. The remaining fights on the undercard passed with little drama. Now it was time for the main event. Mark was the first to enter the arena. He came out to a rousing gospel number played over the thumping PA system and appreciative applause from the partisan crowd of 12,000 fight fans. As he sang and shook his arms out before slipping through the ropes into the ring, he looked fired-up yet composed for the big fight. Michalczewski, the champion and local hero, stepped through the ropes, cool as a genetically modified cucumber, to rapturous applause. After a tedious bout of introductions which included three national anthems (one for the American referee) the first bell sounded.

After a slow start, the fighter currently known as Mark Prince was partying like it was 1999. The first and second rounds were even, both fighters content to feel each other out with exploratory punches. Mark won the third and fourth rounds with a steady stream of punches and a high work rate. But following a cut over the right eye in the fifth, it all started to go progressively southwards.

'Listen to me, Mark,' said Carlie before the sixth round. 'You're burning up energy unnecessarily. Pick the openings.'

Darius had suckered Mark into his game plan. He allowed the challenger to do his best work early on in the fight while he conserved his energy for the later rounds. A championship bout is in some ways like a Test match in cricket – the objective is to score steadily over the duration of the contest. A four- or six-rounder is like a one-day match – score as many points or runs as quickly as possible. There is a particular art and strategy to both kinds of fight.

Approaching the end of the eighth round, Mark had all but punched himself out. In the dying seconds of an exhilarating bout he bounced off the ropes having just taken a right-hander clean on the jaw. He gave one last defiant roar, yelling 'Come on then like a football hooligan confronting a rival mob, before Darius poleaxed him with a text-book left hook. Mark slumped to the canvas, his head bouncing through the ropes and on to the ring apron. For a moment, it looked bad. Mark lay motionless.

'Don't let it turn into a wake. He did himself proud.' Ernie Fossey put his arm around KC as the pair tried to pull back from an early post-mortem of Mark's performance. Fossey was on the money with his remark as the atmosphere inside the dressing room after the fight was like a cold meat and cheese gathering.

Mark entered the dressing room accompanied by a small entourage. The mood was sombre. A male doctor and a female junior MD immediately tended to him. The woman, a redhead around thirty with chunky but attractive legs, was dressed in black and wore high heels. During the fight I had noticed her grimacing at the action as Mark was cut under the eye, and we exchanged flirtatious looks. Now, inside the dressing room her emotions almost got the better of her as her face contorted with an abject expression of compassion and sympathy. Her eyes welled up as Mark groaned under the pain of the stitches and his assorted cuts and bruises. I suppose it was professional ethics that stopped her from crying. The sense of loss was collective. In a small way, Mark's loss was our loss too.

His left eye was badly swollen, distorting his otherwise good looks. A halo of steam rose above Mark's head as the doctor started on the cut over his right eye. It needed six stitches to piece the brow back together. Laid out on the makeshift operating table, motionless and with slabs of grease and sweat swathed across the deep cuts on his eyes and cheeks, he looked like a corpse awaiting embalming.

'My head feels sore, man,' he groaned, slowly dragging himself up. His movement was laboured now, methodical in its economy. Gone was the jaunty pre-fight bounce, the expectation, and the confidence. I wanted to ask him, 'So where is your God now?' not to play devil's advocate or to advance my own cynical beliefs, but purely to provoke a reaction at this most intense of moments, to test his faith in God. Common sense, respect, fear and courtesy, however, kept me from overstaying my welcome.

'I feel like I've let myself down.' Mark was fighting back tears. 'I've let you all down who came here to support me.'

Time seemed to stand still in the dressing room as Mark's tough exterior began slowly to peel away revealing a vulnerable, broken young man. After the stitching he stood up and Cham embraced him. Mark mumbled something and a watery glaze covered his bloodshot eyes. He wore a tortured expression, like a red-hot branding iron was stuck in his back. His face crumpled up and he broke down in tears, consumed by the honesty of his emotions and the realisation of his defeat. Cham held him tightly like a loving brother, and our fallen hero, oblivious to the bystanders in the room, blurted and mumbled indistinguishable words of pain and sorrow and cried uncontrollably like a toddler who had just dropped his ice cream in the street. We were all frozen, lost for words.

Brendan Ingle appeared in the changing room dressed in a canary yellow tracksuit. His outfit was so loud it momentarily broke the silence. Ingle offered his commiseration to Mark and told him what a good fight he'd put up. I introduced myself to him and said I'd like to come to Sheffield to talk to him and Naz.

'Sure, come on up,' he said in his lilting Irish accent. 'But wait till after der Naz fight. We're busy with dat one at der moment. But gid me a call afterward.'

Several people were now vying for Ingle's attention, including some weirdo reporter from Holland who wrote occasional pieces for *Boxing News*. I don't think he was a *bona fide* journalist. He was just a fan with a notepad. I met some real anoraks who covered fights in exchange for a press pass and the opportunity to crawl up someone's backside. I was a union man, NUJ thank you very much, and I wasn't impressed with amateurs who put us pros out of business.

The Flying Dutchman popped up from time to time on the circuit. He always came out with dumb jokes that didn't have a punchline or non-anecdotes that trailed off into incomprehensibility. He started with one about how some guy fell off his stool or something, but Ingle, who nodded sympathetically to begin with, soon sussed what was happening and cut him short. 'Er, yeah, dat's great. Look, I got to go now. I'll see ya all later.'

This was the first time I'd been in a dressing room after a fight and seen at such close quarters the immediate after-shock of a fighter's defeat. The scene reminded me of what the American author Joyce Carol Oates wrote in *On Boxing*. 'Boxing is about failure far more than it is about success,' she had concluded. One day I would realise the profundity of those simple words.

Fighters failed in the end because they never knew when to give up. Boxing is the most hubristic of sports. Mike Tyson once said that the only way they'd get him out of the ring a loser was if he was carried out. 'I refuse to lose,' he said. Rocky Marciano retired undefeated, forty-nine and zero. Only death in a plane crash denied him an inevitable comeback. A real fighter had to be carried out on his shield. It was the way of the gladiator.

I wondered whether in the other dressing room somewhere on the other side of the arena Darius Michalczewski's thirty-eighth straight win had as much significance for him as the first taste of defeat had for Mark Prince.

As we strolled back to the hotel, disconsolate, strung out like a busted string of beads, I got talking to Carlie about Mark and the whole religion thing. I sensed that Mark's beliefs, while genuine and from the heart, were a tad naïve. He seemed to buy into the idea too readily, without question. However, I wasn't about to challenge him over matters theological, not at this point anyway. It seemed that broaching the subjects of transubstantiation, resurrection etc. with Mark would be a hard road to travel at the best of times. So soon after a defeat would be pointless, if not marginally dangerous.

'Mark's got his beliefs and you've got to respect that,' said Carlie. 'But he's very fixed about it. He's not prepared to listen to anything that strays from his way of thinking.

'While we were preparing for the fight in LA, he'd say to me the bible says this or the bible says that. Most of the time I wouldn't get into a discussion about these kinds of things. I'd just say, "Yeah, uh huh." Mark's got to realise that there are different ways of believing in something.

'Let me tell you a story. There's this guy, a devout Christian with an unfailing belief in God, and he's drowning in a lake. A guy comes along in a speedboat and says, "Hey climb in, I'll save you," but the drowning guy says, "No thanks. God will look after me."

'Then another guy comes along in a rowing boat and says, "Yo, climb in, I'll help you out," but once again the drowning guy says, "No thanks. God will help me." Then finally, as he's kicking around swallowing water, bubbles coming up and all, a man on a raft comes along and says, "Hey, I'll help you, climb aboard." But still the man in the water says, "No, God will see me through."

'Eventually, the man drowns and he goes up to heaven. When he gets to the pearly gates he says to the Almighty, "God, after all these years as your obedient servant, why did you let me die?" and God replies, "What are you talking about? Three times I sent someone to help you. What more do you want from me?" '

Carlie knew Mark's loss would reflect badly on him. 'I need to take a break from boxing, take a couple of weeks off maybe.' He sounded piqued. 'I wonder sometimes what motivates me to be in the fight game.' Mark had lost and God wasn't to blame. Carlie's strategy, whatever it was, had simply failed. So had Mark.

Carlie knocked on the door, it opened as if by remote control and inside sprawled around the room were Mark's contingent. Mark lay on the bed nearest the door, his hands propping up his swollen head. He bore the expression of an accused man whose trial had just ended and who was now awaiting the jury's verdict. The others looked equally sombre. Carlie stood in the doorway momentarily, arms holding the doorframe, head slightly bowed. When he walked in, I ventured two paces behind him, like an Arab's wife, into the characterless hotel suite. For a moment all eyes were on me and the collective suggestion of those bleak expressions was that entry into the dark atmosphere of the room was not a good idea. I gave an embarrassed smile and slunk out of the room.

I was humbled by Mark's loss and, more importantly, by the nature of it. It seemed as if the prayers, the belief, the genuflection to the Lord Almighty had brought no reward. Loss in boxing for the Christian was indeed a test of faith. Had Mark's God let him down, betrayed him in his hour of need? Where was the Almighty when Darius Michalczewski pummelled into him with vicious body shots and uppercuts?

Could boxing possibly bring me closer to God? Could I find what I'd been searching for all these years – inner peace, a sense of fulfilment, a spiritual awakening? I doubted it. Smashing someone's face in and Christianity, did they really mix? I wasn't entirely convinced. But standing in the lobby of a three-star hotel at 5.30 a.m. I was running out of energy for philosophising.

'Thanks again for your support, man,' said Mark, gesturing with a hand and turning it into an awkward embrace.

'Don't mention it,' I said. 'I'll be there next time, too.'

Disconsolate, head bowed in abjection, the Prince replied, 'Right now I don't know if there's gonna be a next time.'

I felt for the guy. He was twenty-eight years old and not far from being a leaner, fitter image of myself.

'Try not to look at it that way,' I said. 'You've got to bear in mind that you took the fight to this guy all the way from London, right into his own backyard, right into the ring. Shit, just imagine if it had been at White Hart Lane, in your backyard with your people there.'

The lack of sleep, the excitement of the fight, the flying, the travelling and a combined diet of soft cheeses, bratwurst, Chinese and airline food had liquidised my emotions. I told Mark that by the time he'd seen the video of the fight he'd be thinking differently about the future and considering a possible rematch with the German champion. Our cab rolled up and Mark, Carlie, KC and myself headed for the airport. The next thing I knew someone was tapping me on the shoulder and beckoning me out of the car.

'I'm sorry I couldn't bring back the belt for my people in the UK,' said Mark. We were going our separate ways for separate flights back to England. All I could muster was another 'don't worry about it, there'll be other opportunities' line.

'Hey, here's my number,' said Carlie. 'Give me a call when you're in London.' He scribbled down the number on the back of a cigarette packet and gave it to me. We all shook hands and Carlie, Mark and KC rushed to check in their baggage for the flight, which was making its final boarding call. I had a couple of hours to go yet, so I checked in and caught a few zeds in the departure lounge.

A few days later I called the number Carlie had given me and left a message on an answer machine with a woman's voice on it. I tried a few more times but I never got a reply. I later heard that Carlie had quit boxing for good.

As for Mark, he went into semi-retirement and did not return to the ring for another year, a stone heavier at cruiserweight. He won his comeback fight, against a nobody, but obscurity was beckoning him, too. One minute he was the number one contender in a world title fight, performing in front of 12,000 people. The next, he was just another face on the undercard of a small-hall show. All fighters know that boxing is a game of snakes and ladders – up one minute, down the next. After eighteen fights and eighteen wins, Mark had to learn the bitter truth about loss. He had his faith. He had his belief. Maybe fate would give him a second chance. After all, he understood that boxing, like God, moves in mysterious ways.

chapter 9

The Mark Prince fight inspired me to invest in a new leather skipping rope, a pair of 10oz bag gloves, a pair of black suede Adidas boxing boots and some bandages for my hands. I had to get a move on but although boxing was becoming a major component of my life, it was still far from an obsession. Lara thought otherwise. To her, boxing was diverting me away from the happy little family we had tried to construct out of our own insecurities. Lara accused me of 'turning into Mike Tyson'. In fairness, how could I, a reformed street rat, have expected someone from her background to understand for one moment what I was trying to do? She had had her house bought for her, her car bought for her, her life bought for her. She came from a perfect little whitewashed world. My world was dark. Where I was heading, where I came from, was a million miles from her. I should have seen it coming. I should have read it like a telegraphed punch. But I didn't.

About a year after Luca was born, Lara and I started going through what's usually known as a rough patch. My interest in boxing and my attempt to write a book didn't help the situation. Lara saw me as over-ambitious and insensitive; I saw her as over-dependent and insecure. Money was tight, but we were a damn sight better off than most folk we knew. Deep-seated issues of mistrust, resentment and insecurity (among many other problems) started plaguing our relationship and we eventually sought counselling with Relate. After two sessions I bailed out, having decided that scheduled muckraking was doing me more harm than good. Besides what the hell did I need counselling for? I sought inner peace by pounding a heavy leather bag or hitting the pads at the All Stars gym. Sooner or later I'd be working out my anxieties on someone's face. Counselling? Counselling highlighted unresolved issues that both of us, to a lesser or greater extent, harboured as individuals. These issues were not a consequence of our relationship but existed in spite of it. Our baggage was simply incompatible. Our own personal problems underlined our philosophical, cultural and moral differences. We had grown apart, not over months, but years. We thought naïvely, as many couples do, that a baby would bring us closer together and in some ways she did. I always thought that because Lara and I were born on the same day and in the same year we were soul mates, destined to be together forever. Life, however, cannot be lived with hindsight.

Lara continued with the Monday afternoon sessions on her own while I went about the business of, well, being a selfish pig, I suppose. Counselling had become Lara's Holy Grail. 'Me time' she called it. I didn't need counselling. I had boxing to console my thoughts and feelings – and my sessions didn't have to come to an abrupt end after an hour.

Things finally came to a head one afternoon in early October 1998. Lara, Luca and I were walking along Portobello Road when we ran into Tyrone 'Sugar T' Forbes, a former British middleweight amateur champion. Tyrone had won an ABA title while boxing for All Stars under Akay's tutelage and was well known and respected around Ladbroke Grove for his work in the community. In the past, he had helped me with research and contacts for features I had written on the local area, but his elusiveness meant I only ever saw him by chance. He never kept a telephone and was very rarely at home. I thought he could maybe help me with a few contacts in the boxing world so I made a beeline for him.

'Saved by the bell,' I mumbled, spotting Tyrone.

'What was that?' said Lara.

'Oh nothing, darling. I'm just going to have a chat with Tyrone over there. I'll catch up to you later.'

Tyrone was on a street corner holding court with a friend in his usual animated way, chatting about everything and nothing and putting the world to rights. He was one of those people who never ventured into the minutiae of small talk. A conversation with Tyrone was always about big issues, especially ones that either directly or indirectly affected the Ladbroke Grove community. With Tyrone, there was always something on the agenda. A quick chat was never an option.

I left Lara and Luca, promising to return in time for Lara to make it to Tottenham Court Road for her Relate appointment, and joined Tyrone on the street corner. After about twenty minutes of discussing some pressing local issues, I told him about my plan to become a fighter. He seemed surprised but interested and suggested I do some training with him. 'Come back to my yard and we can talk about it there,' he said. We headed back to his place a few blocks away on Elgin Crescent and chatted for a while about boxing, the state of the area, racism, etc. My mobile rang.

'David, where are you?' asked Lara with a hint of desperation. 'Remember, you're looking after Luca?'

'Don't worry. I'll be there in ten minutes.'

Half an hour later, Tyrone was still bending my ear. Tyrone eked out a living as a bouncer at a nightclub on the Finchley Road. He was not the archetypal lobotomised bodybuilding thug covered in tattoos. At thirty-eight, he was in good shape, lean and muscular, but not bulky. For an ex-boxer, door work was a natural sideline. There were very few practical skills a fighter could transfer from the ring to civvy street. Being 'handy' had its own currency in the murky world of nightclub bouncing.

Tyrone's dream was to win a world title but after four fights as a pro, a reckless driver shattered his hopes when he ran down Tyrone and his two children in the street near their home. Tyrone spent the next six months 'in an emotional abyss' of self-pity. The accident had left him bitter and resentful. Then one day, looking out of his bedroom window as he convalesced, he noticed a group of youths throwing stones, kicking cans and playing with hypodermic needles in the square below. He decided it was time to get off his arse and do something for the youths he saw wasting away on the streets in his neighbourhood. Thus began a decade-long battle with the government, local authorities and the Sports Council to support and fund a sports community project designed to get the youths off the streets. 'Organised play, not organised crime, was the motto,' he said. He also did odd bits of personal training of a self-defence nature. The nightclub's manager was one of his regular clients.

'Come down next Wednesday, around three o'clock,' said Tyrone. 'I'll be finished with John then and we can do a little workout.'

I made a mental note of the date and time and headed home. I was ten maybe fifteen minutes behind schedule – OK, maybe thirty. Lara was fuming.

'Thanks a lot,' she said. 'I'm going to be late for counselling because of you.'

'I'm pleased to see you too,' I replied. We were into the home straight now.

I kissed Luca on the cheek and sat her down for her dinner.

These were the best and worst of times. I had the part-time lecturing job on the go, bits and pieces of freelance work and, of course, a modest advance from my publisher to keep us going. Money was not a big problem, for a change. Thanks to the largesse of Lara's father, we had no mortgage to pay. With my income and our relatively low overheads, she could afford to stay at home and concentrate on looking after Luca, an arrangement we had mutually agreed. But sometimes human beings have a need to create problems for themselves, as if contentment were a sin to be punished.

Lara took off for her appointment cussing the ground I walked on. I rustled up a plate of food for myself and continued feeding Luca her dinner. Ten minutes later, Lara was back. We had spent so much time arguing about me being late, by the time she had got out of the house she was running too late to have any chance of making it to Tottenham Court Road.

As Lara strode into the kitchen her face was reddening with rage and white specks of saliva were brewing at the side of her lips. She picked up my mobile from the kitchen table, raised her arm and went to smash it on the floor.

'Oh come on, don't be silly,' I said. I liked to think that I tried to fight fire with water in these situations. Acting the cool cucumber in the face of someone going ape shit, however, can occasionally backfire, especially when you say, perhaps with a hint of condescension, something like, 'You're over-reacting. Why don't you calm down . . .'

'Don't tell me to calm down, you bastard.'

There was a brief stand-off. The atmosphere grew tenser. She started walking towards the kitchen door when, without warning, she turned, picked up my plate and tipped the lamb stew and three veg I was eating over my head.

'Hmm . . . that's nice,' I said.

Lara took Luca from her highchair into the conjugal bedroom. As I stood cleaning myself with a tea towel she returned to the kitchen, picked up my dinner plate and threw it at me. I decided to use a block rather than a duck or slipping motion to avoid having the plate open my face up like a tin of tomatoes.

'Oh that was really clever. Really fucking clever,' I said, noticing my arm, instead of my face, had opened up like a (very small) tin of tomatoes.

Lara grabbed Luca and her handbag and took off in a puff of expletives. I stood in the kitchen surrounded by my lunch, watching blood drip on to the floor. Gravy, bits of vegetable, meat and claret were splattered everywhere – behind the dishwasher, on the art deco fireplace, on the wall hanging from Habitat. Here I was, the fighter, KO'd in one by the missus, with a plate. I had to laugh at the absurdity of it all. I went to the hospital and a Pakistani doctor put two stitches in my elbow. I spent the night at a friend's place, just to let things calm down.

The following week, Lara and I had another blazing row, this time over whose turn it was to have a lie-in. It was the last hurrah. Children were dying of starvation the world over from Rwanda to East Timor. Hurricanes, earthquakes, tidal waves and forest fires were wiping out entire communities. Eight-year-olds in Glasgow dealt smack and fifteen-year-olds in America blew their schoolmates away with semi-automatic weapons. And we argued about who should feed the baby, not if we were able to feed the baby. We fought over the precious kingdom of the king-sized bed, not for the right to govern ourselves in our own land. We were soft. We were spoilt. We had a need to create adversity out of comfort. Eventually this need destroyed our relationship.

chapter 10

Lambeth College was the toilet seat of learning where I plied my trade three days a week as a part-time lecturer. It wasn't the best job in the world but I'd had worse. The college ran two journalism courses, one a sixteen-week NCTJ fast-track course and the other an NVQ course, which lasted a full academic year. The NCTJ was for university graduates only and attracted students whose ambitions lay in newspaper journalism. The NVQ was for anyone who could spell their name correctly and attracted unemployed bricklayers who had been press-ganged on to the course in Peckham High Street. Because of my inimitable skills as a journalist, teacher and guru, I taught on the NVQ course. From the outset, the Generation X of students I taught suffered from terminal apathy and cynicism. They labelled the NCTJ course élitist and routinely cursed their better-qualified counterparts while deriding their own NVQ as short for 'not very qualified'.

While the NCTJ was almost exclusively white, I had an ethnically diverse group that had the linguistic and cultural panache of the 'Mind Your Language' cast. I guess lecturing a bunch of deranged, apathetic and dysfunctional students was bad karma for all the mental torture I had put my teachers through at school. Job satisfaction was not high on the agenda at Lambeth College. The most rewarding thing about working there was going home at the end of the day.

Most of the time I bluffed my way through lectures relying on my charm, wit and the fact that the students didn't know (or couldn't care less) what the hell I was talking about. As far as they were concerned my seminars were a good crack, simply because the rest of the course was about as interesting as watching paint dry. For eight hours a week during my sessions, the students could talk any old bollocks, and that amused them. Unfortunately, my anarchic, self-expressive approach to education proved too challenging for much of the class, as out of eighteen students at the start of the academic year only eight survived the course. Well, eight survived the college to be precise – half of the remainder transferred to another journalism course. My pass rate, to say the least, was piss poor.

Very few students and even fewer of my colleagues were interested in sport let alone boxing but I didn't hold that against them. To them, as for so many people I met, boxing was an anathema. One exception was Antigone Forder, a lecturer on the NCTJ journalism course. Antigone was devoutly anti-boxing, but nonetheless interested in sport; she had to be considering she was married to a sportswriter with the *Independent*.

'I told Mike when he got the job, absolutely no boxing,' said Antigone one afternoon as we sat in the relative tranquillity of the staffroom. 'If he so much as turns on that TV and there's a hint of it, he's out on his cauliflower ear.' I wasn't sure whether 'got the job' meant with the paper or Antigone. By her own admission, she was no ring-card girl. Witty and intelligent, she looked every bit the college lecturer – comfortable shoes, hair in a bun, woolly cardigan, sort of corduroy chic.

Despite her distaste for boxing, Antigone was intrigued by my ambition to become a fighter. She was particularly curious about my physique and, more importantly, my weight.

'So, which weight are you going to fight at, light-heavyweight?' she asked with genuine interest.

'Well, I had considered light-heavy,' I said. 'And then cruiserweight. But . . .'

Antigone's rather pale complexion glowed. She started rocking on her tatty computer chair and then broke into a shriek of laughter, sending her chair wheeling backwards into the wall adjacent to her desk and then forwards again, slapping her thighs like a pantomime dame.

'What's so funny?' I asked but I knew exactly what had sent her flying – the word cruiser. To anyone familiar with the gay lexicon, the harmless mention of cruiser evokes a pre-pubescent tittering akin to the utterance of the word penis during sex-education classes, or bullocks in geography lessons on animal husbandry on the Indian sub-continent.

'I appreciate that cruiserweight does have a certain camp ring about it, which I'd rather not be associated with,' I said dryly. 'I think light-heavyweight would suit me better.'

'I think you're right,' Antigone giggled.

As much as I needed the money, working at the college was a real chore. I had taken on the lecturing job for the extra dough but also as a means of deflecting the 'why don't you get a proper job?' questions Lara had thrown at me before she started throwing plates. I hated teaching. It was a thankless task. Once I calculated time spent preparing lectures, setting exams and projects, marking papers and providing 'pastoral' services to the students, the money I earned bore no relation to the reality of my workload. I found it increasingly difficult to cope with the physical demands of training three, sometimes four, evenings a week in addition to lecturing and working as a freelance journalist – and I was still a long way off the level of fitness I needed to reach to have any chance of surviving in the ring.

On top of my All Stars training, I started doing one-to-one sessions with Tyrone on Wednesday afternoons. For starters, I would warm up with a couple of rounds of skipping. Now let me make something clear, skipping is not kids' stuff. To be able to skip like a pro took a lot of practice and energy. By this stage I was capable of skipping for three minutes at a time, almost without missing a beat. After the warm-up we'd rig up a ground-to-floor speedball in the basement and I'd run through a drill of punches to sharpen my rather blunt technique. Working round the speedball at right angles, Tyrone would have me throw ten left jabs, then ten straight left–right combinations, ten left hooks off the jab (a hook off the jab is simply a hook thrown immediately after a jab in one continuous movement), ten right hooks off the jab and so on and so forth. I would move on, doing pads, skipping and gruelling groundwork routines with a 15lb medicine ball. Tyrone thought I should ditch the weight-loss idea and box at heavyweight. Heavyweight? 'You'll be too fast for those guys,' he'd say. 'Look at your speed.' I was positive that Tyrone was using kidology on me. I couldn't box at heavyweight.

Every opportunity I had I tried to convince him that being my full-time trainer would be beneficial for both of us.

'I can't get involved in boxing right now,' he told me. 'Since I had the accident I can't go near a boxing gym, a ring, anything like that. You've got to realise that my whole world centred on that dream of becoming a champion. I wanted to be there with the Haglers, the Hearns and the Sugar Rays. My dream never came true. For a long time after the accident I wanted to have tear-ups with people in the street if I heard a bell from ringside. That accident traumatised me. I'm only starting to come to terms with the effects.'

Tyrone said that the trauma was such that for years he couldn't watch his fights on video, or any fight for that matter. He slowly progressed to watching fights with the sound turned down; such was the effect of the bell.

'It's medical. I have to deal with the flashbacks, the psychological trauma. When you've got a focus you can get locked in there. I've seen a sports psychologist about it but he got on this weird blood-lust trip,' said Tyrone, doing a nutty professor impression. 'He thought that I had some kind of obsession with violence, that I was psychotic or something. But I explained to him that I boxed because it was a sport that I enjoyed. He didn't understand. I don't think he wanted to understand.'

Neither love nor money were incentives to Tyrone. I tried to convince him that training me full time would do us both some good, but the unresolved issues surrounding his accident meant the task would be even harder for him than it was for me. Still, I was thankful for the few pointers he gave me on those Wednesday afternoons, which added to my overall slow progression.

It had been nine months since the Takaloo fight and the conception of this outlandish idea. But where was the baby, where was the fruit of my endeavours? After all this time, I had little to show for my efforts. The breakdown of my relationship with Lara had temporarily thrown me into a bottomless pit of apathy. I accepted that we were finished but what really ripped through me was my estrangement from Luca. Not seeing my daughter on a regular basis introduced me to a whole new era of psychological torment.

Gnawed by guilt and insecurity, my mind drifted from the task of becoming a fighter; mental fatigue soon led to physical breakdown. On more than one occasion I sprained my elbows overextending my arms while shadow boxing at the gym. Punching at thin air is not without its risks. A combination of bad technique, tension, anxiety and the lack of a solid object to cushion my frantic blows had been the culprit. I also sprained my right hand working on the heavy bag at the gym, got shin splints from skipping, injured my lower back about half-a-dozen times and twisted my ankle three times while running.

The gulf between the physical requirements and capabilities of a professional athlete and a Sunday afternoon kick-about slob were enormous. I realised this one morning while out running around the streets of west London, when my right knee collapsed halfway through my four-mile circuit; I thought my kneecap had slipped down to my ankles. I could barely walk. I had been aware of niggling pains in my knees for several months but had simply put this down to stress on the joints due to being overweight. I thought, naïvely, that once I lost weight the pain would subside. However, the injury was enough to put me out of action for a few weeks. I visited my GP and was referred to the local hospital for X-rays and an examination. I never made the appointment. Finding out I had rheumatoid arthritis was the last thing I wanted to hear at this stage. I figured the injury was a sign that I was overdoing it and took a sabbatical from training while I tried to make some sense of my life. Consequently my weight went up and my stamina went down.

I was like a rusting 1984 Nissan Sunny with a Lotus V8 twin valve engine; it wouldn't be long till a door or the odd bumper fell off. The will was there, somewhere, but the body just couldn't handle the pace. To give myself an extra boost I became a vitamin junkie and started pumping myself with a medley of vitamins, herbal remedies and supplements. Over the course of four weeks I spent around £150 on a variety of pills, most of which seemed to have no noticeable effect.

I'd usually start the day with a 1000mg of vitamin C; one cod liver oil capsule; 1000mg of anti-oxidants (vitamins A, D, E, etc.); 3 x 320mg tablets of brewer's yeast (rich in riboflavin, niacin and thiamine) – by the end of the day I would've taken six more of these; 100mg of kelp, for iodine; and 10ml of ginseng royal jelly. I even took St John's Wort to ease any depressive tendencies.

I tried using 5mg of creatine before and after workouts as a booster but soon stopped after reading in the *Guardian* that college football players in America were dying from taking it. I tried a soya protein powder supplement mixed with skimmed milk and bananas. I took massive 1250mg tablets complete with 'Growth Hormone Releasing Factors' four at a time. They were designed to increase muscle tissue while burning off excess fatty tissue. The manufacturers ominously recommended you took them just before bed. I often wonder if that was just in case you had a heart attack – you could kick the bucket in your sleep and not inconvenience anyone until the morning. Taking these fat burners was like doing a workout in your sleep. I occasionally awoke in the night to find myself glued to the sheets by a film of sticky sweat. Such was the potency of the tablets, they had you doing the rounds while you were in the land of Nod.

My favourite supplement contained a 'performance enhancing' cocktail of wonder weeds such as Daimana, Saw Palmetto Berry, Kola Nut, ginseng and the highly sought-after Yohimbe. While not on the IOC list of banned substances, Yohimbe was prohibited in the UK. The extract comes from the bark of an African tree which, it is said, is

.so potent that a stroke of its bark on the male member is guaranteed to set the old gentleman off into an erectile frenzy lasting several hours. I wouldn't say my penis launched itself out of my pants and into orbit, but I did feel a mild increase in my libido. I later found that in America Yohimbe was widely marketed as a 'natural alternative to Viagra'.

Eventually my sixty-tablet fix ran out. I rushed, I mean I took a brisk walk, back to the health-food shop where I discovered it, but as the spotty-faced shop assistant had previously warned me, they were out of stock and the blanket ban on its use in the UK meant there was no chance in the foreseeable future of getting any more.

A few weeks after my stock of Yohimbe ran out a friend brought some more over from New York. The label promised it would 'increase excitement, enhance pleasure'. I had just separated from my long-term girlfriend. I was now 'in between relationships'. Being single and constantly horny was not the ideal. Nevertheless, I used the thirty-day supply. I didn't get laid; got a sore wrist, though. I decided not to take Yohimbe again for the foreseeable future.

chapter II

I could see Akay and Colin whispering to each other, making gestures while eyeing up individuals in the class. As I went through my stretching routine, I saw them catch sight of me. I could tell they were talking about me. Paranoia stepped in. What were they saying? How out of shape I was? What was that? What were they talking about? Who . . . me? As they chatted, Akay broke into one of his characteristic belly laughs and again he was the Buddha, pot-bellied and cuddly, but with a sly, knowing glance that took in everything in the periphery of the gym. Black Buddha. He appeared to ask Colin a question. Colin shook his head and mouthed, 'He's not ready yet.'

Shit! They were talking about me. Not ready yet? I'm useless, that's what they're saying. It all came flooding back. Boyhood feelings of rejection on the football pitch, the playground, behind the bike sheds . . . 'He's not ready yet.' For me this was tantamount to, 'He'll never be ready.'

I needed clarification. Being rubbish had serious implications for me. After all, if I had no talent and there was no chance I could ever get into the ring, what was the point? Why go on? Jesus Christ Almighty, I'm a loser! That wasn't the way to think. I had to confront the situation.

'What's going on? I saw you two conspiring about me.' Akay and Colin looked at each other and smiled. Colin nodded his pit-bull-like head in the direction of the noticeboard on the other side of the gym.

'Have you seen the red notice?' he asked and before I could reply Akay piped in with his Buddha chuckle, 'No, no, he's not ready.'

Not ready for what? I went over to the noticeboard, hand wraps trailing behind me like an unravelling mummy. Red notice, where's that? Suddenly the bell rang. Grrrrrrrring.

'Come on, let's fill those bags up,' yelled Colin.

Now I had some anxiety to work off on the bags.

'Dave, Dave,' Colin was calling out and nodding towards the punch bags. He used his head like a gesticulating third arm. Finally, I saw the sign. Jesus, it was right in front of me. Now I was blind as well as stupid. The notice said: 'MASTERCLASS . . . sparring is a must!'

Having returned to the fold from my sabbatical, I decided to approach my training with renewed vigour and commitment. The next stage in my evolution as a fighter would be the masterclass, which was now six weeks away. The masterclass was a three-hour, more intense version of the KO circuit with one-to-one training from Akay, Colin and two other coaches combined with more emphasis on boxing technique and ring craft. It cost twenty quid (including food and refreshments) and was All Stars' very own version of white-collar boxing – a brand of pugilism aimed solely at the professional classes which originated in late eighties New York. The greed-is-good era inspired scores of selfish, emasculated, coke-sniffing, middle-aged Wall Street brokers, crooked corporate lawyers, Freudian psychoanalysts and sundry well-heeled yuppies to bolster their flaccid manhood by slugging it out in city boxing gyms. Trainers ensure that these masters of the universe are carefully matched; amateur and professional boxers are strictly prohibited from participating in bouts. White-collar boxing was bullshit – a bunch of fat bastards playing tough guys – but I had to get into that masterclass. If I couldn't hack a few rounds with some forty-five-year-old bank manager called Brian I might as well give up.

The evening's KO circuit was now in full swing. People were skipping and bobbing and weaving their way round the ring to the sound of speed garage and the drum and bass of gloves pounding leather bags.

'Work it, work those bags,' said a new trainer, trying to stamp his authority on the proceedings.

'Dave, get on that bag there.' Colin was urging me on but I wasn't in the mood for discipline tonight. What was I doing here? As I trudged over to the bags, I caught sight of Akay, lurching off towards the changing rooms.

'Boss, boss, hey boss!' He looked round, grinning.

'I'll talk to you soon,' he said, disappearing down the stairwell into the bowels of the gym.

'How are you doing?' asked one of the regulars.

'I'm knackered,' I said. 'It's this damn cold. I feel shit, my timing, coordination . . . everything's gone.'

'Don't worry about it. How long have you been coming now?' he asked.

'This is about my fifth or sixth week. Some days you have it and others you don't.'

'Don't worry, man. You're ahead of it. You're ahead of the game. You look like a natural.'

Who was he kidding? I was feeling hung up about my shape, weight, physique, age, bank balance . . . I had become touchy. When friends and colleagues referred to me as 'the boxer' I felt ridiculed. Maybe they were only joking but I resented their sarcasm. I resented those who thought I couldn't pull it off. I was being mocked for doing something I thought was highly courageous, novel, interesting – something that merited praise not derision. I was unique, not a freak. This was serious shit. I demanded respect, just like Rocky Balboa before he had the rematch with Apollo Creed in *Rocky II*.

The weeks passed and I bided my time, bobbing and weaving at All Stars three evenings a week until Akay finally gave me the nod for the masterclass. At first I was excited more than anything else at the prospect of getting some live target practice. For someone who has never boxed before, ignorance was indeed bliss. A masterclass designed for white-collar boxers was hardly the Rumble in the Jungle. I had more to fear from my ex than some wannabe boxer. As the day of the masterclass neared, however, I became more anxious, not through fear of injury but fearing I would possibly make a complete arse of myself.

In preparation for my big day, Tyrone gave me a few pointers on sparring. 'If he's a brother, go for the face,' he said throwing a quick combination of punches at an imaginary opponent. 'White guys . . . go for the stomach.' Tyrone reasoned that black fighters were vain and preoccupied with their looks, and as such did not like it in the face. White fighters, on the other hand, all looked like Cabbage Patch dolls, so they were easy about getting a broken nose. The abdominal area was, in Tyrone's opinion, a weak spot because 'white guys drink too much beer'. I tried to convince myself that there was method in this madness.

Apart from Tyrone and of course those at All Stars, I had kept news of my impending sparring session off the agenda when it came to talking to friends, family and colleagues. I figured they would only add to any anxieties by scaremongering and, being outside of boxing, would offer little or no practical encouragement or advice.

That Saturday I got to the gym on time – a first. I have a tendency to be punctual when I'm nervous. The masterclass was due to start at

12.30, immediately after that morning's KO circuit had finished. Before the class started, I had time to customise a plastic gumshield I had bought that morning specially for my big sparring session. To shape it to fit, I had to dip it in boiling water, shove it in my mouth and bite on it while moulding it with my fingers around my upper gums. Chewing on a hulking piece of plastic irritated the roof of my mouth and made me want to retch. I resisted the temptation to throw up – honking all over the gym would've made me look *too* nervous.

As we went through a variety of routines, exercises and tuition on boxing technique, Akay called us one by one into the ring for sparring. There were twelve in the group. The four women sparred with each other, as did a couple of the old boys; the rest of us went in with amateurs from the boxing club. I was the last to go.

My sparring partner was Ramsey, a six-two nubile light-heavyweight with ebony skin and fine chiselled features. I often saw him at the gym, finishing off his routine just as the KO classes were starting. He looked like a 12½ stone Lennox Lewis, complete with a mesh of dreadlocks which he kept under a tight black cap. He was one of those boxers who dispelled the commonly held belief that pugnacity inevitably led to a face like a baboon's backside. Ramsey had the elegance and comportment of a Masai warrior or Nubian chieftain. He had a warm engaging smile, a refreshing change from the icy stares and bad intent of many boxers I had met. As a stereotype of a black man, Ramsey looked more like a fast bowler, basketball player or sprinter than a fighter.

Colin laced up my gloves and fastened my head guard. I felt boxed in wearing that sweaty clump of leather on my head. I asked Colin to take it off. He refused. The bell went. Ramsey and I circled each other. I had no idea what to do. I had no strategy or game plan and, as time was running out and we were the last pair to spar, none of the trainers bothered giving me any instructions.

Ramsey was long and awkward. Every time I went for him, he seemed to slip out of reach. He seemed impossible to hit. This made me feel powerless, and worried. Finally, I managed to step into his range and could feel my gloves narrowly make contact with his. I took a stride forwards and then trod on his left foot, immobilising him for about two seconds. This was unintentional; I lacked the foresight and guile for such a manoeuvre to be deliberate. I was tempted to look down as I felt his toes crunch beneath my feet, like I'd trodden on a small snail or a large cockroach. Ramsey seemed to glance down, too. He looked up and our eyes met embarrassingly like two people exposed by a simultaneous *faux pas*. I slapped in a jab which caught him full in the face and tried to double up with another. The second volley missed and as Ramsey leant back, his extensive gait arced up making him seem two or three inches taller. He grinned, acknowledging my shot. I took some comfort in this, as it seemed to validate some degree of ring craft.

In the second round, I tried to work behind the jab and popped one or two pathetic slaps on Lennox, I mean Ramsey, but he seemed to be constantly out of reach and on the move. Having negotiated the first round with relative ease, bravery got the better of me and I chanced my arm with a right-handed haymaker that connected only with the speckles of dust floating above the ring. I telegraphed the punch so far in advance, Ramsey knew I was going to throw it even before I did. The wild swing sent me off balance and Ramsey countered immediately with a left hook, which I heard before it connected flush on my jaw – phhhhhhhusssssssshhhhhhhh. It sounded like a kite taking hold of the breeze and then PHWACK! I rocked to one side. For a split second, my balance was in question. Whether it was a mark of Ramsey's benevolence or an inability to react fast enough, he didn't follow up with any more blows. Had he done so, my view of the canvas may have been somewhat different.

My first reaction was to go forward, hands up, and come at Ramsey in a show of defiance. If that was his best shot, I wanted him to know that it had had a negligible effect on me. Of course, this was a lie. He had caught me clean and I was still feeling the effects well after we stopped sparring. In the thirty seconds or so of the round that was left, I could feel my eyes streaming, my nose running (thankfully not with blood) and my vision frosting over.

The bell sounded. I glanced round the gym looking for some sort of reaction from the others but everyone was now grabbing mats for the final session of groundwork. I went over to the corner and Colin jumped up on to the ring cordon to take off my gloves.

'Grab a mat, Dave,' he said as I leant against the ropes swallowing huge mouthfuls of air. I was breathless, my mouth was dry, my eyes were watering, I felt a constriction on my chest and my heart was doing ten to a dozen. 'Come on, people, let's get a move on,' cried Colin. I jumped down from the ring, grabbed one of the bottles of water by the spit bucket and drank about half a litre in two seconds. 'Let's go, Dave,' yelled Colin. The monkey was on my back.

I was disappointed with my performance. I didn't know what to expect, but this wasn't it. Still, I had acquitted myself adequately enough for a rank novice and did better than the film producer with tattoos who took home a busted nose and bloodied vest courtesy of one of Akay's best amateurs, Martin 'The Banger' Mubanga.

Amazingly, I had little recollection of what happened in those six minutes of boxing. I knew I had taken a few good hits – a hefty clump to the nose, a decent body shot and a hard jab which had left a bruise on my top lip that looked like dried hot chocolate – but everything else was a blur. It was as if all that nervous energy had produced amnesia, or was it that two rounds of boxing had already left me with Alzheimer's disease? I found it amazing that professional fighters could give television and press interviews immediately after a fight, complete with a blow-by-blow analysis of the action. Yes, taking a bit of a licking had certainly given me a new appreciation of boxing. Crucially, I could now make a decision – either pack my bags and settle for a less enduring future or throw caution to the wind and fight on. My experience, while less than sanguinary, had elicited enough pain to make me reconsider my position on boxing. The punishment I had taken for all of 360 seconds had not deterred me. Although the aches and pains of combat had left me with more self-doubt, I had to fight on. Life outside the ring would still be a struggle, even if I chose to give up.

chapter 12

Acton Town Hall, 7 December 1998. Soon after my sparring session, I caught a cold. I correlated this wretched illness with the telling blow I had sustained, as the bridge of my nose still ached and my nasal passage seemed permanently caked with coagulated blood and mucus. The weather had not helped; winter had stamped its grim authority in earnest. Colds, flu, runny noses and assorted respiratory infections accompanied me on the crummy public transport system which ferried my tired ass from home to work to the gym, from one dive to another. I hadn't trained for a fortnight. An old friend, Rick, had suckered me into going to this particular show on the pretext that it was an unlicensed boxing match. No such luck. It was, as the flyer said, 'a night of professional boxing'. At the last minute, Rick stood me up so I wound up going with three of his friends whom I had never met before – Robert Pereno, his girlfriend and a chick named Floss.

Outside the town hall I had my first encounter with 'Big' Ned Rawlins, a thirty-eight-year-old hustler-cum-promoter-cum-manager who was working the small but growing crowd that had gathered around the main entrance like a ticket tout. Ned was the promoter that evening and he had a wedge of cash in one hand, maybe £400 or £500 in tens and twenties, a small docket of tickets in the other, and a mobile phone sandwiched between his left shoulder and chin. He wore a full-length black duffle coat with the hood up which, on his 6ft 4in frame, made him look like the grim reaper.

'Yeah, I'm there now . . . no, no problem.' Ned spoke into the mobile in a deep Black Country drawl mixed with cockney slang. Our small group headed by Robert stood in front of him on the steps of the Town Hall like a bunch of groupies waiting for an audience with some minor pop star.

'Hi, Ned,' said Robert and the big man stepped forward and gave him a gangster hug.

'All right Robert, how ya doin', mate?' Robert introduced the girls to Ned first, both of whom he gave big hugs and slobbering kisses. Finally, Robert introduced me. Thankfully Ned was less tactile.

'This is David, the journalist I was telling you about who's writing that book on boxing,' said Robert.

'Oh yeah,' said Ned, extending a long arm. He grabbed my hand and seemed to scowl from under his hood. 'I wanna word with you later.'

His mobile rang as people milled round him, thrusting cash and unsold tickets into his hands from different angles. Robert handed over some cash for the tickets Ned had previously given him and I thought perhaps if I kept quiet I might be able to blag my way in for free after all.

'Where's the rest of the cash?' asked Ned, looking at a crumpled handful of notes and some soiled unsold tickets.

'I've got some more to collect inside from a couple of friends and David's got a score for you, haven't you Dave?'

Bollocks. No sooner had I pulled out a crisp new £20 note than Ned's massive paw was engulfing my hand sucking the twenty out from my flimsy grasp.

'Nice one, Dave,' said Ned who by now was juggling about four different conversations with punters, Robert and a squawking voice on his mobile.

This was the first fight I'd actually bought a ticket for in years. I had become so accustomed to getting freebies and press passes that I slightly begrudged having to fork out twenty quid for my unreserved seat in the main hall.

Inside the art deco foyer of the Town Hall the crowd was appreciably larger than the one outside. The usual hardcore, shaven-headed fight fans were there clad in Reeboks and MA1 flight jackets. Before the show started there was a one-minute silence for Brendan Kelly, a twenty-eight-year-old fighter from Hammersmith who had recently died of a heart attack. His picture loomed large on the front of the programme I had just bought. It also had a eulogy to the young prospect who had had just four fights, all wins. The last line was written by his manager, Jim Evans. It read: 'Tonight he will be looking down on us with that big smile and thinking, "Yeah, I finally made it to top of the bill." '

The minute's silence was broken abruptly by the ringside bell and a round of applause signalled the beginning of the night's action. About a hundred people were on the stage, elevated high above the rest of us.

Most of them seemed to be partisan; friends and relatives of the fighters.

A posse of doorman types came bowling into the arena like a funeral cortege in a hurry, wearing black overcoats or Crombies, cashmere and leather jackets. 'Sweet as a nut,' I heard one of them growl into a mobile. 'Sweet, sweet.' Other characters mingled with the crowd, slapping backs and giving warm handshakes, their fat fingers emblazoned with rows of chunky sovereign and Krugerrand rings like nine-carat knuckle-dusters. Others had swallows and shooting stars tattooed on their hands (signifying whether they were an East Ender or a 'sarf' Londoner). A black dude with a 58-inch chest wearing a camelhair coat chewed a cigar and scanned the crowd menacingly. There were dark-haired spivs in shiny suits, peroxide blondes in leather mini skirts, fighters in trouble. 'Let's have a big round of applause for the murmur murmur murmur . . .' crackled the PA in between bouts.

The usual array of hungry-looking punks were paraded into the ring for the night's entertainment – a guy called Israel wearing green shorts with 'Zulu' emblazoned on the waist; a black version of the Dick Tracy character 'Flathead'; two bony super-featherweights knocking the shit out of each other to raucous applause and laughter; and then there was Ned moving through the crowd being tailed by a camera crew. 'Box him,' he'd say as he handed out fliers for an after-show party in the Leopard Lounge on Fulham Broadway. Ned was pacing up and down the aisles like an expectant father as his protégé, Barry 'The Braveheart' Hughes, went about the business of getting his lights punched out in the ring. I didn't know Barry personally but that was the beautiful thing about boxing. All you needed was a limited personal investment in a fighter, such as being the friend of a friend who knew him, and you had the liberty of becoming emotionally attached to the event. When you know the person whose life is on the line, the spectacle becomes all the more engaging.

I saw the way fighters were embraced by their womenfolk after a fight. It was always the women who got in first. The fighters were like those World War II soldiers you'd see in the old Pathé newsreels coming home to celebration, adulation, big hugs and kisses – real man stuff.

I had been to scores of these small-hall shows by now. The York Hall Bethnal Green, Brighton Town Hall, The Elephant and Castle Leisure Centre – the cheesy décor, plastic gangsters, watered-down pints and rowdy crowds were all part of the deal wherever you went.

The heat finally turned up. It always did at these affairs. After a few fights and several pints, the atmosphere changed. 'Stick the bastard,' someone cried as a chorus of 'ooh-ooh' monkey noises echoed round the hall. A fighter in white glittery shorts who had a massive eye, like one of those Japanese Manga cartoon characters, got bashed to raucous applause; an air horn went off and someone cried, 'Shut the fuck up.' The crowd was stamping its feet in the aisles in maddening unison. It was like an Auto Windshields Cup-tie. I had to get out of there. Maybe I had to get out of boxing altogether.

chapter 13

On 1 January 1999, I weighed 14 stone 8lb. I had spent the holidays on my own, feeling sorry for myself. On Christmas Day, I consumed a roast beef joint and all the trimmings, a box of Belgian chocolates, a bottle of Bulgarian red and assorted nibbles. I was inclined to comfort eat when I got depressed. I had been piling on the pounds over the festive season but managed to exorcise some of the Christmas food demons and stay under 15 stone. Weight. What a preoccupation! Maybe it was time for the dreaded Hay diet, you know, that way of eating that stops you from mixing carbohydrates with proteins – very effective, very boring; or maybe Dr Atkins' 'New Diet Revolution' where you eat just fats and proteins; or Dr Barry Sears' 'Zone Plan', the diet that allows you to eat anything you want; or what about the cigarette diet where you smoke forty tabs a day, get cancer, waste away to nothing and achieve that skeletal figure you've always wanted. Christ, my life had become an entry in *Bridget Jones' Diary*.

The start of 1999 signalled a time for revolution not resolutions. I felt the pressure mounting for me to pull my finger out and hit this boxing thing hard. I'd spent the better part of a year slumming it in boxing and getting nowhere fast. In my own defence, it had not been until the latter part of 1998 (when my publisher had generously started to bankroll this operation) that I was able to afford to embark on a career in the ring. But even though I now had funds, those in the fight game who were prepared to take me seriously were either trying to convince me or naturally assumed that an amateur fight was my best bet. Tyrone said I should go for a heavyweight bout as an amateur. Akay said if I could drop down in weight to light-heavy he'd consider training me, again on the basis of an amateur fight. This was not what I had expected or wanted. An amateur fight . . . no, no, no.

Having no one to show faith in me, no mentor, raised increasing doubts about my own capabilities. Maybe becoming a fighter wasn't such a good idea after all. Maybe subconsciously, I was finding ways of putting off my day of reckoning because I knew I couldn't handle it. Damn, the training, even at white-collar level, was hard. Boxing was no joke. I remembered when I got the idea to do this thing, when I saw Takaloo box in Cheshunt. I sat there thinking arrogantly, 'I can do that.' I had underestimated boxing and overestimated my talent. How the hell did I think I could get away with this? Here I was, a jumped-up little media whore, thinking I could be Joe fucking Louis in six months, when it took the average man years of blood, sweat and tears to become even a second-rate pro. I was living in a dream world. No wonder Lara kicked me out. No wonder I spent Christmas Day all alone in a bedsit in Notting Hill. I was a loser.

If I quit now perhaps I could still save face and hightail it with the remainder of my advance. Surely my publisher would understand? I wasn't so sure if I could really go through with this. It wasn't just a case of having the desire, raw talent or potential. Dedication, commitment and discipline were also necessary. Discipline is the cornerstone of boxing. Without it, the sport is reduced to the status of a violent fairground attraction. To be disciplined, however, required a full-time trainer and I still didn't have one.

The economics of boxing dictated that somewhere along the line I had to become a cash prospect in order to get a fight. Someone had to earn something out of me. The trainers I had approached were not interested in me because there was no money in it for them. For one, my career in the ring was going to be very shortlived and none too profitable. Secondly, considering my age, lack of fitness and inexperience it was not wholly unreasonable for a trainer to think I wouldn't make the grade and thus was a poor investment.

My chances of making it as a fighter lay not just in my ability to survive four or six rounds with a seasoned pro, but also in my financial viability as a prospect. To take on a complete nobody like me was admittedly a risky proposition for a promoter. What if I walked out there under the bright lights on the big night and froze – KO'd with one punch in the first round! Jesus, it didn't bear thinking about.

Anyway, my pride aside for a moment, the potential for embarrassment was immense. Everyone involved with me would wind up with egg on his or her face. Still, the novelty of what I was attempting meant I could potentially sell a truckload of tickets to the hordes of friends, family and acquaintances who would just love to see me take a beating.

Bums on seats – that's what promoters were after.

Despite my lack of training, I hadn't been idle. I had been occupying my time boozing, nightclubbing and looking for a new ex-girlfriend. It seemed as though my daughter, my relationship, my life had indirectly fallen victim to boxing. Now I was depressed and unsure where I was heading with this thing. Nothing was working right. My training was unstructured and infrequent, I was slipping into bad habits and losing my sense of direction. I needed a break, someone to give me a chance. I was desperate for some guidance.

After a couple of unsuccessful approaches to moneyed individuals whom I tried to hustle into forming a syndicate on my behalf, I arranged to meet 'Big' Ned at his temporary 'office', a bar called the Revolution in Chelsea's King's Road. I got the impression that if anyone could fix me up, Ned could.

Ned extended that long arm of his which seemed to stretch halfway along the bar and gave me a knuckle-busting handshake.

'Ha, ha, ha . . . Dave, my man!' He was a man whose bonhomie and hedonistic ambition stood in equal measure to his generous frame. 'Big' by name, big by nature.

'What are you drinking, Dave?'

'Orange juice,' I said.

'Ha, ha. I like it. Laying off the booze, eh?'

'Well, you know how it is, Ned . . .'

Ned lit a cigarette, puffed on it like a teenaged smoker and ordered a double whiskey and lemonade for him and an orange juice for me. He shuffled behind the bar and started needling the staff with friendly jibes. He looked right at home.

'I spend a lot of time in here. It's close to everything. I'm local, the ex-missus is local . . . everything's local.' We sat down at the bar and quickly got into his weekend exploits. 'I went to Beach Blanket Babylon and the Fez club on Saturday. Met some blonde bird . . . she was with her boyfriend, but she wants some beast sex. Hahahahaha . . .'

'Sounds like she's got a case of jungle fever then, Ned,' I ventured.

'Hahahaha . . . that's right. Jungle fucking fever. She's got it! Hahahaha,' Ned broke into guffaws of laughter and gave me about four or five clenched fist handshakes in quick succession. He became pensive all of a sudden. 'What did you think of wee Barry at that Acton show?' he asked. I gave him my honest opinion, which was that I thought he could have had the fight sewn up if he had not lost his concentration.

'His hair seemed to get in his face and put him off,' I said. 'What's he doing now?'

'I've had to sack him, knock him on the head for a bit. He thinks he's the champ already. He's got this fucking bird, she's no good for him. I've told him to go and train at Howard's gym in Sheffield but he wants to go and train in Glasgow. If he goes up there he'll get nicked. All he wants to do is go knocking people out.'

Ned explained that Barry, like many fighters, wanted to live life in the fast lane and being in his hometown with all the accompanying distractions could prove detrimental to his career. Tearaway boxers were not a going concern and Ned had other irons in the fire. He was developing an idea for a power station that runs on perpetual motion. He had originally conceived the idea while serving as a marine engineer in the navy. Despite having never produced a technical drawing or having any knowledge of quantum physics, he had apparently gained the interest of several academics and scientists. 'If this thing comes off, I'll be the richest nigger in the world,' he said.

The science of the concept was too difficult to comprehend as Ned dazzled me with a well-rehearsed story about the billions of megahertz the thing would produce and its energy-saving properties. Ned spoke as though the power station's construction were a foregone conclusion. He had a way of making it sound like a piece of cake. In fact, Ned had a way of making everything sound like a piece of cake.

"Ow much do you weigh?' said Ned, shifting the conversation and lunging forward to grab a chunk of my stomach in his vice-like grip. Before I could answer he broke into a customary fit of laughter.

'Oh fucking hell, man! You gotta lose a few pounds. How tall are you?'

'About six one and a half,' I said.

'Get yourself down to cruiserweight. I bet you eat like a bastard, don't you?'

'Well, I do like my food I suppose.'

I could sense the click and whirr of Ned going through some devious thought process as he started sizing me up. He beamed and ordered some more drinks.

'Dave's gonna be a boxer. I like it, I fucking like it,' said Ned, laughing. 'You wanna get up to Howard Rainey's gym in Sheffield, the Don Valley Sports Academy. Betty, this woman who's got a lodging house for fighters, would look after you. She'll do your cooking, cleaning, washing, everything. You'll be sorted. Howard'll train you up and in six months you'll be one of us.'

The Don Valley Sports Academy – it sounded a bit dubious, a bit pseudo. But it was obvious Ned was keen on my idea, and despite having little knowledge of him or this Rainey character, I instinctively trusted his opinion. For the next few minutes Ned raved about Howard, a fifty-five-year-old maverick who had been a fighter, mountaineer, an inventor of running machines and all sorts. He started training amateurs in the Lake District in the 1970s before moving to London where he coached in a variety of amateur clubs. Howard trained Barry 'The Braveheart'. But the jewel in his crown was Colin McMillan whom he had trained to become WBO world featherweight champion before a serious shoulder injury eventually ended his career.

'You've got to meet Howard. He can do anything. He's one of the best trainers in the world.' He took a big gulp of whiskey from his big tumbler and continued with the sermon according to 'Big' Ned. 'You got to do a trial for the British Boxing Board of Control,' he said. 'Basically, you do two or three rounds of sparring in front of the officials, just so they can see you know what you're doing . . . so that you don't make a fool of yourself in the ring. Once you get through that, you've got your licence. Sweet! You're a brother so you know how to stand your ground,' he continued. 'Just throw a lot of jabs.' Ned got off his barstool and threw a flurry of quick, stiff jabs that made his body jolt as if he were having a spasm. Ned had boxed as a heavyweight for about seven years but was forced to quit after doctors discovered he had a heart murmur and his licence was revoked.

'Howard'll train you up. Give it six months and you'll be ready to take someone's fucking head off. You never know, you might be good enough to go in three or four months' time.'

Now we were talking. I was impressed with Ned's enthusiasm and his positive approach following some of the negative reactions I had previously encountered. As he had been involved in the Acton show and managed Barry 'The Braveheart', I suggested maybe he could manage or promote me.

'Why not?' he said gleefully. 'I'll get you someone to fight. After you win it . . . after you win your first fight . . .' – this sounded encouraging, if somewhat premature – '. . . you'll want to fight again. It's a great hype for a promotion. We'll get you someone to fight. You'll win, don't worry about that.' This was now sounding a little too encouraging. Ned paused and chuckled conspiratorially, his eyes beaming mesmerically into mine. In a nanosecond 'I' had become 'we' suggesting some shadowy syndicate would be vying for a piece of the action. And what about 'You'll win, don't worry about that.' Was Ned just geeing me up?

The big guy took another large swig of his drink, emptying the glass. He rattled the ice cubes in it and looked over at the barman.

'Give us a whiskey and lemonade will ya, Jay?'

'That'll be five pounds, please,' said the barman. Ned looked nonplussed.

'What are you talking about?' said Ned. The pair went into a convoluted exchange about Ned's bar tab, bike parts and sundry items of trivia.'If you don't give me the drink, you'll . . .' Ned made a coded gesture. 'What are you saying? Give me a fucking drink.'

The barman reluctantly poured another whiskey and lemonade while Ned answered yet another call on his mobile. 'Yeah . . . what? Yeah . . . I'll be there in twenty minutes.' Ned knocked back the drink and ushered me out of the bar.

'Look, Dave, I gotta run, mate. Take down Howard's number and give him a bell. He'll work you hard. He won't beat the crap out of you but he'll work you hard. You'll get fit up there all right. You'll also get a lot of respect from the fighters up there for doing this.'

We walked down the King's Road for a few minutes and just as we were parting company my mobile rang. 'Hi, it's Diana, Rick's girl-friend . . .' Ned slipped down a side street and I carried on talking to Diana. She had bad news. 'Rick's been sent to jail for twelve months for tax evasion,' she said.

'Shit,' I said. Apparently, he owed Her Majesty £30,000 in unpaid taxes. Naughty boy. Rick was arranging my attendance at the Holyfield–Lewis jamboree and for a moment I thought my big fight ticket was blown. Diana, however, gave me the number of one of Rick's friends, a ticket tout named Blue. Blue reckoned he could get me into Madison Square Garden – for two hundred smackers . . .

We arranged to meet in the dark, dank underpass of Vauxhall tube station, as good a place as any I suppose to hand over two hundred quid for a bookmark-sized piece of paper. Blue arrived at 3.00 p.m. – bang on time. We recognised each other immediately from our descriptions over the telephone (tall, dark and handsome. Oh really? So am I) and exchanged convoluted clenched-fist handshakes like a couple of LA gang-bangers. Blue had dark, ebony skin, soft features and casual, country-club garb accentuated by a chamois coloured suede jacket. He was definitely a smooth operator.

'Do you wanna do it here?' he asked in a silky cockney drawl. Stereotypes aside, I felt overly conscious of the image of two well-proportioned black men cutting a cash deal in an urban subway. 'Or we can go back to my office, my car's just around the corner.'

I had no real reason to be mistrusting of Blue. After all, he was a friend of a friend and had come on recommendation; but I had never paid such an obscene figure for a fight ticket, or any ticket, even an airline ticket. As a journalist I had become accustomed to freebies, discounts, junkets, and here I was shelling out two hundred notes for a 'brief' (as they say in the touting business) that had a face value of a hundred dollars, or roughly sixty quid. I would be in level five, up in the gods. I'd probably need a telescope to see the action in the ring, but I didn't care. I had to get to that fight for the atmosphere, the sense of history in the making. After months of floating with the flotsam and jetsam of the small-hall scene I was yearning for a taste of the big time, just a glimpse of the glamour end of the fight game.

If I was desperate to get to Madison Square Garden for the fight so were thousands of others. The venue would hold some 21,000 fans but the allocation for the UK was 7,000 resulting in a massive black market for tickets. This was the 'fight of the century' – well, at least since the last 'fight of the century' – and every serious fight fan wanted a piece of it. The previous defining moment in world championship boxing was when Mike Tyson unified the heavyweight title in 1987 by defeating 'Bonecrusher' Smith and then Tony Tucker, making him the undisputed heavyweight champion of the world.

I begrudged handing over £200 in crisp, new bank notes. I thought about what the money could buy for my daughter and felt guilty. I wasn't rich. Could I afford it? Not really. But could I afford not to be part of 'Crowning Glory' the hyperbolic name given to the event by its promoter, the ubiquitous Don King? Others with more money to burn or less guilt would pay up to £1,500 for a ringside seat.

As soon as tickets had gone on sale on 30 November, the American public and touts or 'scalpers' as they are called there, immediately snapped up thousands of cheap seats, devouring the $100 and $250 places within days. The fight was still two months away. Don King's hype was muted, quiet like a sleeping lion yet to roar. Save for the big-money seats, the fight was already a sell-out. Two hundred pounds! Was I insane? By this time I was flat broke again. It would have to go on the credit card – more interest to pay on yet another credit-card bill. But Blue needed payment in cash. 'A cynic is a man who knows the price of everything and the value of nothing,' said Oscar Wilde. This was no time to be cynical.

We reached Blue's car, an early nineties, maroon soft top Golf Gti. He got in the driving seat, physically and metaphorically. I was still uncomfortable about the price tag and although I knew I was going to cough up, pride dictated that I try at least a quarter-baked attempt at haggling. It was no use; it was a seller's market.

'Dave, I wouldn't even be doing this if it wasn't for Rick,' said Blue. 'I got people queuing up. I'm doing this as a favour.' Some favour. We talked small for a while, me clutching the 'bottle' (touting parlance for the money), Blue fingering a stumpy wedge of tickets. I didn't want to let go. I felt as though an old pet was being put down – £200, goodbye my old friend, my old chum.

Once I had that little strip of card in my possession, I was on my own. If there was anything snide about it, I could kiss those two hundred smackers goodbye. After all, the ticket could have been obtained by mail order using a stolen credit-card number (this was a common scam run by the more unscrupulous ticket touts). Alternatively, it could've been counterfeit. A fight of this interest was sure to attract the odd rogue printer or two. I grilled Blue about the validity and origins of the ticket.

'It's kosher, man,' he stressed. 'I've got my reputation to think about. I only deal in the real McCoy.'

From our conversation I learnt we had a few mutual acquaintances. So I had no need to worry, did I? Blue after all was a friend of a friend. I handed over the cash. Jesus, I handed over the money and took the ticket. It looked genuine, but then so did Michael Jackson before he discovered wet-look perms and plastic surgery. I prayed that I wouldn't reach Madison Square Garden on 13 March and find out that seat 8 row E in section 424 was occupied by half-a-dozen other schmucks.

chapter 14

The situation had hit rock bottom with Lara. We were barely talking and when we did it was through gritted teeth. She still insisted that counselling was the be all and end all, the shot in the arm for our non-existent relationship, but I remained resistant to any more of that psychobabble. It was patently clear that we could not, or would not, resolve our differences, so Lara raised the stakes and threatened to return to her hometown of Coventry and take Luca with her. Coventry! Jesus H Christ! What in Hanuman the monkey god's name had Coventry got to offer other than terminal boredom? The city's greatest contribution to the tapestry of English culture is that it's the one place where sad fuckers with no friends are 'sent to'.

I made up my mind. I could no longer go on doing things by half measures. I'd jack in my job and make for Sheffield, throw myself headlong into my work. I could return to London at weekends to see Luca and the breathing space it would provide could be just the thing to inject some life back into my relationship with Lara. It would also give me the solitary environment and focus I needed to dedicate myself to boxing.

I was apprehensive about going up to Sheffield to train. I knew doing it this way would take me to a whole new level. To date, I'd been play boxing, deluding myself that somehow I could magic my way into the ring without too much effort. It was impossible. The only way for me to complete what I had set out to do was to throw myself 100 per cent into boxing and this meant leaving all the distractions of London behind. I'd had just a couple of rounds of sparring. Where was that going to get me? As Joyce Carol Oates said, 'People play football or golf, they don't play boxing.' This wasn't a game. I needed to get serious. I needed to stop avoiding the inevitable showdown with myself.

I'd had it with college. My students were revolting, both in the descriptive and active sense. After a meeting with my class and the head of department – forty-five minutes of slurs, insults, undue criticism and excuse giving – I'd had enough. The students could fry for all I cared. For five months, I'd played Jack Nicholson to their ragtag bunch of *One Flew over the Cuckoo's Nest* crackpots. I was through with their excuses, lies, deceit, lack of commitment and dedication, their insecurities . . . everything!

The remaining dozen or so stragglers left on the course comprised a menagerie of social dysfunction. They didn't need a lecturer; they needed a fucking psychoanalyst. These guys should have been in group therapy, not college. I had a violent alcoholic; two neurotic worriers (one of whom I'm certain was just a nervous breakdown away from stalking me); a possible smack freak; two Walter Mitty characters whose glowing on-paper credentials bore no relation to their piss-poor performance in class; a giggling dolly bird – mutton dressed up as lamb – who still believed a mini skirt and stilettos were the best career tools a gal could have; a monosyllabic teenager (what's new); and a serial victim who leapt from one crisis to another. My favourite, though, was a Nigerian chick. She was so hung up at me for not responding to her low-cut tops and subtle advances that she showed me the finger and told me to 'piss off' one day in front of the whole class, all because I wouldn't give her the bus fare for a field trip I had organised.

That was it. They could keep their foibles and idiosyncratic behaviour and find someone else to entertain them for £18.73 an hour. The case for Sheffield was strengthening by the minute. I picked up the telephone and made the call.

'All right, mate, how are you?' Howard spoke with a deep, laconic growl, very rough, very smooth. He sounded like he smoked for a living. I told him a bit about myself, my meeting with Ned and the nature of my project. He sounded interested and refreshingly unfazed by the idea. I had a half-term break the following week so I asked him if I could come for a few days 'in camp' to test the water.

'Yeah, come up, we'll sort you out. We've got Clinton Woods preparing for the European light-heavy. Terry Dunstan has just come back from sparring with Lennox Lewis. He got the sack for nearly knocking him out.' I was impressed. 'Don't muck in with anybody, mind you. Wait until you get here. We'll sort some digs out for ya. I might be able to put you up at our place.'

Before I hung up, I reminded Howard exactly what my mission was. There was no underestimating the short-term memories and even shorter attention spans of people in boxing. Howard, however, seemed sharp.

'How old are you?' he asked.

'Thirty . . . er . . . thirty-one actually,' I said. I was often tempted to lie about my date of birth, just like Archie Moore and Sonny Liston. The onset of age was now more important than ever. Fighting was a race against the clock.

'No problem,' said Howard. 'Don't worry, we'll straighten you out.'

Sheffield, 22 February 1999. The cab wound its way through a series of modern developments and council estates, empty pubs, tatty buildings and decaying churches before breaking into a stretch of road lined with small industrial units and a disused paint factory. It was just after 6.00 p.m. In the city centre, the rush-hour traffic was still breathing life into the metropolis but by the time the cab hit the dimly lit streets of Darnall I had reached a dead part of town. This was my first glimpse of *Full Monty* country, a land of broken dreams and desperation where unemployed steelworkers stripped for the wives and girlfriends of other unemployed steelworkers.

The cab pulled up outside a dilapidated building in Worksop Road. Over the entrance a torn banner flapped in the wind and rain. It read: 'Welcome to the Don Valley Sports Academy and Ringside Bar'. The fare from the railway station came to £3.90. Apart from muttering, 'This is it,' the driver hadn't said a word during the twenty-minute journey. I gave him four quid and told him to keep the change.

I walked through two sets of double doors into a club bar and immediately met some strange looks. The place was empty but for a barmaid and a few pallid locals who were sitting round a table having a conversation about nothing.

'I'm looking for Howard Rainey,' I said. More strange looks. Had I come to the right place? A moment of uncertainty passed.

'Are you a boxer?' asked one of the locals, sizing me up.

'Of sorts,' I said, trying not to be too surly, too southern.

'I'll show you the way,' said another local, leading me to the back of the club. I walked through an anteroom of cast-iron free weights, exercise machines and grotesque pin-ups of female bodybuilders until I reached the boxing gym where several scrawny-looking youths were hammering away at punch bags. The gym was a decent sized space – around a thousand square feet. It had high ceilings, yellowing white-washed walls and, along one side, large opaque windows that looked out on to the street below. It was bright(ish), lit by several mangy fluorescent light fittings, and was sparsely decorated with old fight posters. It bore all the grubby hallmarks of an authentic boxing gym. Broken training apparatus, bowling balls, tools, busted punch bags and ripped-up crash mats were strewn everywhere and the familiar musty aroma of stale sweat, leather, Olbas Oil, Deep Heat and bowel movements hung in the air. A reconstructed hi-fi system blasted out mind-numbing dance music which accompanied the overall din of ropes crashing, fists smacking bags, shouting, swearing and belching.

The most conspicuous features of the gym were the two boxing rings. They were around 13 foot square, considerably smaller than the standard 16 to 22 foot ones used for fights, and cobbled together with rusting scaffold poles and fraying ropes. To complete the Third World aesthetic, they were laid not with canvas, but grey office carpet which was scuffed and ripped in several places. Bungee cords and a variety of straps were attached to the rings. Over one of them, suspended by four ropes and a makeshift pulley system, was a metal frame housing a grid of thin rope separated into sixteen shoulder-width square sections; it looked like the head of a gigantic lacrosse stick. It all seemed very unconventional.

'Howard, there's a fella here for ya,' the local shouted at three men who were leaning against the ropes watching two youths spar. 'Eh Howard! Oh for fuck's sake . . . That's him over there.' He pointed to the biggest of the three men, a huge lump with wild grey hair and glasses, and then disappeared back into the anteroom towards the bar.

I approached the trio at ringside, heading straight for the big man. I felt apprehensive. Walking into a boxing gym for the first time is always mildly intimidating. Usually there is a palpable sense of tension, the product of too many big egos in too small a space. As I stepped forward one of the men glanced at me and nudged the big man.

'Hi Howard, I'm David,' I said, extending my hand. Howard's wife Lorna had earlier told me on the telephone that I couldn't miss him. 'He's six foot four with a boxer's face,' she said. She forgot to mention that he was 18 stone and built like the proverbial brick shithouse. He took my hand in a massive paw and shook it gently.

'Hello Dave.'

Howard didn't just have a boxer's face, he had *the* boxer's face. It was part hangdog Robert Mitchum, part Joe Palooka, the 1940s boxing comic-strip hero. He had an exquisitely broken nose, so misshapen it looked like someone had dropped an anvil on it. Howard's face had more character than Robert De Niro at a gurning contest. He also had incredible teeth – all six of them – tombstones eaten away by the passage of time, fists and cancer sticks.

'Where have you trained before?' Howard asked, continuing to scan the goings-on in the gym.

'I've done a bit at All Stars, in the Harrow Road,' I said.

'Oh you know Akay? Nice fella. I spent a bit of time at his gym. How is he?

'Ebullient.'

'You what?

'He's fine,' I said. 'I used to go to the Peacock in Canning Town as well.'

'Fucking poser's gym. I bet you've never seen anywhere like this before, have yer?'

'I can't say I have.'

Howard gave me a mini tour of the gym, demonstrating some of his innovations along the way. The rope grid in the number two ring, for instance, was designed as an aid for bobbing and weaving, rolling, and training head and lateral movement. Then there were a number of leg devices he had invented for stretching; wobbly boards for balance; specially designed speedballs . . .

'See that kid over there.' Howard gestured towards a light-skinned black guy in his early twenties, around six two and 185lb. He was beating up on a heavy punch bag like it owed him money.

'That's Danny Daley . . . the next Roy Jones. Bags of fucking talent.'

'Yeah, but he's only had one fight and thinks he knows it all,' added a guy who had come to join us.

'This is John,' said Howard. 'He'll be in your corner for your fight.' John Naylor was one of three coaches who trained the amateurs on Monday, Wednesday and Friday evenings.

'So you're the fella Howard told me about . . . the one who's writing the book?'

'That's right.' I gave him the spiel on the book, a thirty-second blurb.

'Where you stopping while you're in Sheffield?' said John.

'At Howard's place,' I said.

'What . . . in Manor?'

'Yeah, Manor. I think.'

'Ha ha ha ha ha . . .'

'What's it like round there?' I asked.

'If you want my honest opinion, it's a shithole.'

Lorna had made grilled chicken, jacket potatoes and salad for dinner. As Howard led me through the backdoor of the house into the kitchen (the front door was never used) he paused on the doorstep, held one nostril and expectorated a stream of phlegm.

'Oh, you're an animal,' said Lorna, greeting us.

'Piss off,' replied Howard and pecked her on the cheek.

'If you're going to stay here, we're not going to put on any airs and graces for you,' said Lorna, immediately establishing the ground rules. 'If you're going to be here for the foreseeable future, treat this place like it's your home.'

A petite but feisty 'sarf' Londoner, Lorna was a striking contrast to Howard. She didn't have a boxer's face for one, or grey hair. She had long brown hair and all of her own teeth which took over her face when she smiled. At thirty-three she was young enough to be Howard's daughter and energetic enough sometimes to behave like it. Where Howard was laconic she was loquacious; where he was thoughtful and patient, she was impulsive and impatient. As a couple they made an interesting pair. Lorna was as much part of 'the camp' as Howard and a real Jacqueline of all trades. Apart from counselling some of his 'boys' over their love lives and petty insecurities, she looked after those boxers who chose to stay at the house in the days or weeks before a fight. 'My sofa's seen more fighters than Madison Square Garden,' she joked. She called herself the 'chief cook and bottle washer' and practically managed Howard's life, acting as his PA, PR and unofficial agent to a couple of fighters. That was Lorna Rainey.

'Some people think I'm a mug but I learnt a long time ago that the man I fell in love with was more in love with his work than me and the only way to deal with it and not get left out of his life was to get involved.'

Lorna said she'd been drawn to Howard's legs. That's how they met. She was leaning over the balcony of her flat in Lambeth watching 'the legs' go by. She eventually collared him. Women like her are good at getting what they want. They had only been married a year when I arrived. Young love.

The Rainey house was a modest three-bedroomed semi on the New Manor estate. The walls were thin and the carpets were thick. The dining room was adorned with pictures of Howard with Frank Bruno, Roberto Duran, Colin McMillan and scores of other fighters – champions, contenders, prospects – guys he'd trained or come to know over the years. Apart from the pictures, there was nothing remarkable about the house. Well, there was the mess. Piles of dirty washing, ironing, toys, TV remote controls, cushions, ashtrays, shoes, clothes, odd bits of paperwork and sundry other items of crap were strewn everywhere. If a burglar broke into the Rainey house, he'd swear someone had beaten him to it.

Lorna's boys, eight-year-old Scott and twelve-year-old Simon, were the laziest pair of brats I'd ever encountered. What they got away with I would have been hung, drawn and quartered for as a boy. The moment they walked through the door they contributed to the underlying chaos and mayhem in the house by discarding their dirty clothes on the living-room floor, throwing half-eaten plates of food about and jacking up the volume of the TV. 'Will you shut up!' Lorna yelled at them as they badgered her with requests for Playstation games, Nike trainers and movie tickets.

Over the next few months, for the duration of my stay, I would be staying in Scott's room, an eight by six box with a single bed. I had a little teak-effect bedside cupboard, a couple of shelves for my books and three PVC containers to store clothes and personal effects. There was no wardrobe. The room was small and simple but it was better than the alternative which was sharing the larger room with Simon.

The Rainey household was mad and I was mad for getting myself institutionalised in it. I thought I'd be like a young Mike Tyson being thrust into the bosom of Cus D'Amato's home in the Catskills, adopted for boxing. But unlike Cus's place, which I guess reeked of peace and tranquillity, my new home was full of disorder and mayhem. It reminded me of 'The Royle Family', the hilarious BBC comedy series set in the living room of a northern working-class family where relatives cackled and bickered with each other over egg and chips and mushy peas.

Despite feeling at odds with my new environment, it was kind of homely being with a family like the Raineys. They even had a dog, a Staffordshire bull terrier called Scrap who made it his life's work from the time I arrived to sire a litter of puppies with my left leg. But in Sheffield, far from my friends, my daughter, my family and the familiarity of London, holed up in a tiny bedroom in an unforgiving part of the country, I felt foreign and out of sorts. Still, I always felt like an outsider, wherever I went. This sense of alienation would help me complete my mission. I had no ties here, no distractions, nothing to divert my attention from the matter in hand. I was two hundred miles away from home in another world where I could lose myself and become a fighter.

That night Howard treated me to a seminar on musculature, blood oxygenation and VO2; and countless anecdotes on boxing, like the time Frank Bruno showed up at the now defunct Thomas à Becket gym on the Old Kent Road. Big Frank had recently won the WBC heavyweight title after out-pointing Oliver McCall. Following three previously unsuccessful attempts at winning a world title belt Bruno had finally reached the zenith of his career. He sidled up to Howard and shoved a grand into his hand. 'I want you to have this, Howard, just to say thanks for all your help,' said Bruno. 'What's this?' says Howard. 'A thousand fucking pounds!' Bruno is taken aback. 'Sorry, Howard. Isn't it enough?' 'I don't want your fucking money, Frank. Keep it.' Bruno insisted that Howard keep the money. Then came the pitch. 'Do you mind if we have our photo taken together?' asked Bruno. 'You bastard. You just gave me that money so's you can get a fucking picture. Go on then.' Howard has an aversion to having his photo taken.

When a show was on Sky, Howard would leave his boxers and the promoters to do the post-fight interviews. He wasn't into the obligatory soundbite. 'I'd just get me things together, pack me bags up and fuck off,' he said. The limelight wasn't something he craved, which was just as well. The TV people would have had to bleep every other word out of his interviews.

Howard moved on to a little ditty about one of his former fighters, Paul 'Scrap Iron' Ryan. One day he and Howard were talking about religion.

'See, Paul, he's a nice fella and all that,' said Howard, 'but a fucking idiot. I said to him one day, "Did you know that Jesus was black?" "Bollocks," says Ryan. "You what?" I say. "Course he were black," I tell him. "He must've been. He were from the Middle East." "That's fucking rubbish," he says. "Jesus weren't fucking black, I've seen photos of 'im." What an idiot!'

Howard also spoke about sparring with Muhammad Ali when Ali was in Britain preparing for the Jack London fight.

'He gave me his robe as a memento,' he said, chuckling. 'And I fucking dyed it. I didn't like the colour.' He also pulled out the gold stitching that spelled out the great fighter's name. 'It wasn't my name, was it?' Howard lost the robe by the wayside. 'Imagine that now. It'd be worth a fortune.' I remembered seeing somewhere in the *Guinness Book of Records* that an Ali robe once went for $157,947 at auction. Howard said he never bothered to keep mementoes or have his photo taken with people from the fight game until recently. He was never particularly sentimental about such things.

Howard told me about Professor Sir David Warren, the foremost authority in the country on knee injuries and one of Howard's idols.

'I could do with him looking at my knees,' I said.

'Mmm. You've got hamstring problems. That's what's affecting your knees. I noticed it in the gym earlier today.' My knees had been a sore point for some time. 'Go over there and walk towards me,' said Howard gesturing fifteen feet across the living room. 'Yep. Hamstrings and gluteus maximus. I'll sort it out in the gym tomorrow.' But the temptation to try and break my legs straightaway was too great. 'Do you ever get lower back pains?' asked Howard.

'Yes, occasionally,' I replied.

'That's because your back is compensating for your hamstring. Lie down there on the floor.' I got on my back and followed his instructions as he told me to bring my knees up to my chest alternately. 'Now grip the sole of your left foot and extend your leg.'

My flexibility was atrocious. I was as stiff as a cadaver coated in creosote. I repeated the move with my right leg. Same thing.

'Right, get on to your stomach,' said Howard. Why wait until tomorrow to sort it out? 'This might hurt a bit.' As I lay face down Howard perched on top of my extended left leg and brought my right leg up to a right angle at the knee. I could feel him kneading and drilling into the back of my thigh with his elbow, working the muscle as if trying to move a ball bearing around under my skin.

'Can you feel that?' he said as I made the odd muffled shriek, trying my utmost to suppress the pain.

'Yeah, yeah . . .' I mumbled. It was agonising. More was to come. I repeated the stretch with the right knee up to my chest, but amazingly this time when I extended my leg there was greater flexibility.

'Wow, that's incredible.' I paced around the living room for a spell and felt much lighter on my feet.

'Right. Now get down on the floor again. Get on your side, left leg under right. Point your right toe down and straighten your leg. Come on, straighter. Now move your foot around in a figure of eight. That's not a figure of eight it's a fucking circle. Right, that's it. Straighten your leg. Keep your leg straight. Right, where can you feel the tension, inside or outside of the thigh?'

'Outside.'

'Get on your back.' Nothing had prepared me for what I was about to experience. 'Hold on. You're gonna really feel this.'

I lay on my back with my right leg pointing straight up in the air. Howard grasped it as if he were about to toss the caber. With his right arm he pulled my leg in at the knee, on the patella, while bending my foot inwards towards the floor. The pain was excruciating. At one point I thought the application of his 18-stone bulk would snap my leg in two like a dried twig. This demonstration of muscle manipulation-cum-sadism seemed to last an eternity. I thought this man was truly the son of Satan. But when I stood up, I felt remarkably light on my feet.

'Shit. It's like I've got a new leg.'

'Stretching. It's all done by stretching,' said Howard slipping back into his seat with a cigarette. 'These fucking coaches out there haven't got a clue.'

Perhaps I had finally found one who did.

chapter 15

The following morning I left the house early and ventured out into the streets to survey my new neighbourhood. When I asked Binda the local newsagent for a copy of the *Guardian* he laughed. All that was available was the *Sun*, the *Mirror*, the *Daily Sport* and the local rag. I bought the local rag.

Manor had all the hallmarks of suburban decay – gangs of teenaged yobs in sportswear, drinking cheap lager and hanging out on street corners with their stolen mountain bikes; a fat couple with their fat children ambling up the road carrying scrap metal, their huge backsides wobbling behind them; boarded-up shop fronts decorated with graffiti – 'Tracy loves Danny', 'Mark's a poof'; boy racers wheel-spinning their way out of the Springwood pub car park in their beat-up Ford Fiestas; unkempt grass verges littered with rubbish indicating the local authority had long given up hope of preserving the social fabric of Sheffield's roughest neighbourhood. Even the ice-cream man sold cigarettes and Rizla papers. Not far away lived the local drug dealer and over the road one of Simon's twelve-year-old buddies was on smack.

Every other night a South Yorkshire police chopper would circle high above Manor, playing cat and mouse in the ritual hunt with joyriders and burglars. Lorna joked that she could rest easy in her home because the law was always nearby. This was a land of 'Police, Camera, Action' and 'Newsnight' special investigations into poverty in the nineties.

Politicians used rhetoric like 'dependency culture' and 'poverty is a scar on the skin of the nation' and came up with schemes like the 'Sure Start' for families and the 'New Deal' for the unemployed. But talk was worthless on the streets of Manor. Here, as in all the pockets of poverty in Britain, the task was one of containment. Contain the unemployed and dispossessed; give them just enough money for booze, fags and chips to keep them happy, temporarily, until some mandarin comes up with another bright idea. The problems were too vast even to contemplate tackling. There was a cultural rot going on. What it meant was the junkies, the joyriders, the slags and lads hanging around aimlessly on street corners controlled the Manors of this world. This week's scandal was that a local twelve-year-old girl was pregnant. The father was fourteen. The story hit the national press and then, like the hopes of the community, faded away.

After my reconnaissance of the area I went back to the house and contemplated suicide. What the hell was I doing in this godforsaken place? I'd lived in worse places, but not much worse.

Lorna did one of her 'specials', a full English breakfast consisting of lashings of scrambled eggs, sausages, bacon, baked beans, plum tomatoes, mushrooms, several slices of bread, tea and orange juice. Coronary heart disease was optional. Then we sat down to watch the 'Jerry Springer Show' on cable. Howard had the obligatory fag in his mouth. He was like a smoking bear. The only time he wasn't smoking was when he was shovelling food into his mouth, or that's how it seemed. He had obviously never grown out of the oral phase.

'Jerry, Jerry, Jerry,' said Lorna diving on to the sofa. 'I love Jerry Springer. Not the one you get on ITV. That's not the real Jerry. Sky One. Now that's proper Jerry.' The three of us became transfixed by the images on the screen. The segment we were watching was entitled 'I want to break up your marriage' or something like that. A woman was berating her son-in-law, continually getting up out of her seat on one side of the stage twenty feet away to harass the guy. She delivered a tirade of abuse, most of which couldn't be heard for bleeping. In between the hoopla of the hysterical audience we saw snatches of Jerry sitting among the great unwashed, head in hands, as the two participants traded insults. Howard and Lorna gazed at the screen, mesmerised. 'She's a prostitute . . . she even offered me sex,' said the guy of his mother-in-law. He looked like Noel Edmonds. 'You haven't had a fucking job in six years, you dummy,' she countered; and so on and so forth. Eventually there was the obligatory mass brawl.

'I don't watch it for the stories,' said Lorna. 'I just like the punch-ups.' Maybe daytime chat could replace boxing as the country's number one full-contact spectator sport. Howard was silently absorbed by the shenanigans for some time. Suddenly he piped up, 'I like her,' referring to one of two women who were now rushing each other on stage.

The show finished. It was time for work. Howard, Lorna and I set off to meet Mick, one of Howard's partners in the running-machine invention, and David who had reputedly inherited £19 million and, it was hoped, would bankroll the operation.

'Mick could tell you a few stories about boxing,' said Lorna as we sauntered into the office of the iron works where the machine was in its final stages of development.

'Horizontal champion, me,' said Mick, a former fighter in his mid-fifties who'd also been a boxing promoter. No sooner had we sat down than Howard started telling jokes.

'An IRA terrorist walks into a pet shop and says, "You've got three minutes to clear out, we're gonna blow the shop up." So the owner says, "But what about the tortoise?" ' And there's more.

'Two things people know Howard for,' says Lorna. 'Bad jokes and cigarettes.' Howard's ability to cane a packet of fags was legendary. Akay, who worked with Howard for a spell, confessed that while he was a fine man and a good trainer he couldn't have him at All Stars for any longer than a short spell because his chain-smoking conflicted with his dislike of tobacco. True to form, Howard finished another joke and instantly lit a cigarette. He consumed packets of twenty Sovereigns like a kid gobbles jellybabies. He seemed to spend half his time stopping at petrol stations and tobacconists to buy cancer sticks.

'Right, hop on there, son,' said Howard, several bad jokes and cigarettes later. With your eyes half closed the running machine looked like the rack. The basic concept was that you lay on your back on a bench, hooked your feet into two rubber bands which were connected to rollers and off you went. It was a strange sensation, running in a horizontal position. The bench rocked from side to side as I built up steam.

'That's it, keep going, faster, faster,' said Howard. Lorna joined us in the small workshop.

'You're knackering him out,' she said. My legs were turning to lead as Howard banged on the bottom axle of the machine to adjust the torque.

'How's that?' asked Howard.

'It's getting heavier,' I replied breathlessly.

'Come on, get your arms going as well,' he said, urging me on.

'Lie down and relax,' chipped in Lorna. 'You don't run looking at your feet, do you? Put your head back. Relax.' Relaxing this wasn't. I was sweating uncontrollably. My legs felt like jelly. I was slowing down. It was becoming impossible to move any more.

'Come on lad, keep going,' barked Howard. I tried a few more plodding steps and gave up.

'I've had it,' I gasped. I squeezed my upper thighs. They were numb. I stood up and nearly keeled over.

'What do you reckon?' asked Howard.

'That's something else,' I said. Saddam Hussein had nothing on this guy.

Howard was on a mission with his running machine. He figured each one would have a cost price of around £600 and retail for about two grand. He not only wanted to make piles of cash out of them but he genuinely wanted the project to be of public benefit and to provide employment for local people. Hope – we were all riding on it. Howard had his running machine, Ned had his perpetual motion power station; and I had my fists and a laptop computer.

I hung out with Lorna for a while, drinking cups of tea back at the house, and then headed into the city centre and spent money I didn't have. Howard was off on another adventure when we returned to the house, so I had the pleasure of an escort to the gym on foot and public transport from Simon.

'I've got a decision to make this evening,' said Simon. I was trying not to listen. 'I've got this girl who fancies me. She asked me out last week and I told her I'd give an answer tonight.'

'Tell her to piss off,' I said.

'You what?' Simon looked at me in the way kids do when adults say things they don't understand. If this little oik was going to engage me in conversation, I may as well give him my tuppence worth – of bullshit.

'Yeah, tell her to sling her hook. She's probably a little scrubber anyway.'

'Yeah,' said Simon vacantly. I thought, sensing I was a freak, he'd shut up. He continued talking. 'Me last girlfriend were all over me. She were kissing me all the time . . . it were right embarrassing.' Kissing you? Tsch!

Simon carried on with his juvenile nonsense as we headed for the bus stop through a sprawl of housing estates and across a muddy stretch of grass where a playground once stood. In its place were the remnants of a bonfire. A kid came up to us on a dirt bike and started talking about stolen video games or something. He was about eleven years old and had no helmet on.

'That's my best mate, Adrian,' said Simon.

'What's he on?' I mumbled.

'You what?' replied Simon.

'Don't answer a question with a question,' I said. We carried on much in the same vein until we got to the gym.

'This is Clinton,' said Howard. 'Clinton the boxer meet Dave the journalist.' Clinton was preparing for his big shot – the British, Commonwealth and European light-heavyweight title in Sheffield on 13 March. He was better looking than the average boxer, six foot two, slim with a touch of the Steve McQueen about him. No wonder there was talk in the gym of TV appearances and sponsorship deals.

'You're fighting in a couple of weeks' time,' I said.

'Yeah,' said Clinton.

'Are you coming up for the fight?' asked Howard.

'I'm going to be in New York for the Holyfield–Lewis fight. But I'll be thinking of you while I'm there.'

'No you fucking won't,' said Howard, smirking.

On the other side of the gym, I noticed a small boy crying and packing his training gear into a bag.

'What's up, what's the matter?' asked Andy Marlowe, who ran kick boxing classes on Tuesdays and Thursdays. Andy used to work Clinton's corner with Howard, but their relationship had soured and the partnership had dissolved. The boy explained that he had been sparring with Simon during Andy's class and had a broken tooth and a busted lip as a result. I joined the small group that had formed round the boy trying to console him. It was very touching.

'Don't worry about it,' said Clinton, offering his words of wisdom. 'One day you'll be able to knock 'im out.' Simon came over.

'I feel bad,' he whispered to me. 'Andy told him to keep his guard up but he didn't listen so I kicked him in the head and chipped his tooth.' Simon demonstrated the offending move, a left side sweep kick.

'I put my guard up and you hit me in the mouth,' the boy said, still sobbing.

'No I didn't,' said Simon. 'I kicked you.'

'You punched me deliberately,' insisted the boy. Such were the slings and arrows of the gym.

chapter 16

Lorna was balancing the telephone on her shoulder and flicking through a black Filofax for Frank Maloney's number. She thought Maloney, a relatively small-time promoter but Lennox Lewis's manager, might be interested in staging my big fight.

'You got to be one hundred and twenty per cent into this thing,' she said, lecturing me on my motives for becoming a fighter. Lorna had been probing me all morning about the book; she wanted to see some of my material, i.e. evidence of my 'commitment'.

'Where's that bloody number . . . Anyway, like I was saying, you'd be jeopardising your health and the confidence of others if you didn't take this seriously. You can't just walk away at the end.'

Walk away? You're damn right I would walk away. I put my life on hold to come to Sheffield and become a fighter, for the purpose of a book. I loved fast food, boozing, partying . . . I wasn't going to give all this up forever. I wasn't interested in being a boxer *per se*, but I was willing to temporarily forego one or two luxuries because I accepted sacrifice as intrinsic to the assignment. Once this was over, I would be back to my old tricks. What was Lorna suggesting, that I make a career out of boxing, give up big breakfasts, sex, chocolate, late nights, alcohol, sex, drugs, ice cream, sex, permanently? Dream on!

As much as I sympathised with Lao Tzu's philosophy that 'a man's expectations should be further than his reach', at thirty-one years six months and fifteen days old I was pushing it by attempting just one professional contest. I was painfully aware of the old aphorism, 'we live beyond what we enact'. I was a writer not a fighter. Moonlighting in the ring on a permanent basis was out of the question.

Lorna was not the first person to whom I had to justify my *raison d'être*. I had to repeat the same old spiel about my desire to write an 'inside story' as a participatory journalist so many times that I'd found myself constantly revalidating and re-evaluating my motives. Was there more to this than writing a book?

I had met many people over the past few months who doubted my ability as a writer and as a fighter and who thus could not get their heads round what I was trying to do. I felt this sense of cynicism coming from Lorna, too. She was full of working-class bravado. It was as if she was trying to put me through some sort of litmus test to see what I was made of, and how genuine I was. She seemed to doubt that any writer would or could put themselves through months and months of blood, sweat and tears just to write a book.

'You're not doing this just for a book, are you? You've got something to prove . . . to your dad . . . to yourself?' Mention your father or, heaven forbid, your mother and people go off on a Freudian trip. Was Lorna trying to do an armchair psychoanalysis on me? That was my job.

'Hmm. Maybe I have got something to prove,' I said. 'But haven't we all? Life is one big acid test.'

'Just make sure you do this for yourself,' said Lorna, finally locating Maloney's number. She made the call, but li'l Frank was in New York handling Lennox's affairs for the forthcoming big fight.

I really thought I was pushing it going this far. There was no way I was going to have more than one fight, no way. And Lorna didn't reassure me that I'd get that far, what with her tales of boxing woe, of fighters pooping their pants right before a fight.

'I hate boxing,' said Lorna, 'the business side of it at least. I love the fighters, though. Howard's got this one fighter . . . Scott Lansdowne . . . have you met him? Lovely boy. Anyway, on his pro debut he stayed here with us and woke up in the morning of the fight vomiting, absolutely shitting himself. He was shaking all day. I had to reassure him. I cuddled that boy all day.'

Scott won his pro debut and I'm sure Lorna played more than a small part in getting him through what must have been an ordeal. But was 'absolutely shitting yourself', shaking and vomiting all day the price you had to pay to get through your debut? I'd now been to so many fights and felt enough of the tense, anxious atmosphere to get nervous just watching fighters go through the motions. A little bit of knowledge can be a dangerous thing.

After Lorna's sermonising, Howard and I headed for the gym in his beat-up motor, 'Titanic' as Danny called it. What was left of the car was a 1988 Vauxhall Carlton, black, rusting, with the near side rear brake light held together with pink gaffer tape. Howard used the front passenger foot-well as a dustbin and the floor was covered with an assortment of sweet wrappers, old newspapers, cigarette butts and empty soft-drink cans. The first time I got in that heap Howard noticed me looking down at my feet with some disdain. 'Don't fucking worry about that,' he said. I wouldn't say I'm a clean freak but I am a stickler for personal hygiene and I was still deprogramming myself from the effects of a girlfriend who listed 'cleaning' as a hobby on her CV.

The gym was empty when we arrived and I quickly changed into my sweats, ready for my first day of training.

'Take your shoes and socks off and get on a couple of those bowling balls over there,' said Howard. I had seen a couple of guys doing this the day before and mimicked them by holding on to the ropes and feebly balancing on the balls. Howard said the idea of the exercise was to massage the meridian points on the soles of your feet, thus increasing your flexibility.

'Right, let's see you shadow,' said Howard.

All of a sudden, I felt really self-conscious and awkward. At All Stars, I could get away with poncing about in the crowd of other half-witted novices, but now I was under scrutiny. I could feel Howard watching my every move, analysing each clumsy step, each wooden punch. I alternated between the bowling balls and shadow boxing for a few rounds, then Howard threw me a couple of straps attached to about two and a half feet of bungee cord. 'Get these round your ankles,' he said. He told me my feet were too wide and the straps would help me with my stance and balance. I shadow boxed some more and then moved on to a heavy black leather bag. It was the hardest thing I had hit since accidentally putting my fist through a door at home in London while demonstrating the finer points of the noble art to a girlfriend. I hit the bag like a sissy. I was trying to punch holes through it but hardly any punches seemed to connect properly.

'What ya doing?' said Howard. 'Don't worry about trying to take it off the fucking wall. Work on speed and technique. The power'll come in time. For the moment, I want you to just work on that jab. We'll take it easy . . . one thing at a time, Captain.'

The jab is the meat and potatoes of boxing. It's the most commonly used punch and usually the first one a boxer learns. The jab is based on the principle that the shortest distance between two points is a straight line. By shooting out a straight left jab (or a right for a southpaw), a boxer is able to gauge the distance between himself and his opponent, in readiness for either an offensive or defensive manoeuvre. Doubling the jab repeatedly keeps an opponent off-balance and puts a fighter in an ideal position to throw follow-up punches such as a straight right or a left hook. The majority of combinations of punches generally start from a jab. A bad jab not only makes it harder to throw hooks, uppercuts and right crosses, but it also weakens a fighter's balance and defence, making him vulnerable to counter punches. This is why it is essential to develop a solid, technically proficient jab.

After rapidly breaking into a sweat and feeling sapped of all strength, I moved on to a lighter, longer bag and then on to a floor-to-ceiling speedball. I finished training and as the day moved on, a slow procession of young amateurs and old pros appeared.

'That kid you're fighting on Friday night, Danny, he's from Hull Police,' said John Naylor.

'Hull Police? All the more reason to knock the bastard out,' replied Danny. Another trainer, a 250lb lump with a massive head and long greasy hair, overheard the conversation and ambled over.

'Aye, that Hull lad'll be a strong, brave fella. Thou knows what those police kids are like.' The lump walked away and went back to pad work with one of the amateurs. Amateurs and pros alike were always referred to as 'kids' or 'lads' regardless of age.

'Big strong lad!' said Danny incredulously. 'What the fuck does he know?'

Danny removed his T-shirt, baring his chiselled, angular physique. I noticed some of the younger amateurs staring at him furtively, with an almost envious appreciation. He bounded up to Howard and started badgering him with questions about what he should do in the fight, how he should stand, throw punches, etc. Howard appeared aloof. His eye was on something else. Nevertheless, he reassured the young buck – like a knowing father – that everything would be OK so long as he does as he's told. Armed with this minor confidence-booster, Danny strode around the gym posing, looking at his smooth-skinned reflection in the mirror, doing Muhammad Ali impersonations and pontificating about his second excursion into the ring in two days' time – 'Hull Police? I'm gonna knock that motherfucker out!'

Minutes later a well-built guy with what looked like soot on his face walked into the gym.

'Justin, meet David. David, meet Justin,' said Howard, going on to explain that Justin Fleming, a welder by trade and a former amateur fighter with many fights to his credit, would be one of my main sparring partners. 'He's a nice lad, our Justin. Can't fucking fight, but a nice kid.' Justin told me he was dragged down to a boxing gym when he was thirteen. He's thirty now. Howard said he could have been a contender according to his former trainer, Brendan Ingle, who coached him at his St Thomas's gym across the city in Wincobank. In those days, when Prince Naz looked up to Ingle like a father, Justin used to 'bash up' Johnny Nelson in sparring. Nelson was currently the WBO world cruiserweight champion. He fought nobodies for twenty-five grand a pop. Justin welded industrial crushing machines for four hundred quid a week.

Two regulars in the gym, 'the Rotherham lads', gave me their appraisal of Justin when I told them I was going to spar with him.

'Aye, he's a right fucking animal,' said one.

'Have ye seen 'im spar?' said the other. 'Fucking mental. Non-stop.'

I noticed Justin sizing me up, trying to figure me out. His shoulders were massive and looked padded like a gridiron linebacker. He looked like you could put a yoke on his back and have him ploughing fields.

'Young David's up here to write a book,' mumbled Howard.

'Oh yeah?' said Justin, twirling a bandage around his wrist and knuckles. 'So what's this book about, then?'

'Boxing,' I said. 'Howard's training me to have a fight.' Justin's face dropped.

'Yeah? You got some bottle, ain't ya? 'Ere Howard, can we spar today?' He grinned, showing a large gap where a front tooth used to be.

''E's not ready yet, Just. Another month and you can have a piece of 'im,' said Howard.

'You got some bottle,' Justin repeated. He still seemed stunned at the idea of me, some soft southern writer, coming up to the Steel City to become a fighter. ''E's got some bottle, ain't he Howard?'

'We'll see,' said Howard dryly. 'We'll see.'

When I first arrived at the gym Howard had mentioned that John Naylor would be in the corner for my fight. John was of course an amateur coach and as such was not permitted to work as a second or trainer in a professional bout. Howard, like so many before him, had assumed that I was intending to have an amateur fight, even though I thought I'd made it clear when I first spoke to him on the telephone. After the grilling Lorna had given me that morning, I gave her a synopsis of my book so she and Howard could fully appreciate what I was trying to do. I couldn't afford to waste time with any more misunderstandings.

'Howard ... HOWARD.' Lorna was having difficulty getting

through to Howard, who was slouched on the sofa. Howard was deaf in his right ear. According to Lorna, this was a legacy of his days as a fighter – too many blows to the head – although Howard always strenuously denied it. When his mobile went off in the gym, a chorus of 'HOWARD, YOUR PHONE'S RINGING' rang out and seconds later, somewhat surprised, he'd say, 'Oh yeah,' and pull it from the waistband of his jogging bottoms. Once he'd made it to the sofa, remote control in hand, Howard would get lost in the multi-channel edutainment world of cable TV. Entranced by the mating rituals of the Borneo orang-utan, absorbed in the intrigue of the Roswell UFO incident, Howard would zone out and disappear far from the madding crowd of Lorna and the kids.

'Howard, Howard . . . HOWARD! I'm TALKING to you!'

'Uh?'

'You do know that David wants to have a *professional* fight, don't you?

'You what?'

'Oh, for Christ's sake, Howard,' said Lorna, turning her attention to me. 'I wasn't quite sure what you were trying to do at first.' Neither was I, come to think of it. 'But after reading that stuff you gave me it all makes sense.'

Lorna threatened to turn off the TV – that got her Howard's attention.

'David wants to have a professional fight, Howard, not amateur.'

'Hmm . . . professional. No problem. It'll take a few more months . . .' he paused for thought – and more thought. 'No problem.'

Howard lit a cigarette, shifted in his seat, and went back to his orang-utans, Egyptology and UFOs.

chapter 17

The following morning Sky Sports arrived at the gym to interview Clinton. Sky was the only TV network in the country showing any serious interest in boxing. ITV were screening Shea Neary in his WBU title fights and the Beeb were flirting with highlights of boxing on *Grandstand*. Channel 5 showed the odd fight or two. It was a far cry from the time when legions watched Frank Bruno on *Midweek Sports Special* and made him a household name; and a record-breaking 18.3 million saw Barry McGuigan fight Danilo Cabrera on BBC1 for the WBA featherweight title. That was in 1986.

As Clinton prepared for his big TV break, his promoter and manager Dennis Hobson Jr made sure the sponsors got their money's worth. The sportswear firm Diadora furnished Clinton with tracksuits, trainers, baseball caps and the like so naturally he had to wear the gear on TV and for photo calls. At the back of the gym Diadora had a fifteen-foot banner with their logo emblazoned on it; Dennis made sure the Sky people hooked their camera up so Diadora got the necessary product placement in the background.

Dennis was a thirty-seven-year-old scrap metal dealer with ambitions beyond muck and brass. He reminded me of Jim Davidson. He was always grinning inanely like the cat that got the cream and cracking snide jokes at someone else's expense. His wide-boy style wasn't everyone's cup of tea but I thought he was a typically loveable rogue, always chasing 'the birds' (the younger the better), wheeling and dealing non-stop on his mobile. When the mood took him he even sparred with some of the lads in the gym, including Clinton. He co-owned the gym with his father, Old Man Dennis (who had introduced him and his millionaire brother Andrew into the scrap game), his mother Pat and a couple of silent partners. Of the ten or so pros who gravitated around the gym, Dennis promoted and managed half.

The Hobson clan were well known in the City of Steel. They were to Sheffield what the Ewings were to Dallas. Senior was a reformed gambler who had spent over a million pounds on the gee gees, dogs and whatever else took his fancy. He had apparently been the first man in Sheffield to own a Rolls-Royce Silver Shadow.

Dennis had his sidekick with him, a retard in shabby, greasy clothes with a face like a duck. Everyone called him 'Tosser'. Tosser did 'odds and sods' for Dennis's scrap metal business. Danny said the real reason he had him around was so he had 'someone to take the piss out of when he's bored'.

As the Sky people went about setting up their cameras and sound equipment, Tosser inspected one of the cameras like a she-ape picking nits from her young. Minutes later Danny strolled into the gym and upon seeing Tosser immediately started to gee him up with juvenile comments.

''Ere Tosser, have Sky come to film ya for the Discovery Channel?' said Danny.

'Fuck off,' replied Tosser, which was pretty much the extent of his vocabulary.

'Look at them trousers. He's not changed 'em in the three years I've known him,' said Danny to anyone who'd listen. 'Look at him. He's like a village idiot.'

The cameras started rolling and Clinton went into a monologue about how he 'got back into boxing to keep fit and stay out of trouble' after he'd 'got into one punch-up too many'.

'He's really come out of his shell. He's much better with his interviews,' Dennis whispered to me as Clinton casually answered questions.

Later in the day I escaped into Sheffield town centre with Danny for a binge at McDonald's. Even though he never stopped talking (usually about himself) and was a constant irritant, Danny had an endearing quality about him. Perhaps it was his vulnerability, coupled with a sense of insecurity and honesty, character traits that most fighters seem to have in abundance.

'I grew up with smoking,' said Danny as we munched our way through our 'extra value meals' and drank thick shakes. 'When I were a kid, I used to think that it were me old man's natural smell. I'd smell the weed coming through the door and say, "Yep. The old man's 'ere." '

Danny's mother was a schoolteacher and his father 'something in the music business'. He got into boxing after trying martial arts and bodybuilding and he thought he could go all the way if he could stay off the street. Danny told me of his exploits as a 'street *bwoy*', juggling girls, money, all sorts. Then there were the gang fights, banging chicks in the backs of cars . . .

'If it weren't for Howard, I wouldn't be in that gym,' he said.

That evening Shaun Stokes, an overweight welterweight who looked like a fat Jack Kid Berg, showed up at the Raineys' place. I had seen Shaun at the gym; he'd given me some funny looks. He always looked miserable or 'mardy' as they say in Yorkshire. At twenty-nine Shaun was in semi-retirement, i.e. he had quit boxing after his last fight and was now waiting for his next fight. Shaun had come to talk to Howard about pebbledashing his house.

'I'm gonna get him to pebbledash the garden shed first, just to see how he gets on,' said Howard.

I left the boys to talk about pebbledashing and went up to my room to read *This Bloody Mary* from my small collection of boxing books. Flicking through the pages, I drifted off, daydreaming, visualising myself sitting in the corner of the ring. It's the fight. A hand is thrust in my mouth and yanks out my gumshield. Howard is coolly giving me instructions. I feel a gentle slap round the face. Water is poured over my head. I take a swig from a bottle, spit it out into a bucket and the gumshield goes back in my mouth. 'Seconds out . . .'

A fight was a long way off but that didn't stop me from going through the motions in my head, constantly. What would it be like? Would I cope? How will I look? Will I make a complete fool of myself? These thoughts, fears, were with me every day.

Howard had earlier remarked that I was 'looking sharp'. 'In six months' time you'll be sparring with Danny and giving him hell,' he said. 'Give it nine months, fight at Christmas and you'll win for sure.' His words were encouraging. But nine months? I didn't have that sort of time. I was already behind schedule. My publishing deadline was the end of October. I figured if I really worked hard, I could get a pro fight around the end of the summer, barring any mishaps. I would soon come to realise that this was a fantasy.

After just three days of training, my body ached like it never had before. 'You really need at least a year to get properly fit,' Howard had told me, emphasising the need for me gradually to wean my body on to the daily grind of hard training. Howard said that for the first few months of training I should not overdo it.

A combination of intense exercise, stress, lack of sleep and adjusting to a new environment made me rundown and, buckling under the northern weather, I came down with the flu. I lay on my bed blowing, puffing and breathing heavily. I broke into a cold sweat. A mild fever was starting to get a hold of me, twisting me in knots. I refused to succumb to illness. After three days I was done in. 'Soft southern poof' they'd all say if I didn't make it to the gym the following day. I was determined to show these people I had heart, so I resigned myself to continuing training even though my body deserved a rest and I'd rather be in bed with a cup of tea and a good book.

The gym was all but empty and eerily quiet apart from the faint creaking of a punch bag swaying on a chain. Clinton and a young cruiserweight called Mark Hobson, a paid sparring partner from Bradford, stepped into the confines of the ring. The buzzer sounded, breaking the silence. They touched gloves and began to fight, tentatively flicking out jabs, weighing up each other, trying to find their distance. After a couple of rounds they'd warmed up and the reality of the pain game kicked in. Small welts and bruises appeared on their sweaty brows and cheeks as the sparring became more intense. A trickle of blood oozed from Hobson's nose courtesy of a straight right hand. Clinton had what looked like a split lip.

As the sound of 'Ooosh ooosh' punctuated the silence of the gym with each punch thrown, I made a mental note of each fighters' patterns, mistakes, idiosyncrasies and subtle techniques as I shadow boxed in the adjacent ring. Sparring provided an ideal opportunity to look and learn. Watching the pros fight at such close quarters was a boon to my education and I paid keen attention to their footwork, head movement and the combinations of punches they threw. I learned as much, if not more, watching sparring than actual fights. For one, seeing guys like Clinton spar day in day out gave me the opportunity to analyse individual styles and emulate oft-repeated moves.

In between rounds they'd spit on the floor beside the ring. Buckets were a rarity in the gym. Clinton backed Mark up into a corner, lacing him with body shots. There was a lot of heavy breathing. The ropes around the ring groaned like the rigging on a schooner in high seas; more heavy breathing. During these sparring sessions, Howard would lean on a corner post of the ring, quiet but for the odd exclamation or critical comment. Occasionally he'd gesture with his arm for one fighter to move anti-clockwise, away from the other's right fist. Dennis Hobson Sr eyed the sparring intently, keeping a close watch on his investment.

One of the barmaids stared at the champion like a teenaged groupie. I dropped the rope grid down over the ring and did a few rounds of bobbing and weaving between the lines and then got to work on the 60lb heavy bag – a solid black leather number. As I slugged away at the bag, sooty-faced Justin arrived and after warming up began pounding vicious rights and lefts into the next bag along from me.

Mark's girlfriend sat poker faced, watching from the sidelines. She was in her early twenties, pretty with long brown hair and about eight months pregnant. She gently rubbed her tummy as Mark continued to fight off the back foot with Clinton stalking him round the ring. After five rounds Howard said customarily, 'That'll do yer,' and the pair slipped through the ropes and out of the ring. Clinton moved on to the heavy bag.

I had survived my first week in Sheffield. I still felt like a foreigner, detached from my new surroundings, but I felt comfortable. There were no lynch mobs, no disgruntled locals who hated cockneys, no North–South divide. The North wasn't that bad. It was set.

'I can't believe thou's never boxed before,' said Justin, grinning as I jabbed at the heavy bag. 'Look at him . . . never fucking boxed before!' The three-minute timer buzzed and I stared at myself in the mirror. I was wearing a Lonsdale all-in-one. It was the kind favoured by wrestlers and Mike Tyson, only Mike looked marginally better in his. I threw a flurry of uncoordinated punches into thin air and felt really self-conscious. 'You fucking look the part,' said Justin.

'All I've got to do now is fight the part,' I said.

According to Justin the word in the gym was that I had noticeably improved in the few days since I arrived. I was encouraged by the support I got from most of the guys in the gym. I was of course something of a novelty, a 'nobble' as Howard would say, but I could sense a genuine appreciation from those around me for my cause. In a funny sort of way I felt a strange sense of belonging in the gym. My arrival there and the sense that I had finally cracked the egg I'd been boiling all these months made me reflect on the rollercoaster life I'd led and the events that had catapulted me into boxing. I cried in my little bedroom later that evening just thinking about where I'd been, what I'd achieved and where I was headed. Tears would be the watermark of my experiences over the coming months.

Maloney's people had got back to Lorna to say they were interested in speaking to me about becoming a pro. Bingo! And there was positive feedback from the gym.

'Don't tell Howard I told you this,' said Lorna, 'but he said he thinks you've got "fucking talent". Howard doesn't say things like that lightly.'

The deal was I paid £30 a week for my board and lodging. This was strictly a business arrangement. Maybe Lorna would say anything to keep those tenners rolling in. Did I really have 'fucking talent'? I could see the Raineys were in financial straits. They needed me. I needed them. We'd get on like a house on fire.

Danny Daley, Howard's answer to Roy Jones, won his second fight that night at the Moat House hotel in Doncaster. He pulled off a neat performance, flooring his opponent twice in the third round, first with a right uppercut and then with a short left hook, but not before he got wobbled himself.

'He hit me and I saw stars. First time I've ever seen stars,' said Danny. 'I just backed off and got it together and came back at him. Yeah, he rocked me. But I dealt with him in style.'

After the fight Howard and I returned home and I stayed up until 4.30 that morning talking with Lorna. I thought I had problems, but she had more baggage than Luton airport. 'My attitude is everyone's got baggage, Dave. You've just got to pick someone whose baggage you can handle.' Some of her revelations came as a shock. She'd had a tough life. The night before she'd had a blood clot on her leg, a recurring problem which was the result of a stroke she'd had a few years earlier. The blood clots caused her to have frequent blackouts. She had to take something like thirty tablets a day to keep her breathing. On top of that she'd had a nervous breakdown four years earlier, which resulted in her spending three weeks in psychiatric care. Thank God for Prozac. 'I've had all sorts done to me. I've been hung out of a fifth-floor window, dragged across the street by my hair, beaten black and blue. I've had a gun held to my head . . .' As I say, I thought I had problems.

chapter 18

Madison Square Garden, New York City, 13 March 1999. Limousine after limousine pulled up outside the main concourse of the 'spiritual home of boxing' on 7th Avenue. The beautiful people sashayed from their chrome and leather interiors on to the sidewalk. The hustle, the bustle, the bump and grind of the big-fight crowd was alive with a pulsating energy. The Big Apple hadn't seen anything like this since Smokin' Joe Frazier went fifteen gruelling rounds with Muhammad Ali and won. On that night in 1971, 21,455 fight fans paid $1,352,961 to see one of the greatest fights of all time. A ringside seat cost $150 and Frank Sinatra took photographs from the press bench. On this night, another sell-out crowd of 21,284 paid over $11 million to see one of the most dubious decisions of all time. A ringside seat cost $5,000 and given the chance, Don King would've sold photographs of his mama from the press bench.

Seventh Avenue was awash with fur coats, gold chains, trilby hats, mobile phones, cops, canes, camcorders, leopard skin, high-class hookers, pimps, pushers, cigars, Cuban heels, diamond rings, Rolexes, reefers, fishnet stockings, kilts, reporters, high-rollers and low-riders and conspicuous consumption in myriad guises. The faint smell of marijuana, expensive aftershave and exhaust fumes hung leisurely in the air as a cast of thousands paraded along the sidewalk and ducked in and out of the passing traffic in a Technicolor burst of zoot suits, sequinned strapless numbers and assorted fancy dress. I felt like I'd stumbled on to the set of *West Side Story* or Spike Lee's *Malcolm X*. The glitz and the glamour of the big-fight scene was a far cry from the spit and sawdust of the small-hall shows I'd become accustomed to in the UK.

Here I was, an Englishman in New York. It had been nearly twenty years since I'd last walked the city's mean streets; but now I was surprised to find that the Big Apple was no longer a tough nut. Mayor Giuliani's administration had in recent years introduced a zero tolerance policy towards crime that had resulted in legions of muggers, beggars, pickpockets, peddlers and panhandlers being swept off the streets. New York was now one of the safest cities in America, in fact the world. When I was a boy in Brooklyn, for a year I was terrorised by the worst the city had to offer. Nowadays, even the old neighbourhood of Flatbush and the crumbling tenement blocks where I lived on 141 East 21st and 49 East 19th Streets didn't seem that bad. (That said, a week after I hit town the cops shot dead a couple of hoods who robbed a liquor store around the corner from where I used to live.)

I planned to have an extended trip, to reacquaint myself with the city. I did the shopping and sightseeing number and visited my old neighbourhood including Walt Whitman IS 246, my alma mater. While trying to dig up my old school records, I met one of Whitman's longest-serving teachers, Mrs Macnamara, a short grey-haired grandmother type in her sixties. She introduced me to some of her colleagues. 'This is Davis [sic] Matthews from England. He was a student here nearly twenty years ago. He's a writer. Can you believe that? He went to this school and he's a writer. We do have some success stories after all!'

Mrs Macnamara gave me a mini tour of the ground floor. I still felt nervous walking around those corridors. I'd been mugged in and around the school several times as a kid. She told me that recently one of her pupils had been stabbed to death over a drug deal. She bitched about Bill Clinton – 'the President's a jerk' – and the school – 'this place is the lowest of the low'. She was right on both counts. In 1999, out of 235 middle schools in New York, Walt Whitman was ranked 219th with just 22.6 per cent of students at or above the required grade level for reading. As for Bill's track record . . . well, it speaks for itself.

On the day of the fight, I met with some old pals from London (identities changed to spare them the indignity of a) prosecution and b) divorce proceedings). Eddie, Marcus, his brother Steve and Ronnie were all staying in the Metro Hotel, a comfortable three-star joint off Broadway. They were also in town for the big fight. Then there was Kevin and his mate Will, a stockbroker who worked on Wall Street. In the New York vernacular, these were my 'homeboys'. I liked to think of them simply as the Lads – hedonistic, working-class fellas with high disposal incomes, an aversion to any form of responsibility and a predilection for excitement. They would travel from the Birmingham NEC to the Hilton Las Vegas for big title fights and a good time; they'd show up at stag dos in limos clutching bottles of champagne. The previous week they flew from London to Newcastle for the Calzaghe–Reid middleweight title fight. The Lads liked to think they were players. Real *Lock, Stock and Two Smoking Barrels*-type players. They'd paid £400 apiece for their Holyfield–Lewis tickets, which had a face value of $250. Add the hotel accommodation, flights, partying, drugs, booze and sundry expenses and they'd probably blown five grand a head for the weekend.

'I'm out of it,' said Steve, staggering out of the Metro Hotel into the street. 'I've got to go for a walk and freshen up.' Steve was still feeling the effects of his first night in New York City. The Lads had been to a club called Webster's – four floors of hip-hop, R'n'B, dance and Brit-pop. They'd got slaughtered on too much booze and coke. The bender had started the moment they'd got on the plane at Heathrow. Steve had 'bottled' (i.e. inserted in his rectum) several grams of cocaine for the weekend's jollity. Everyone had got high on his supply.

'He fucking irritated the arse out of me on the flight over,' said Eddie as Steve disappeared into the milieu of Broadway. 'Every five minutes he was climbing over me to get to the toilet for a line.'

Booze, coke, whores – it was all part of a weekend away for the Lads. These animals knew how to party hearty, no expense spared. Where they got the money from for such a lifestyle was anyone's guess. They didn't have what you'd call 'regular' jobs.

Eddie and I went for breakfast. On the way to the diner we passed a tramp dressed in a greatcoat, hooded sweat shirt and Yankees baseball cap. She wore a Reebok sneaker on her right foot and one by Guess? Jeans on her left. She had a kind of vagrant chic about her. Only in America. In Notting Hill she'd look like just another trustafarian.

'You're getting a bit thin on top, Davy boy,' said Eddie as we left the diner.

'I know . . .' Jesus, the secret was out. Thanks for the hereditary baldness, Dad. The only comfort I took from going bald (apart from major savings on shampoo bills) was the nebulous link between baldness and high levels of testosterone. Eddie had a full head of hair so I quickly changed the subject as we carried on surfing through the flotsam and jetsam of lower Broadway.

One schizophrenic, four junkies and a bag lady later, we reached our bar-room rendezvous with the rest of the crew. The Lads drank beer. I had cranberry juice. I was determined to lay off the booze and the drugs regardless of the company I kept. The barman set up more drinks and the talk was of boxing, booze and birds.

'When I went to Vegas for the Bruno–Tyson fight,' said Marcus, 'I was pissed up on the plane, in the hotel, at the fight. I was so drunk I couldn't see what was happening. After getting lagged up last week I decided this time around to take it easy, pace myself . . . before I get completely fucked!' Raucous laughter.

Kevin said the previous night, while the others boogied the night away at Webster's, he and his broker friend got a couple of hookers from the Yellow Pages. Five hundred and eighty bucks they cost in total, including coke.

The day progressed and the excitement started to sink in. I was high on the expectation of the big fight. The Lads were just high. A few of us found ourselves bumming around the Garden in the late afternoon. I cussed the name of Don King. He'd screwed me for $15 for an official programme; fifteen bucks for nothing more than a glossy arse lick to Teflon Don with a few fight facts thrown in. Eddie bought about half-a-dozen copies; one for himself and the rest as souvenirs for the folks back home – at $15 a go! Was I tight, or just out of touch with the realities of sports capitalism? Despite the price tag the vendors in their little booths on the concourse were doing a roaring trade. Soon they were sold out and a couple of hours later the hustlers who had bought the early stocks were back on the same concourse selling the same programmes to suckers for $75 a pop. Only in America.

The Lads went back to the Metro to freshen up, sink more beers and snort more coke before showtime. I tagged along and stayed clean. Honest. About three fights into the undercard we returned to the Garden.

The concourse was now teeming with people. A group of young girls were handing out little Jamaican flags. We passed the first sentry post of security guards into the Garden and broke through a throng of fight fans in the foyer. We examined our tickets to work out where our seats were and joined the sea of Lewis supporters dressed in a rainbow parade of football colours milling around. The 7,000 who had ventured over from the UK constituted a mini invasion. New York welcomed the British fight fan with typical American hospitality. Why wouldn't they when all that lovely sterling was piling into J.C. Penny, Macy's and various outlets of Footlocker? As we stood trying to figure out the way to our seats and the probability of sneaking me into the $250 enclosure, I felt a tap on my shoulder.

'Hey, Dave. What's up? We fucking made it, man! Jimmy came

through!' Gabriel and Tony greeted me like a couple of old swells. They were ex-pats from Leamington Spa whom I'd met on the JFK–Manhattan airport bus. The pair ran a yacht repair shop on the west coast and had flown over from LA without tickets for the fight in the hope that they'd score from one of the many 'scalpers' outside the Garden. They were swaying in front of me, their faces beaming with that ruddy glow that only farmers and drunks have. While Tony grinned inanely like a banjo-playing hick, Gabriel held a ticket aloft and then kissed it longingly. This was lurve.

'A hundred and fifty bucks,' drooled Gabriel giving that piece of cardboard another wet one for good measure.

'What a result,' I said. 'Where'd you get the tickets?'

'Jimmy's, man,' said Gabriel his face sweaty and reddening. 'A hundred and fifty bucks. Jimmy came through! Jimmy, I fucking love you!'

Jimmy, from what I could make out, was the owner of a bar somewhere in Manhattan. A friend of a friend had put Gabriel in touch with him and he and Tony had bought the tickets. They had paid $150 for tickets with a face value of $100 on the night of the fight. This was the undisputed heavyweight championship of the world, the greatest prize in sport. It had been sold out for four months. Something didn't add up.

'Where are you seated?' I asked, trying to sneak a closer look at one of the tickets. Tony pulled out a thin strip of card and showed it to me. Gabriel was dancing on the spot like a crack addict about to hit the pipe. He was ecstatic. I took one look at the ticket and knew it was a fake, and not even a good one.

I didn't have the heart to steal their thunder, especially as they thought they had better seats than I did. Apart from some fairly obvious indicators, the tickets lacked the lightly embossed words 'Madison Square Garden' which ran diagonally across its face as a sign of authentication. They'd never get past the second set of security guards with those tickets. At the second sentry point the tickets were more closely scrutinised and also checked against an ultra-violet light.

I imagined the inevitable rejection; that sinking feeling of being ripped off followed by drunken despondency. They'd have to watch the big fight in a small bar. There'd be the desire to wreak revenge on Jimmy hastened by the feeling of hopelessness once it had sunk in that he's probably in with the mob and could have their heads blown off as soon as look at them. Finally, there'd be the realisation that they'd been stiffed and there was sweet FA they could do about it. I felt mildly sorry for Gabriel and Tony. Still, at least I wasn't in the shit.

'Well, I've got to catch up with my mates,' I said, edging away. 'Enjoy the fight.'

'Yeah, you too, Dave,' replied Gabriel and with that he grabbed Tony's shoulders from behind and the pair did a conga in the opposite direction and disappeared deep into the crowd.

I caught up with the Lads but they soon slipped through one of the security cordons leading into the section of the auditorium where their seats were. Those bastards didn't even try to work me in. I cussed them and ventured up into the gods to my seat, four rows from the very back of the auditorium.

The undercard was in full swing and the arena was slowly filling up. Don King was booed and hissed like a pantomime villain every time his fat frame, resplendent with his gawking face and shock of hair appeared on the massive overhead video screens above the ring. For years the public had been fed the line that King was a scumbag *par excellence*. He had spent time in the slammer for kicking a man to death. 'Don, I'll pay you the money,' were his victim's last words. He'd come a long way from running a numbers racket in Cleveland to become the P.T. Barnum of boxing.

'This is the fight the world has been clamouring for,' said King in his pre-fight hype. 'Finally, for the first time in seven years we will have an undisputed heavyweight champion of the world on 13 March at Madison Square Garden, the Mecca of boxing.

'I have never worked harder to make a fight happen,' he added. 'In the end, it's all worth it for the people.' It had all been worth it for King, too. Teflon Don's golden egg was the US pay-per-view rights which he split fifty-fifty with the distributors. The fight generated an estimated 1.2 million buys at $49.95 a throw. Add to that another $8 million worth of foreign pay-per-view sales and the $10 million he hustled from Madison Square Garden to stage the fight. Subtract Lewis's $11.5 million purse, Holyfield's $20.5 million cut, five or six million in expenses to referees, cornermen, judges, sanctioning bodies, advertising, etc., and what have you got? As they say Stateside, 'Do the math.' King made a nice little earner.

I bit into a $4.99 jumbo hotdog. (Lorna told me I could eat what I wanted providing I returned to Sheffield no heavier than 14½ stone.) 'LENNOX BABEEE!!!' bellowed a fat drunk sitting behind me as an image of Lewis flashed up on the overhead screen. The arena was nearing capacity as heavyweights Mario Cawley and Johnny 'The Quiet Man' Ruiz slugged it out in the ring. The distant rumble of the crowd rose to a crescendo as Cawley was knocked down in the second round only to beat the count with seconds to spare. 'Saved by the bell,' muttered the guy next to me. Cawley went on to get knocked out in the fourth round. There were some good fighters on the undercard – Ruiz, Fernando Vargas, James 'The Mighty Quinn' Page – but no one was really interested in them. The big one was just too big to allow more than a passing interest in the undercard.

An Englishman in a Norwich City football shirt lit up a cigarette. Within seconds a short bull-dyke security guard was on the case.

'Excuse me, sir, but smoking is not permitted in the auditorium.'

'Why aren't you allowed to smoke?' snarled the Englishman.

'Fire department regulations.'

'Are you going to tell everyone in here to put their cigarettes out?'

'Only those in my section, sir.' The Englishman put out the cigarette, grudgingly.

A thumping serenade of rap and R'n'B rang out. The MC gave a roll call of celebrities over the PA. The star-studded audience included firebrand civil rights leader Reverend Al Sharpton; John F. Kennedy Jr; comedian Jerry Seinfeld; movie stars Michael Douglas (ringside), Michael J. Fox and Jack Nicholson (ringside); basketball legend 'Magic' Johnson; husband and wife actors Sara Jessica Parker and Matthew Broderick; hip-hop supremo Puff Daddy; Rolling Stones Keith Richards and Ronnie Wood; film director Spike Lee... At most of the fights I had previously been to the only celebrities to be found were the odd soap extra and that guy who plays DC Burnside in 'The Bill'.

A Canadian maple leaf and the Stars and Stripes flew over the ring but curiously there was no Union Flag. The minutes ticked away to the big fight. An image of Evander Holyfield wearing a baseball jacket and cap bearing his clothing label, 'Holyfield Warrior', appeared on the overhead video screen. A thunderous boo rang out from the British supporters dotted in clumps around the arena, momentarily drowning the applause given to Holyfield by the Americans. The Americans tried to rally with cheering for Holyfield but conceded defeat when Don King appeared on the overhead screen yet again followed by the obligatory booing. 'There's only one Frankie Warren... one Frankie War-ren... there's only one Frankie Wa-rr-en.'

Chants of 'LOOO-ISS, LOOO-ISS' reverberated round the Garden.

Lennox was our knight in shining shorts, the gladiator steering our chariot of dreams. British fight fans had not warmed to Lewis in the early days because of his transatlantic upbringing. Born in London to Jamaican parents, his mother Violet took him as a small boy to Ontario where he grew up and learned to box. Under the Canadian flag he got to the 1984 Olympic quarterfinals and at the 1988 Seoul Games he stopped Riddick Bowe in the super-heavyweight final to take the gold medal.

In 1993 Lewis became technically the first English heavyweight world champion since Bob Fitzsimmons in 1897 after Bowe (by then undisputed heavyweight champion) ceremoniously dumped his WBC belt in a dustbin live on TV rather than face a mandatory defence.

Lewis's first defence was against national hero Frank Bruno whom he stopped after seven laborious rounds in Cardiff in 1993. He then overwhelmed Phil Jackson in eight rounds in Miami but was spectacularly knocked out by Oliver McCall in two rounds at Wembley in 1994. Three years later he regained the title from McCall during a bizarre episode in which the American champion had a nervous breakdown in the ring a couple of rounds into the fight. Lewis successfully defended his title against the 6ft 8in Henry Akinwande, after the Nigerian was disqualified for repeatedly holding. His warm-up for Holyfield was a tough points win over the Croatian Zeljko Mavrovic who weighed in at 15 stone 4½lb compared to Lewis's huge 17 stone 5lb.

Now aged thirty-three, the WBC champion had got what he'd been waiting years for – a crack at thirty-six-year-old Evander Holyfield, his IBF and WBA belts and the chance to unify the heavyweight division.

'Ladies and gentlemen,' announced the MC Jimmy Lennon Jr. 'Let me welcome you to Madison Square Garden in New York. The most famous arena in the world . . .' We were now minutes away from the moment we'd all been waiting for.

'. . . there's only one Lennox Lewis, he's walking along, singing a song walking in a Lewis wonderland . . .' A fella with a ZZ Top beard wearing a red morning suit, Union Jack waistcoat and black top hat swaggered into the seating area, spilling beer from a plastic pint glass. He yelled a stream of expletives at the overhead screen when another image of King and Holyfield appeared, following up with another song, 'Rule Britannia, Britannia rule the waves, Britons never, never, never shall be slaves!' The Garden management apparently hadn't realised the folly of making alcohol available to the English.

Suddenly the bull-dyke security guard reappeared with a man looking for his seat. The pair counted up and down the rows until their gaze rested on me. No, it couldn't be.

'I need to see this guy's ticket,' she said to the man as they hovered down the aisle towards me. 'It's your lucky night,' she said, eyeing me like she'd caught a live one. 'May I see your ticket please, sir?' I showed her my ticket.

'Is there a problem?' I asked.

'No problem,' she replied. The bull-dyke looked at my ticket, then the man's ticket. I looked at the bull-dyke, then the man. 'Thank you, sir.' The bull dyke escorted the man back up the aisle mumbling something about seating allocations and duplicate tickets.

'LOOO-ISS, LOOO-ISS, LOOO-ISS.' The crowd erupted as Lennox, an impressive 6ft 5in and weighing in at 246lb, entered the arena to a booming Bob Marley anthem playing on the PA system. A minor fracas occurred as Lennox, dressed in red trunks with gold trim but eschewing a robe, squeezed his way through the crowded arena entrance surrounded by his brother Dennis, manager Maloney, trainer Steward and an entourage of seconds, minders and flunkies. As he jigged and shadow boxed in the ring, a shaven-headed Holyfield, giving away two and a half inches and 31lb, emerged wearing purple shorts with red trim and a purple and white robe with 'PHIL: 4-13' on the back. A rousing gospel number rang out and Holyfield sang along in praise to the Lord. After the pre-fight formalities, the bell sounded. Round One.

'Whack him round the ear, Lennox, it's only plastic,' someone cried as Lewis and Holyfield tentatively played their opening gambits. The pair jabbed, posed and feinted until the end of the round when Holyfield picked up Lewis and threw him to the canvas. Referee Arthur Mercante Jr brought the fighters together for a friendly warning after the bell rang.

Lewis took the second round. Holyfield had prophesied a third-round knockout – God had told him so in a dream. He would become undisputed heavyweight champion of the world, and who was he to argue with the big guy upstairs? As the fighters rested after the second round, there was growing anticipation around the arena. 'This is when Holyfield said he's gonna take him out,' I heard someone say behind me. It was like sitting through a movie in readiness for the infamous throat slashing or head turning scene or something. Everyone knew it was in the script for something to happen in the third round.

The crowd roared as the bell rang. Holyfield ran at Lewis like a man possessed. There was a collective groan as 21,284 spectators shuffled to the edges of their seats. The pair grappled as Holyfield tried to get inside. Mercante warned Lewis for pushing and he looked in trouble as Holyfield, true to his word, bombarded him with a series of uppercuts and hooks slipping under the 84-inch Lewis jab and forcing him on to his back foot for most of the round. Don King must have worked some of that old black magic during the 180-second onslaught. Lewis survived the third to go on to score big in the fifth, a round in which 21,284 pairs of frustrated eyes could see Holyfield's bulbous head ready to be taken off his shoulders, but Lewis could not. Instead of punishing the American when he had him pinned against the ropes Lewis preferred to paw at him like a grizzly bear playing with a half-cut possum. Holyfield later mocked Lewis's punches as 'pitty patty shots'.

The Associated Press scoring system had Lewis winning nine rounds to Holyfield's three. The result thus seemed a foregone conclusion. The judges at ringside had other ideas. Eugenia Williams, the IBF judge, controversially scored the fight 115–113 in Holyfield's favour. Boy, was she going to pay for that. The Venezuela-based World Boxing Association had assigned Stanley Christodolou of South Africa who scored the fight 116–113 for Lewis and the Mexico City-based World Boxing Council had assigned British referee Larry O'Connell who amazingly scored the fight a draw at 115–115 but later admitted his scorecard was wrong and that Lewis won the fight. O'Connell as much as Williams cost Lewis the fight. Given the overall distaste for draws in such big fights, O'Connell must have been blind or stupid to conjure up such a decision.

Amid the chaos of the ring many of the crowd were on their feet stunned by the decision, looking displaced like passengers who had just emerged from a road traffic accident. I could not believe it. A draw. A fucking draw! The buzz at ringside was that almost immediately King and the presidents of all three sanctioning bodies had agreed to a rematch within six months. Well, they wouldn't get my money for a rematch even if they held it in the Don Valley gym.

According to the official fight stats Lewis had connected with 348 punches over twelve rounds compared with Holyfield's 130; Lewis had nailed Holyfield with 65 per cent of his 'power punches' compared with 36 per cent for Holyfield. How could it be that a fighter threw and landed more punches than his opponent yet scored a draw on one card and a loss on another? Raucous booing followed the decision; even the American fans joined in.

Fighters get robbed inside and outside the ring all the time. That's the nature of the beast. Unless you knock a guy out there's always that margin of error that allows a bad decision or two to slip through. But not since Muhammad Ali's questionable points win over Ken Norton in 1974 had a championship been in more dispute.

'The people deserve an undisputed world heavyweight champion which has not happened in nearly a decade,' King had said. But we didn't get that, did we Don?

I had travelled 3,000 miles not as a drooling Lewis acolyte, but as a fan who just wanted to be part of an historic moment, a witness to the 'Crowning Glory' of probably the last undisputed heavyweight champion this century. It was supposed to have been different this time. There were to be no ifs or buts. The speculation would finally end and one man would walk victorious from the ring with an authentic claim to his place in the pantheon of boxing gods. Yeah, right.

Most of the boxing I'd seen for the past year or so was devoid of glamour, lustre and the mystique of celebrity. This was supposed to be as good as it got – Madison Square Garden for God's sake, the Undisputed Heavyweight Championship of the World, $4.99 jumbo hotdogs. But where was boxing now? A result like this could send boxing back into the dark ages. Talk was that the characters had gone and that the sport was now just a sideshow heading toward the ignominy of WWF wrestling. Kids didn't see boxers as role models any more. They wanted to be footballers or golfers. They wanted to play tennis. Tennis! The 'Crowning Glory' of Evander Holyfield versus Lennox Lewis was supposed to restore credibility to a much-maligned sport. It had failed miserably in its task.

After the fight the British fans spewed out into the streets dejected but still enlivened by the prospect of days of heated debate about the fight's outcome. I ran into the Lads on the concourse. All we could do was shake our heads in despair. We'd had a vague plan about celebrating in style in the eventuality of a Lennox win. There was even talk of a contact getting us into his post-fight party on West 18th Street. But a draw seemed a tad unworthy of jubilation. If this had been anywhere else but America, I'm sure the Union Jacks and John Bulls would've ripped Madison Square Garden apart. My 6,999 compatriots had evidently seen the Rodney King video too.

Back at the hotel, the Lads were still smarting about the fight. They were also arguing constantly about cocaine. They started fighting. Steve smacked Marcus in the mouth in an outpouring of brotherly love.

Eddie grabbed Steve by the throat. Steve threw a drink in Eddie's face. I chatted up a Canadian chick at the bar. I realised that I couldn't handle this sort of lifestyle, not just physically, but spiritually as well. I aspired to be a professional athlete. I no longer smoked, drank, took drugs or got into punch-ups. I guess I was no longer one of the Lads.

The day after the fight the *New York Post* wasted no time or words on its analysis of the fight. 'ROBBERY!' it proclaimed on page one, with the sub-head 'Sham decision costs Lewis undisputed title' sprawled across a massive photo of Lewis landing a left jab on Holyfield's jaw. The back-page leader read 'D-RAW DEAL' – not only a play on words but also on Holyfield's 'Real Deal' nickname. This had the sub-head 'Judges rob Lewis of Holyfield's two titles'.

The *Post* reported the following week that Eugenia Williams, a forty-eight-year-old single mother of two who had trained as a boxer and model, had filed for personal bankruptcy on 25 January, six weeks before the fight. She was over $70,000 in debt and had some twenty credit cards to pay off. Things were beginning to look decidedly fishy. As a $39,200-a-year accountant for the Atlantic City government, perhaps you'd expect her to have had a better check on her personal finances. She was paid $5,150 to judge the fight by Don King, who covered each judge's fees, food and travel expenses, along with their accommodation. This was customary and indeed there was nothing unusual in this sort of arrangement.

In an abrupt telephone conversation, Williams told a reporter when asked about the bankruptcy, 'I don't know what you're talking about. They told me not to answer any more questions.' She did not say who 'they' were. Williams was appointed as a judge by the New Jersey-based International Boxing Federation (IBF), one of the three sanctioning bodies to provide officials for the fight. Since 1989 she had judged more than ninety fights including twenty-seven 'world' title bouts.

'She is either biased, incompetent or worse,' said HBO matchmaker Lou DiBella.

'People are entitled to their own opinion,' retorted Williams who, after days of silence, came out swinging at the crowd of reporters gunning for America's most hated woman. 'I called what I saw. I have no problems with that. I didn't make any mistakes. I get paid to do a job and I did it the best I could. I stand by what I scored.'

I started to feel sorry for Williams after the hammering she'd got. She was the scapegoat for a fight which, in all honesty and with hindsight, did not turn out to be the much-hyped 'fight of the century' we had all naïvely expected. Williams claimed that her view at ringside was partly obscured but British fight fans know that there's an historical 'us and them' situation when it comes to British and American fighters. British fighters get stiffed by American judges all the time. It's not just a boxing thing. It's a cultural thing. As an American judge on American soil scoring a fight involving an American who had two world championship belts to his name, what did we expect if not loaded judgement from Williams?

'I'm ashamed of our country,' said three-belt light-heavyweight champion Roy Jones Jr, himself a victim of biased judging at the 1988 Seoul Olympics.

On a partisan level, I could see the mean-spirited method in Ms Williams's madness. Larry O'Connell, on the other hand, was the real joker in the ringside pack – a British referee scoring a draw when Lewis had done enough to win the fight. O'Connell should've had his passport taken away from him. He should've been deported to whatever rock he had originally crawled out from under because his assessment of the fight was not only injudicious, myopic and insulting to the millions of fans the world over who in some shape or form paid good money to watch it, but his spinelessness seemed to exemplify a weakness in the British character when it came to facing up to the Americans. The British press accordingly gave him a right good pasting.

Williams and Co. had caused such a stink that within days of the fight there was a special state Senate hearing into the fiasco at Madison Square Garden. Manhattan District Attorney Robert Morgenthau announced a criminal investigation which promised to examine any possible criminal activity that may have influenced the outcome of the fight. It was just the first of three investigations into the fight initiated by the State of New York. The bigwigs in the City That Never Sleeps, after all these years, had finally woken up to something that the rest of us had known for a long, long time – boxing was, is, and I suspect always will be, a dirty business.

Part Two

A hurting business

chapter 19

My new home, 29 March 1999. I had arrived back at the Rainey house around 1.30 p.m. with my world in a kitbag, a backpack, two carrier bags and a holdall to find Lorna in the middle of a minor crisis.

'He's an absolute bastard,' she said to the nextdoor neighbour, Kennedy, who was sitting at the dinner table, dumbstruck at Lorna's reaction to his news, his chair gently creaking under his 6ft 2in, 18 stone bulk. 'It's embarrassing for me because I made the recommendation.'

Lorna made tea and toasted bagels and explained that one of Howard's former charges, a heavyweight named Scott Welch, had recently sublet Kennedy's flat and accidentally gone off with the keys. Unless they could find him and get him to send the keys back, Kennedy would have a £265 bill to replace the locks and, according to Lorna, the front door and God knows what else. The situation was resolved, of course, but in the face of all that flapping, I took off for the gym. When I got there it was empty but for Howard and Justin, who was jumping rope.

'Was thou at the bus stop on Prince of Wales Road half hour ago?' he asked.

'Yeah, I was,' I said.

'I thought it were you but I weren't sure. I could've given you a lift. I didn't quite recognise you, though. Sorry about that.'

'Never mind,' I said. Why do people bother?

Howard and I spoke briefly about my trip to New York and the Holyfield–Lewis fight before he ushered me into the gym's grotty little changing room to get ready for training. From the cramped shower cubicle a dark, muscular, 6ft 3in figure emerged. It was Terry Dunstan.

While I had been away, Terry had returned to camp after eight weeks in Pennsylvania sparring with Lennox Lewis in preparation for the Holyfield fight. He was a real class act. He had been British, Commonwealth and European cruiserweight champion and an outright winner of a Lonsdale belt. To do that you had to have made three successful defences of a British title. Later it was amended to four defences because of the £4,000 cost of producing each belt. Terry holds the record for the fastest stoppage in a British cruiserweight title fight – forty-four seconds against John 'Buster' Keeton in 1996 – and he holds the record for the fastest knockout in European title history. It took an amazing one punch and sixteen seconds to flatten Alexander Gurov of the Ukraine at the Elephant and Castle in February 1998. A month after that record win, however, Terry was himself knocked out by Imamu Mayfield in the eleventh round of an IBF world cruiserweight title fight. 'He went down like a sack of potatoes,' Howard told me. 'Twice he was knocked down. He had to be helped to his feet. But he wouldn't admit it. Fighters never admit defeat.'

Lorna said that Howard had cried himself to sleep the night Terry lost to Mayfield. He blamed himself for the defeat. Terry and Howard had trained together for fifteen years. The pair had met after Terry, aged fifteen and a promising basketball player, decked his coach following a training session at Crystal Palace. Naturally he was dropped from the team, so he ditched his hoop dreams to take up boxing at St Monica's gym near his home in Vauxhall, south London, where Howard was head coach. Their relationship was more father and son than trainer and fighter, which in part was due to similar familial experiences. Terry's father had left when he was seven 'because of his womanising'. Howard, too, had had little to do with his father when he was young. Later in life the pattern was repeated when divorce separated Howard from his son Peter, with whom he maintained a distant but close relationship.

Terry's reputation preceded him, both inside and outside the gym. Because of his experience, ability and long-standing association with Howard, before I'd even met him I understood he was the *de facto* 'king of the gym'. He didn't take to strangers in the camp too readily and as Lorna had predicted he was sceptical of me at first.

'So you're the writer, then?' he said, eyeing me up and down.

'Yeah, my name's David. You must be Terry.'

'Yeah. What you gonna fucking do about it, son?' he said, grinning. I laughed. I assumed he was joking. We chatted for a bit, me explaining the nature of my book, and Terry explaining how he was going to knock out various characters in the boxing world.

'People think boxing is all Rocky Balboa and big pay days,' said

Terry. 'That's bollocks. I literally got two years left at the top and then I want out. I want to buy some property – New York, Miami, London. My mum's literally the only thing that keeps me in this country.' The word 'literally' was to Terry Dunstan what 'Know what I mean, 'arry' was to Frank Bruno.

Terry beefed a lot about the boxing establishment, especially Simon Block of the British Boxing Board of Control, Frank Warren, Panos Eliades . . . Among fighters, he had a particular loathing for cruiser-weight archrival Johnny Nelson, with whom he had developed a long-running feud following a spat in a local nightclub. Terry was like a time bomb waiting to explode. He had a mental hit list that was second to none. I figured it was potluck what kind of mood you could catch him in in the ring. I made it my mission from then on to avoid sparring with him for as long as I could.

In terms of the gym pecking order, as a three-belt champion, Clinton was, on paper, the 'king of the gym'. None of the other active pros in the gym at that time were titleholders. Consequently, this created an air of grudging admiration but also mild envy. The amateurs, the novice pros and those who had never won honours looked up to Clinton as an inspiration, a role model if you like. After four and a half years as a pro and twenty-two contests, Clinton was finally on the road to making a full-time living from boxing. No more signing-on, no more buses to the gym, no more council flat.

For others such as Terry, who were waiting for a second chance, a break, or simply redemption, Clinton's success was viewed with a tinge of resentment. There was no doubting Terry's ability to take Clinton. After all, he had a height, weight and reach advantage. He had also been in with world-class opposition, something Clinton had yet to experience. But he didn't have the belts or, more importantly, the opportunity to earn good money.

To keep the equilibrium in the gym, Howard never let Clinton and Terry spar together. Clinton didn't fancy the odds. He said that he thought Terry took sparring 'too personal'. I would soon come to understand what he meant. In contrast, Terry was always dying to get his hands on Clinton. 'Howard won't let me spar with him because he knows what I'll do to him,' he told me.

Howard knew all the petty little private wars that went on between the guys in the gym. While he kept the peace by keeping certain fighters apart, he wasn't averse to using some propaganda to stoke up a little fire in a boxer's belly. For instance, a favoured routine was to wind up

Terry over the mats we used for groundwork. Actually, they weren't mats but carpet remnants, shoddy brown chequered rags, not fit for the dog to sleep on. There was one strip, however, that stood out. It was newer than the rest, a plush green piece of Axminster and very comfortable.

Whenever a group of us hit the floor to do our groundwork and Terry picked up the Axminster, Howard would be straight on his case. 'Axminster's for champs, Terry,' he'd say sardonically, snatching it away and handing it to Clinton. 'When you're a champ, you can use it.'

For my first day of full training, Howard put me through two one and a half hour sessions (a regime that would continue for several weeks) doing a combination of eight rounds of shadow boxing, eight rounds on the heavy bag, four rounds on the floor-to-ceiling speedball and light sparring. I worked on my balance on the 'wobbly board', a two and a half foot square piece of hardboard with about eight inches of the top of a sawn-off gas bottle bolted to one side. The idea was to stay on the board and make like you were surfing. 'I've got twelve-year-olds shadow boxing on that,' said Howard the first time I stepped on it and promptly fell off. The wobbly board was deceptively difficult and took a while to master, but eventually I got there.

Although the months I had spent training at All Stars and with Tyrone had given me a useful grounding, everything I had learnt before was history. It was back to basics – footwork, coordination, movement, balance, timing. Howard would do seemingly crazy things like shove a broomstick down the back of my T-shirt and shorts and strap it to my leg with gaffer tape. I'd have to shadow box trussed up like this for several rounds to encourage me to straighten my back and adjust my stance. In addition, he would strap my ankles together with a two-foot bungee cord to stop me from adopting too wide a stance. Sometimes I felt like a complete idiot bound up like this but I soon came to realise that Howard used the same methodology on all his new charges, regardless of their experience or ability.

Howard was famous in the fight game for his unconventional training techniques. He had a reputation for getting fighters to do exercises with bungee cords and caribinas (a legacy of his days climbing Ben Nevis and the Matterhorn) which others in the fight game frowned upon. He was seen as eccentric and while boxing accepted people for all their idiosyncrasies, the traditions of the sport, in Britain at least, were rooted in a lot of conservative and often outmoded ideas.

Even cynical pros, who tried to avoid the embarrassment of some of his more extreme techniques, were made to wear eyepatches, blindfolds, bungee cords on waistbands, iron boots, roller blades and assorted gadgets designed to improve movement, technique and power. It all seemed off-the-wall at times but I respected Howard and admired his invention and radical approach to training.

Howard broke down every stage of my early development into individual components, working on a punch-by-punch basis. Whether it was how I threw a left hook or a right uppercut, the technique, the style I had learnt in London had to be unlearnt. For starters, Howard and I concentrated specifically on my jab and basic footwork, just as I had done before I had left for New York. Howard would have me stand against a wall of the gym, left side on, and throw jabs along it backwards and forwards until my arm ached and my brain drained with the repetition. It would then be back on the bowling balls, again jabbing away while trying to maintain my balance. Then the same on the wobbly board and so on and so forth.

After two days of training, jabbing away ceaselessly at a heavy bag, and fighting thin air like a man possessed, Howard threw me to the sharks. He wanted me to spar with Clinton Woods, the new European, British and Commonwealth light-heavyweight champion. Naturally, I couldn't wait . . .

Learning how to hit a punch bag is one thing. Learning how to hit a moving target who's trying to hit you while, to use the boxing credo, you 'defend yourself at all times', is a completely different proposition. Unlike many martial arts, to learn to box requires full-contact training almost from day one. Becoming a boxer is largely a matter of trial and error, as I was about to find out. The gym is the proving ground and the ring is where you serve your apprenticeship. Unlike karate or jujitsu, disciplines with a multitude of complex moves and techniques, boxing has a simple credo that is learnt not through theory but through practice. To learn to box you have to fight.

My encounter with Clinton was to be my first sparring session at the gym. Apart from for the two rounds at All Stars, which hardly counted, I was a crude novice. Clinton had stopped the former light-heavyweight champion Crawford Ashley less than a month earlier in the seventh round of their confrontation in Manchester on the night I watched Lennox Lewis and Evander Holyfield fight in New York. I was about to spar with a hungry and ambitious newly crowned champion.

I gloved up. Howard fastened my head guard and smeared Vaseline across my nose, cheeks, eyebrows and chin. Only in boxing could a man ask another man to apply Vaseline without getting his balls stroked.

I stepped between the ropes. My heart was pounding. I looked at Clinton but he made no eye contact. He had a poker face. He shrugged his shoulders repeatedly and bent his neck from side to side to loosen up. He was walking anti-clockwise round the ring. I followed suit. Seconds passed. I felt as though I was approaching the gallows. Clinton was the hangman. This time around, the sense of nervous anticipation was palpable – I knew exactly what to expect and that made matters worse. Having had a taster of two rounds with Ramsey, an amateur of limited ability, my imagination started to run riot. On that occasion, I had my nose temporarily enlarged and won a fattish lip. Clinton was a professional and a champion to boot. It would be a result if I were still standing after two rounds.

As the buzzer sounded heralding the start of the round, fear gave way to anxiety. I moved tentatively round the ring, flicking out the odd jab and trying to look something like a boxer. I was naturally tense. Space was tight in the thirteen-foot square ring. Everywhere I turned Clinton was there in front of me, eyes peering into mine, peppering me with rapid-fire jabs. His left fist was like a Gatling gun. I now understood the rationale behind sparring in a small ring. Less space made you work harder and gave you less room to relax; it disciplined you into producing a high work rate so that when you boxed in a larger ring the extra space increased your mobility.

In spite of my inflexibility I managed to throw a couple of ragged combinations and even tagged the champion with a clean right cross. 'Nice shot,' he said generously. He kidded me for much of the first round, blocking and slipping most of what I threw, occasionally throwing in a stiff jab to shake me up.

In the second round, Clinton upped the pace after I caught him with a couple of lucky shots. Despite my inexperience, I could still pack a punch. Maybe he felt that he'd got caught carelessly and had underestimated my ability. At one point he glanced over at Howard. He seemed frustrated by my style (or lack of it) but nevertheless caught me with some good shots, especially a couple of hooks to the body. The punches didn't really bother me. I could handle the body punches; the face was different. I found it harder to catch him in the body than the head. I used my one advantage – about 2 stone – to swing him around and push him on to the ropes and into corners whenever I got the chance but I could never capitalise with a really decent punch.

I had no idea what to do. I just played it by ear and mugged my way through the motions. Howard had given me no instructions whatsoever. He just stood propped up by the ring post watching silently. What was I supposed to be looking at – Clinton's eyes, his hands, his feet, what? What was I looking for? What should I do? Every now and again I'd remember a move I'd seen a fighter do on TV or at a show. I'd try to emulate the fancy footwork, the slip, the slide, but somehow it didn't come out right. As a boxer, I was about as useful as an IOU from Lord Lucan.

I was scrapping, street fighting with gloves on. This wasn't the real deal. My left shoulder was wilting from jabbing, my back was aching and I was as hot as a whore's knickers. Howard could see I was flagging and at the end of the second round cried out in a gravelly voice, 'That'll do yer.'

'One more round,' said Clinton looking at me for affirmation as I leant across the ropes panting ferociously, trying not to cough my guts up.

I was sweating my nuts off. Perspiration ran down into my eyes and blurred my vision. I felt hemmed in inside Simon's old head guard, which Howard had loaned me. Jesus, it was so tight. People in S&M clubs in London paid good money for this sort of thing. I could hardly breathe. Was I about to have a heart attack? High blood pressure ran in my family. My father had not too long ago had a triple bypass operation. Occasionally I got chest pains, particularly when I was under a lot of stress. I'm going to die, I thought, right here, right now. I am going to have a massive heart attack and keel over. Alternatively, I'd collapse from exhaustion, my gumshield would slip into the back of my throat and I'd choke to death. Encumbered by these ridiculous gloves, I'd claw at my throat, uselessly trying to pull this lump of plastic out while everyone gathered round, gawping at me as I foamed at the mouth and choked on my own vomit. I would've been happy for it to end there and then. I mean it. What was I doing? Who was I trying to kid? There was no way I could ever get into the ring with a professional fighter and survive let alone secure even a draw. As for a win! Come on. Let's be serious. It was a good idea at the time but this psychotic project had no legs and I didn't have the arse for it. I'd just pack it in now, say my farewells and jump on a train back to the smoke. I'm sure my publisher would've understood if I'd turned up at his office with a broken nose saying, 'Look old boy, I gave it my best shot but I'm afraid this boxing lark is not my cup of tea. Sorry old chap, no can do. Do you fancy 100,000 words on "gardening, the inside story" or maybe a 400 page gonzo cookbook?'

I had worked flat out but I knew that the pace we were sparring at was a walk in the park for Clinton. Realistically, I wasn't fit for this business and maybe it would take me an eternity to get into shape. He still had three or four gears to go whereas I had stalled somewhere between opening the car door and putting the key in the ignition.

'Yeah, why not? Let's have another,' I heard myself say in my best 'I don't give a rat's arse' voice. I was intent on proving I had brass balls. This was a big mistake.

I got battered like a cod fillet in the third round. Clinton pounded me repetitively with his stiff left – rat-a-tat-tat-tat, all over my face. I seemed to have no answer. 'Come on, come on,' he said, becoming increasingly frustrated by my lack of fight. Did I have no balls? Why couldn't I fight back? My left arm by this stage was gone completely and I covered up as best I could, moving into him in some crazy attempt to soak up some shots and counter to the body. Counter to the body? What a joke! What was I thinking of? This guy just kept on coming. He was all over me, hitting me with gratuitous hooks and crosses to the head. The thought of being knocked out crossed my mind. Something told me to hold it up. I couldn't go down, especially in my first sparring session. Go down? I could hear Howard now. 'Well, Captain, you tried but you were fucking crap. Keep pushing that pen, son.'

My ego wouldn't let me go out like that. I'd never hit the deck in my life. No one had ever put me over. My pride made me unbearably stubborn at times and it was occasions like this when that sense of pig ignorance and obstinacy kicked in. I held on, glancing at the three-minute timer, praying for the suffering to end. My fitness let me down. It wasn't the blows – the pain of these is momentary – but the lack of stamina grinds you down, sets you up for the kill. If Clinton had really wanted to, he could've taken me out of the game, no problem.

Conserving energy was an art. Experienced boxers knew how to make you do all the work, wear you down and then pick you off. Positioning in the ring was an important factor in conserving energy. If you could dominate the centre of the ring and keep your opponent on his back foot on the outer reaches of the ring, he was using more legwork and potentially more energy than you were. The same could be said for picking your shots. Throwing punches willy-nilly cost you in later rounds. I had so much to learn; too much it seemed.

I crawled out of the ring, dragging myself through the ropes. My breath, my breath . . . I could hardly breathe. I was gasping for water. My mouth felt drier than an Egyptian's sandal. No one had offered me a drink throughout those three rounds, or did they and I couldn't remember?

'That was good sparring,' said Howard as he peeled my sweat-soaked gloves off. 'Well done.'

'Are you kidding?' I panted. 'I hardly laid a glove on him and I took too many shots and . . .'

'Listen,' said Howard in a fatherly tone. 'You don't know what he was trying to do in there, do you?'

The words were lost on me for a moment. I still couldn't breathe and I certainly couldn't think straight.

'For all you know he might've been trying to knock you out, right? But you're still standing.'

'Yeah, but . . .'

'Listen. You showed something in there and that something is moral fortitude. That'll do yer for today.'

I had no experience in the ring but I'd managed to get through three rounds with the newly crowned British, Commonwealth and European light-heavyweight champion and was still on my feet even though I was uncoordinated, off balance, rigid with fear, tense and immobile. At least I wasn't a coward. If the realisation had come that I had no guts, no balls, no heart, I would've been finished. In boxing, there is no escape for the coward. He can be saved from a beating, but not humiliation. Boxing is the only professional sport where men score points for vicious intent. As Jackie Bowers had told me, 'you have to want to fight'. You have to be prepared to hurt and be hurt. This was a hurting business. In the ring, aggression begets aggression leading to an inevitable outcome: pain. Boxing is a profession of violence.

Reluctance to use one's fist of fury inside the ring, no matter the circumstances, is seen (ironically by opponents of boxing) as 'unsportsmanlike conduct'. You must not only defend yourself at all times but you must demonstrate a sufficient level of hostility towards your opponent to make a contest. Inflicting physical and mental punishment on opponents and, in return, accepting the same in kind is what fighters devote their entire lives to perfecting. Anything short of this two-way form of communication is not acceptable, not sportsmanlike.

In order to 'bring me along', i.e. build my confidence and develop my ring craft, Howard would have me 'move around' with guys whom he trusted not to take advantage of my inexperience. For the rest of the week, my sparring partner was Scott Lansdowne, the heavyweight with the nervous disposition. Scott was a twenty-five-year-old nightclub doorman who made the 150-mile a day round trip five, sometimes six, days a week from his home in Leicester to Sheffield to train at the gym. He had had a relatively short amateur career with only six or seven fights to his credit as a junior. When I first arrived on the scene, he was still a one-bout professional, but having trained with Howard for the past year he was a lot better than his record suggested. Scott was around 5ft 10in and weighed a good 16 stone. He was built like a white version of Mike Tyson, stocky with massive calves and thighs. I thought he was a dead ringer for John Belushi, the American comic who died of a drug overdose. I mentioned the resemblance to him. He wasn't too impressed.

Compared with Clinton, Scott was an easier target to hit. His short, stocky frame meant I could punch down at him and get more power into the shots I landed as he tried to slip inside my reach to catch me with body shots, while at close range I managed to land a few blows about his head and body. Having had only one professional fight compared with Clinton's twenty-two, he was a far less wily opponent. But what he lacked in experience he more than made up for in terms of power. The first time we sparred together I wound up with a bruise the size of a small hamster on my left arm after he had repeatedly targeted it with chopping right hooks. I thanked my lucky stars he wasn't aiming for my face. In the early days Scott would land very few shots to my head. This wasn't a testament to my defensive skills or natural ability as a fighter, it was simply the case that Howard would give Scott instructions not to 'load up' on me so I became accustomed to and comfortable with being in a ring. As time went on and I gradually improved, Scott, like all my sparring partners, became less benevolent.

Scott was a southpaw so I had to concentrate on moving around him clockwise to avoid the big left-hand punches. The vast majority of fighters are orthodox, i.e. right-handed, which is why many have an aversion to fighting southpaws. Orthodox fighters spar almost exclusively with other orthodox fighters. Consequently, they are programmed from an early age to move anti-clockwise to avoid the stronger right hand of an opponent.

Sparring was the cornerstone of a fighter's training. The ring was where I would learn my craft. I took some comfort in the fact that everyone found getting into the ring hard in one way or another. You had your good days and you had your bad days.

'You're either a fighter, you go out stealing or you do a nine-to-five.' Terry was in the ring leaning against the ropes pontificating. 'Danny,

Getting ready for another hard day at the office – Don Valley Sports Academy,
Sheffield. (*Michael Bale*)

Taking a breather at the Peacock Gym, Canning Town, London. If I knew back then what I know now I would've taken up golf instead of boxing. (*Michael Bale*)

Who ate all the pies? Striking meaty 15½-stone pose at the Peacock in February 1998. (*Michael Bale*)

Sparring without a head guard. Not a wise idea ... unless you fancy a cauliflower ear as a souvenir. My trainer, manager, landlord and friend Howard Rainey looks on in the background, unconcerned. (*Michael Bale*)

Getting some post-spar advice from my sparring partner, Shaun Stokes. (*Michael Bale*)

Today a punch bag, tomorrow the world! (*Michael Bale*)

Documenting and analysing my experiences in boxing meant that I often suffered from what my trainer called 'paralysis by analysis'. In making the transition from writer to fighter I had to learn to act instinctively, not journalistically. Philosophising is best kept out of a boxing ring. (*Michael Bale*)

Me and my shadow. In the fourteen months that I spent training and living with Howard and his family we developed a friendship that transcended boxing. (*Michael Bale*)

Going through the pre-fight medical examination. As the doctor takes my blood pressure, checks my breathing and tests my eyesight I'm trying to focus on the task at hand and get into 'the zone'. (*Phil Fisk*)

The bombshell. I weighed in at 12 stone 10½ lb – five pounds heavier than I had weighed the day before. My opponent, Matt Scriven, had *apparently* weighed in the day before the fight at 11 stone 9lb. I was expected to come in no heavier than 12 stone 8lb. Because of the discrepancy in weight, the fight was in jeopardy. (*Phil Fisk*)

After drawn-out 'negotiations' the fight is on and I make my grand entrance into the ring. (*Phil Fisk*)

Taking instructions from Howard after the first round. I was so focussed on fighting that most of what my corner told me between rounds went in one ear and out the other. (*Phil Fisk*)

My most effective weapon in the fight was my left jab. Trouble was, my opponent had an equally effective chin. (*Phil Fisk*)

Stand still so I can bloody hit you! (*Phil Fisk*)

Bingo! In that moment of vicious intensity when a gloved fist connects remorselessly with flesh and bone, a professional fighter is in his element. (*Phil Fisk*)

After more than two years of research, fourteen months of intensive training and six rounds of boxing, it's all over. As for the result… (*Phil Fisk*)

I've heard it said that professional boxing is a crazy business. Well, do I look mad? (*Phil Fisk*)

do you want to be a thief or a playboy?' Danny had got busted up in a car crash a couple of nights earlier and had been yapping on about it all day. Before he could reply, Terry's attention turned to Ben Coward, a young middleweight known in the gym as the 'World Champion Shadow Boxer' on account of his great style but lack of dedication. I finished my three rounds with Scott. Clinton stepped into the ring and they continued sparring as I looked on from the sidelines.

'Ben, sort it out, mate. No word of a lie, I used to be a fat bastard like him.' Terry looked at Howard as he barracked Ben. 'Now I'm a lean, mean fighting machine.'

'Ben, gloves on,' said Howard.

'Scott, double the jab, double the jab,' said Terry, now barracking Scott. 'For fuck's sake double the jab.'

'I heard you the first time, Terry,' said Scott, stepping away from Clinton.

'That'll do yer,' yelled Howard as the buzzer signalled the end of the round.

'One more,' said Clinton.

'No, I want him in with yer.' Howard pointed to Ben and the round robin continued on its merry way.

By Good Friday I had figured out how to stay on the wobbly board long enough to shadow box a three-punch combination before falling off. In one week of intensive, professional training, I had learnt more than in a whole year of haphazard activity.

'See those bowling balls over there?' said Howard, pointing to the side of the ring. 'If you look at the earth from outer space, it looks exactly like that. Amazing that, ain't it?'

'You what?' I said, falling off the wobbly board again. I decided shadow boxing on solid ground was a better idea.

'How old are you?' asked Howard, scrutinising my movement.

'Thirty-one,' I said.

'You could be Central Area champion in two years,' said Howard. 'Not a world champion, though,' he added rather sarcastically,

'Well, there's no bloody point in carrying on then, is there?' I quipped.

Here I was with just a couple of weeks of elementary training under my belt and I was being told I could win a Central Area title. A Central Area title! That was effectively the next step towards challenging for a British title and a Lonsdale belt. After that came Commonwealth and European titles. And then . . . Today Don Valley, tomorrow the world! Was this more kidology? Did Howard honestly think I was that good?

His penchant for taking the piss and speaking in riddles often made it difficult to tell with him where sarcasm ended and sincerity began. Nevertheless, this apparent vote of confidence was certainly a boost to the ego and the thought of having that level of potential was, in the beginning at least, enough to keep me motivated.

Wherever Howard was in the gym, he had an eye on what you were up to. I occasionally caught him using the mirrors to spy on me and the other fighters. He certainly wasn't a hard taskmaster, but if you slipped up he was a monkey on your back. 'Go on, let it go and turn that fucking fist,' he'd bark at me, and I hit that bastard heavy bag like there was no tomorrow – BAF! BAF! 'You'll be a puncher,' Howard said casually as I moved round the heavy bag hammering it with straight right hands. Puncher was the term used for a fighter who could bang, the kind of guy who dealt with most of his opponents by knocking them out. I liked the sound of that. Me, a puncher!

At the end of my first full week of training I returned to London as usual to see Luca and pay a visit, out of courtesy, to Big Ned, just to let him know how I was progressing. I arrived at Ned's bachelor pad just off the Fulham Palace Road on Saturday evening to find him half-dressed and wrestling with a mound of clothes, newspapers, tools, videotapes and sundry crap littered around his living room.

'Dave, my man, come on in. Don't worry about the mess, mate, I had a bit of a big night yesterday.'

'Yeah, I noticed,' I said, scanning the room.

After about eighteen seconds Ned aborted the obviously pointless exercise of cleaning, got dressed and disappeared into the kitchen to rustle up some food. Pots and pans banged away and five minutes later he re-emerged with a tray containing two bowls of steaming hot pasta.

'I'm blowing all my dough on this gig,' I said, digging into the food and moaning with my mouth full about the cost of travelling to Sheffield, training, board, etc.

'You need a fucking sponsor, mate,' said Ned. 'Someone to take care of you, get you some of that folding gear.'

Folding gear – there was an expression I hadn't heard in a long time. It was such a charming phrase, and a much more evocative euphemism for money than 'filthy lucre' or 'spondulix'. Come to think of it, so was 'here's a cheque for several thousand pounds'. As we ate, Ned gave me the low-down on his weekend's sexual gymnastics and I thought maybe, just maybe, if I sculpted and fine-tuned my body into a lean, mean fighting machine, I could hire myself out as a gigolo to rich old birds at the weekends.

'I could get on to Colin Hart at the *Sun*,' said Ned. 'Smashing fella. He'd love this coup. You could get a nice little earner, he gets his story and the *Sun* gets loads of publicity. Everyone's happy. Sorted.' Ned had a curious way of putting a sardonic mockney spin to his speech. 'In fact . . . ,' he paused for thought momentarily, 'you could even fight for the British light-heavyweight title. Fucking hell! What a coup! This could be history in the making, brother.' We made a fraternal clenched-fist handshake as Ned acknowledged the magnitude, the coolness and the pecuniary advantages of such a coup.

The idea sounded good in principle, but I already knew enough about Ned to fathom that many of his bright ideas didn't always go to plan. Howard had told me that not all of Ned's promotions had been profitable. Forewarned is forearmed. This tale, along with the vicissitudes of the Barry 'The Braveheart' Hughes saga, made me think twice about being overly enthusiastic about Ned's commission-based schemes.

'I'll definitely give it some thought, Ned,' I said, trying to sound interested yet noncommittal. 'But not until I've spoken to a few people first, eh? These things have a habit of, er . . . blowing up sometimes.'

I didn't have long to catch the last train back to my pied-à-terre in Ladbroke Grove so I made my excuses and got ready to leave.

'Have you got a pair of sparring gloves?' asked Ned. My whining about training equipment had obviously struck a chord.

'No, I haven't actually. I've been borrowing everyone else's.'

'Hang on.' Ned was gone four or five minutes and I was beginning to wonder whether he'd return anti-climactically with a list of boxing equipment stockists. Instead he appeared in the living room beaming, holding a large carrier bag. 'I knew I had 'em somewhere. Here you go, mate.'

I looked in the bag and pulled out a pair of nearly new 14oz sparring gloves, which were 4oz heavier than competition gloves. They were navy blue and red with an archetypal boxing logo that read 'TITLE'. They were much larger than the bag gloves I normally used and looked even bigger than the sparring gloves I had donned back at the gym. I felt touched that Ned should make the gesture; after all we hardly knew each other. Nevertheless, I took the gloves on the basis that they were on permanent loan. Having just sat down and eaten with someone who had more angles than a Rubik cube, the old cliché 'there's no such thing as a free lunch' sprang to mind. I thanked Ned for the gloves, stuck them under my arm and took off into the night.

chapter 20

By the end of April I was surprised that Lorna was still fattening me up with her 'specials'. I thought by now I should've been on a strict diet of raw egg whites, unbuttered toast, muesli, salads and various rabbit foods. But Howard assured me that for the time being my weight was the least of my problems. Occasionally I'd suffer pangs of guilt about my calorific intake and skip lunch, which was easy because there was hardly anywhere of merit to eat in the vicinity of the gym. But all too often I'd make up for the lack of lunch at dinner by scoffing second helpings of roast lamb, broccoli, peas, carrots, roast potatoes, parsnips, Yorkshire puddings, gravy and all the traditional English fare that Lorna could muster. A pudding nearly always followed dinner – bananas and ice cream, fruit trifle, chocolate gateau, apple pie and custard were household favourites. I also regularly snacked on chocolate bars, biscuits and late-night bowls of cereal.

My increased physical activity made me acutely appreciative of food. Regular, coordinated training also allowed me to indulge without necessarily gaining weight. Whereas in the past I had trained and gained weight, I learnt from Howard that by consuming at least six litres of water per day I could gradually bring my weight down without a radical change in diet. Water literally flushed a lot of crap out of the system and in the process made the body more fuel efficient by helping to transport glucose in the blood to the muscles used in exercise. In the short term, while my body needed the extra energy to cope with the intensity of my new training regime, I could eat almost what I liked. Food also gave me comfort from the aches and pains of training and as such, from a psychological perspective, it was important to eat well and not starve.

Gradually, my enthusiasm and thirst for learning helped me push through the inevitable pain barriers I encountered. After a while, the pain became a secondary consideration and I accepted it as par for the course, much in the same way I accepted the possibility of brain damage or death as an occupational hazard. My primary and overriding concern was not to embarrass myself. I suppose there were those in the game who actively got off on receiving a good hiding. I never met anyone like that, or at least no one who admitted to it. But the injuries and the marks attained from combat in the ring were like battle scars, badges of honour to wear with pride. Mark Brooks, a promising eighteen-year-old whom Howard had poached from a rival amateur club, even had a fetish for bruising. 'I don't know what it is with me but I just love having black eyes,' he confessed. 'I think they're great. I can't explain it. They just make me feel really hard.' Strange.

Fat lips, bruises, abrasions, cuts and swellings – they all told a story. Of course, not all the marks a fighter carries are from battles in the ring. The outside world is full of other dangerous obstacles. 'A few year ago before I were boxing,' said Clinton, 'I were up in Skeggy [Skegness] with me mates. I had this hat on with "Kiss me quick" printed on it. Some bloke runs up to me and nicks it. I said, "All right, give it us back then, mate," and he said, "Come on then, I'll fight you for it." I start squaring up to him and the next thing I know someone's glassed me from the side.' He showed me the cut under his left eye. 'Nine fucking stitches I had to have in that . . . the bastard.'

Once I'd had a few head shots and got a measure of the pain, it became an acceptable part of the job. I suppose the first few million brain cells you had punched out of you were the ones that dealt with the processing of pain, as I found there was a definite correlation between the number of blows to the head and my ability to sustain punishment.

Guys eyed you furtively in the gym, sizing you up, looking for your weaknesses so they could exploit them when the time came. In the early days I was conscious not to make an arse of myself in front of the other fighters. It was important that now I had found a permanent training camp I gained the respect of my peers. I was a stranger in a strange land after all so I was acutely aware of the need to fit in, to be accepted.

Even minor things like the way I wrapped my hands with bandages took on a new importance. I never paid much attention to it before but as I became more professional in my attitude, I treated my hands with greater respect – they were now the tools of two trades. Another reason to pay close attention to my hands was that for a boxer of my build, they were extremely delicate and small, spanning just 22 centimetres from little finger to thumb. I got into the habit of wrapping my hands with intricate loops, taping them up with gaffer or masking tape. For added protection, Howard got me into using foam padding taped across my knuckles; some fighters used sanitary towels as an alternative.

I never found head guards to be a comfort to wear. The sweat seemed to funnel its way into my eyes after a couple of rounds and I always felt my vision was restricted. Every time I took a decent shot to the head it wobbled, distracting me long enough to take another one. But after a while, I realised a head guard was a necessary evil. The bruises and welts I'd get, particularly on the forehead and cheeks, if I didn't wear one were not particularly attractive.

A gumshield is another vital piece of equipment. It stabilises the jaw and thus reduces the risk of fractures to the jawbone and lacerations in the mouth. It also prevents the teeth from breaking or coming loose and possibly being lodged in the throat. The bite surface in particular protects the teeth from uppercuts to the chin and the lip surface deflects the power from punches aimed at the teeth, preventing cuts to the lips, tongue and cheeks. A gumshield also helps to protect the head by decreasing the shock wave of a blow from the jaw to the temporal bone, reducing intracranial fractures. Boxing without a gumshield is thus about as sensible as sticking your nuts in a vice and cranking the handle.

Sugar Ray Robinson hated wearing gumshields and so did I. When I first started using them they felt really uncomfortable and irritated the back of my throat. This discomfort combined with the nervous anticipation of sparring at times made me want to throw up. I'd expectorate for a couple of minutes and then feel fine. I had to learn to breathe through my nose and keep my mouth closed while wearing one. For someone who talks as incessantly as I do, keeping my mouth shut for three minutes at a time was a struggle. Some guys had gumshields specially made by a dentist but I still used standard customisable ones, as I had for the All Stars masterclass. I shaped the shield to my gums by placing it in boiling water and then into my gaping mouth. The theory was that as you sucked the air out of the gumshield and bit into it, it moulded itself around your upper set of teeth. It usually took me four or five attempts to achieve the desired effect and I'd be constantly dunking the gumshield into cups of boiling water and shoving it in my cakehole like a digestive biscuit.

Titanic wouldn't start. Again. Howard kept turning it over and over until what remnants of battery power it had finally faded. What a way to start the week. 'Bollocks,' he said, getting out of the car and mumbling something to Lorna who was standing in the doorway. She immediately snapped back at him and the pair went into a spat for a couple of minutes.

The Raineys were tense that morning as their old friend Professor Sir David Warren was coming up to see Howard regarding his running machine. Howard had briefed me on Sir David – he had been the youngest man in the country to hold a professorship; he had been a head lecturer at Harvard for nine years; and he was osteopath to the Duke of Edinburgh to whom he referred affectionately as 'Phil the Greek'. Howard thought that the sun shone out of David's rear end and spoke about him frequently, with awe.

We got a cab to the gym and within minutes of our arrival, David Warren showed up. I was standing on the steps of the gym with Terry. We were just about to leave for the Full Monty café for breakfast.

'Oh no,' said Terry as Prof. Warren stepped slowly out of the car accompanied by a guy called Rob, a representative of a company that was interested in Howard's running machine.

'Aha!' said Professor Warren, staring Terry square in the face. After all that I'd heard about him, he wasn't quite what I was expecting. He wasn't wearing a tweed jacket or a cravat, and he didn't have a grey beard or any of the stereotypical garb of a professor. He was big, about 18 stone, with a roly-poly frame and walked on crutches. 'Here's the man who answers the phone with a less than courteous manner,' said the Professor. 'What was it you said? "Hello you old bitch" or was it "Hello you old fucking dog?" '

'I think it was "Hello you old dog",' said Terry. 'I don't swear,' he added with what he thought was an innocent smile.

'No, I believe "bitch" was used in there and there was some "fucking" as well.'

I introduced myself to the Professor, interrupting this discourse on Terry's telephone manner. A couple of days earlier, Terry had picked up the telephone at Howard's place and for some strange reason, thinking it was an old girlfriend, he went into what was supposed to be some good-natured insults about the woman's sexual proclivities. As it turned out, it was the Professor on the telephone. Apparently he didn't take kindly to foul language; not unless it was his own. The Professor and Howard talked business for a while and then he disappeared back to London.

Later that day, I sparred with Danny. He said I gave him the 'evil eye'. He didn't know how to handle me. I was unconventional and unpredictable. Danny was young and always out to impress. His main objective seemed to be to try to take my head off. This was the difference between sparring with pros and amateurs. The pros appreciated I was trying to learn. The amateurs just saw me as an easy target. I caught Danny with some crisp jabs and a solid uppercut that rocked him. I got lucky. He got tired, eventually. In the fourth round my left arm seemed to slip out at the elbow and we stopped sparring, much to his relief. I was in agony, unable to move my arm properly. I went home and rubbed Olbas Oil into it and by the following morning it was near perfect again.

After talking with the Professor, Howard came up with another invention – two speedballs swivelling on a bungee cord from the floor to the ceiling. Where he conjured these curious applications from was a wonder.

'Since I've got back into TM I keep getting these brainwaves,' he said. Howard had practised transcendental meditation on and off for about twenty years. When we got home from the gym he'd usually go up to his bedroom for a session but occasionally he'd pull up on the drive and just zone right out in Titanic for half an hour.

TM had helped Howard turn the gym into his own personalised toolshed. At one point the place was packed with blocks of wood on roller-skate wheels, foam surfboards, and all manner of contraptions designed to stretch various muscles. Most of the guys in the gym took these innovations with a pinch of salt. Even though they tolerated Howard's eccentricities and indeed saw the benefits in his most pragmatic dalliances, they were generally far too conservative in their training methods to accept every novel idea he came up with. Every day he'd be sawing, sanding, drilling, hammering a variety of gadgets and devices for training he had invented. Some had their practical uses, others just seemed like experiments which operated in a sort of hit and miss fashion. A lot of the guys thought he'd lost it, especially when he invented a rig for roller-skating. Roller-skating! What did that have to do with boxing?

One day Howard had a cocky young super-featherweight from Newark called Carl Greaves in the ring bound up with bungee cord moving backwards and forwards on a skateboard. He was new to the gym and unfamiliar with Howard's training techniques.

'Oh, he hasn't got you with that one, has he?' I said to gee him up.

'Cool' Carl, as he was known on the circuit, was the holder of a British Masters belt, a fairly insignificant title that had been conjured up by a cadre of small-hall promoters.

'What? Is this some sort of wind up?' said Carl.

'Yeah, it's part of Howard's initiation routine,' I continued. 'Just wait till he gets the tallow and metal shavings on your bollocks.'

'Shut the fuck up will you,' said Howard, seeing that Carl was becoming self-conscious and uneasy about his latest invention.

For Howard, it was often difficult to get fighters who were unaccustomed to his methods to take him seriously at first. Britain was not as radical as the States in terms of training techniques. But every fighter who came to the gym and allowed Howard his indulgences benefited from his weird and wonderful techniques.

Howard didn't have speedballs at the gym, he didn't think that skipping did a fighter much good and he didn't believe that the age-old institution of dawn runs was of any use to a fighter. 'The only reason why fighters used to run first thing in the morning is because a lot of the trainers in the old days were cab drivers. They didn't finish their shifts until late at night so they preferred to train in the afternoon. That's why they'd get the fighters to run first thing so they could recover for a few hours and then train that afternoon.' Howard explained that it takes at least two or three hours after waking for the body's metabolic rate to reach a level where it's in a condition for intensive training.

'All those four, five, six, seven milers – they're a load of bollocks. It takes too much out of you. A marathon runner doesn't train by running marathons, does he? So why should a boxer run for an hour a day when he's going to be fighting for twelve minutes?'

A Yorkshireman and proud of it, Howard's twenty or so years of living in London had tempered his accent. He didn't have the brogue of most of the Sheffielders I came into contact with, those who pronounced water as 'watter' and said sen instead of self. There were little touches of thou and thee or owt and nowt. His old pal Keith Handley, who had tried unsuccessfully to teach me a crash course in Yorkshire dialect, said Howard had a sort of 'northern general' accent, not specific to any area or region, just, well, northern in general. 'I can't do accents,' Howard had said. This was a little too modest even for him. He did an amusing Pakistani accent which careered off into a South Wales brogue and a comical cockney accent which made him sound like Jack Regan from 'The Sweeney'.

He seemed to take a vicarious pleasure out of what we did, like he was reliving his own youth through ours. He also loved spotting talent. Danny Daley for instance was a genuine Howard Rainey protégé – someone he was nurturing practically from scratch. He had big ideas for the kid, thought he could go all the way. I thought from Danny's attitude that he didn't have enough heart to make it, but maybe I'd be proved wrong.

'You're coming on good . . . getting there,' said Howard one evening. I thought I'd sparred badly earlier on. Howard got into a stance in the living room and did a darting sidestep, moving into a position to throw a hook. For an old boy he could still move. That was something I noticed in the gyms. The old boys, the former pros, could still feint, bob and weave and throw a quick combination. Of course, they'd be ruined after thirty seconds but they still had the moves. Even Muhammad Ali still had the moves.

'Now we start upping it,' said Howard crashing on to the sofa and lighting up another Sovereign. 'We'll work on single punches with the pads. I'll do a teaching session next week, just you and Danny, before anyone else gets there.' I was getting the feeling that Howard was really into this harebrained scheme. The old boy was just mad enough to see the point of it all. All the trainers I'd met previously were too conventional, too rooted in a sense of tradition and conservatism. Maybe they just didn't think they could train someone like me to become a fighter, so fear of failure made them avoid the task. Howard didn't seem to have that problem. He didn't seem hung up by ego. He was a very genuine, humble man. I'd learnt from the gym grapevine that he never took payment from an up-and-coming fighter's purse, even though he hardly ever had enough cash to put petrol in Titanic. Howard's rule of thumb was you had to earn a grand before he'd take his 10 per cent. I was forty quid up already.

Later that evening, I went with Howard, Clinton, Shaun Stokes and Vicky, a 180lb sunbed junky who worked for Dennis as PA and barmaid, to an amateur boxing show in Bradford. Clinton took us in his new Fiat Punto, flooring it most of the way. It was a sponsored rental car, a perk of being the champ. He was guest of honour at the show and was going to show off his three belts.

If boxing is exploitative, it can be at its cruellest in the junior amateur ranks, among the kids at the bottom end of the so-called farm system. That is a process by which talented young fighters are nurtured through the ranks from junior to novice to senior amateur level and eventually on to become professionals and thus investments for managers and promoters.

As the clinking of glasses, the clanking of gold jewellery, the rhubarb, rhubarb of conversation reverberated round the ballroom, boys as young as ten went hell for leather at each other, foregoing any skill or technique they may have learnt in the gym. I found it disturbing that the audience of cigar-puffing penguins could roar with laughter and guffaw with excitement at the sight of pre-pubescent boys bashing themselves senseless. They were not a pretty bunch – drunken, overfed greengrocers, black cab drivers, sales reps, low-ranking freemasons, retired coppers and assorted members of the upper working-class and lower middle-class yeomanry.

Inside the show's programme I found the following quote:

Boxing is a science, the study of a lifetime, in which you may exhaust yourself, but never your subject. It is a contest, a duel calling for skill and self-control. It is a test of temper, a trial of honour, a revealer of character. It affords the chance to play the man and act the gentleman. It provides not only physical health, but a natural force. It includes companionship with friends and opportunities to excel in your chosen sport. So go for it, you would-be champions and you enjoy every moment of your chosen sport: but remember we cannot all be champions.

The words seemed corny. But as Clinton displayed his belts, lapped up the applause and signed autographs, they made me think about myself as an athlete. I had always thought that sport, like all art, was useless. It was a construct, subjective, without real meaning. I wasn't like the youngsters I'd seen that evening, arms flailing, swinging wildly, learning to be a boxer. I had served no apprenticeship in the ring and I hadn't been culturalised over years as a fighter. But to survive I had to start believing I was one. The fight game was way too tough just to go through the motions. To be a fighter you had to believe in something; there had to be a meaning to all this. Otherwise you were just a guy in a pair of shorts taking a beating.

chapter 21

Colin McMillan had spent years trying to get a manager's licence. For reasons best known to the Board he had never succeeded with an application, even though he'd won a world title and was a true 'ambassador of the sport'. But recently his luck had changed and the Board had granted him a licence. Colin was now free to negotiate with promoters on behalf of his one and only client, Terry Dunstan, whom he had previously represented in a limited capacity as an agent. Whatever Terry paid Colin, it wasn't enough.

'Bruce Scott's got no fucking medical certificate?' snarled Terry into his mobile. Colin was on the receiving end, literally. I could see the cab driver looking sheepishly in the rear-view mirror. Terry was getting agitated. His eyes became two gaping black holes when he got annoyed, although he seldom lost his cool. He had that way of boiling up yet never letting his rage go over the top. His present gripe was a problem over a fight he was anticipating with Bruce Scott, who at the time was the British and Commonwealth cruiserweight champion. As Terry was the number one contender and mandatory opponent, the Board would have to strip Scott if he refused the fight. That's the way it worked. Scott had claimed medical grounds for delaying the fight and was given ten days by the Board to produce a medical certificate. However, twenty-one days had now passed and the Board hadn't acted. Terry thought this latest knock-back was part of a wider conspiracy to keep him out of the picture. He wanted to confront Simon Block at the Board because they hadn't stripped Scott of his British cruiserweight title and cleared him to fight Johnny Nelson for the WBO title.

Terry wanted Bruce Scott badly so he could get a title and get back to earning decent money. He was still 'in negotiation with Frank Warren' over the deal and hadn't fought for some eight months. In that time he had plied his trade as a sparring partner to Lennox Lewis and Herbie

Hide and worked the door at a nightclub on Fulham Broadway. The most money he'd ever made from boxing was £25,000 for the Mayfield title fight; 4 per cent of this went to the Board, another 4 per cent to the IBF and then there was Frank Warren's cut, training fees, expenses including sparring, accommodation, vitamins and sundries.

I asked Terry why he still bothered with boxing if he thought that the Board and even his own promoter were keen to keep him out in the cold. He grinned and simply said, 'I just like to beat people up.'

Terry did have a sensitive side. He normally saved it for when his girlfriend Nicki was around. They were either lovey-dovey or pistols at dawn, there was no in-between. They'd known each other, in the biblical sense, for less than six months but already the talk was of buying a house together. Nicki was a thirty-one-year-old sassy brunette, heavily tanned, buxom, around five five. She always wore dark clothes, combat pants, too much make-up and those platform sneakers that look like moon boots. She could have been an extra on 'Coronation Street'. Nicki lived just outside Sheffield but was often at the gym, too often for Howard and many in the camp who thought she was a bad influence on Terry.

'I'm not like other athletes' girlfriends or wives,' she told me. 'I've always been into sport myself. I swam for my county, was in all the teams at school. I've been into martial arts since I was nineteen.'

Nicki had left her second husband, an American, for Terry. She also liked to point out that she'd given up 'a Ford Explorer, a jacuzzi, two floodlit tennis courts and a green card' to be with him. She had this idea that Terry was going to win a world title and make 'them' rich. Howard and Lorna suspected she was either a chancer or a great lay. Lately she'd been running rings around Terry. On the other hand, his attitude towards women indicated that maybe it was him who was doing the running around.

'See, boxers, they love a dirty bird,' he said, licking his lips and laughing. He was full of stories about his sexploits. Boxers did love dirty birds, or dirty sex, or just plain old sex. It was the body culture that did it – vanity, narcissism and testosterone. The fitter you got the hornier you got. Why waste all that, especially on one woman? Fighters were womanising, cheating pigs, which is probably why I fitted in. Most of the sexploits I'd hear about in the changing room at the gym, however, surpassed anything I was capable of. They are also unfit to print. Without getting too graphic there was a lot of talk about anal sex, threesomes, infidelity, promiscuity and barely legal bedroom activities.

No one used condoms. A lot of talk was puff, locker-room chest beating, but sometimes the tales were too candid to be untrue. One guy told me how he used to take a beating from another guy in sparring and then go to his house and screw his wife while he was at work.

People were obsessed with sex in Sheffield. Who could blame them? The city was that grim you needed something to do. Sheffield had a fantastic line in massage parlours. They were everywhere. They began appearing in the 1970s following the reign of terror wrought by the Yorkshire Ripper, Peter Sutcliffe. Since then the authorities had adopted a softly softly approach, taking the view that prostitutes were safer on a rubber mattress above a chip shop than on a street corner.

Porn movies were also big in Sheffield, especially the so-called 'amateur' ones. Howard and a few of the lads in the gym had their own swapshop going. He was quite the connoisseur when it came to mucky videos. It was a real bone of contention between him and Lorna. She thought he had a psychological problem. He kept stacks of videos in the house, under the sofa and on top of the wall units, and watched them while she was asleep, sometimes until four in the morning. Often she'd come downstairs and berate him for it but he'd just shrug his shoulders, ignore her and go back to watching them as soon as she went back upstairs.

A sexual proclivity I never encountered in boxing, at least explicitly, was homosexuality. Occasionally a rumour would get around that a particular figure in boxing was gay, but usually these rumours were circulated purely to slight someone's character, especially if they were an ex-business or training associate or a rival fighter. Despite the apparent incongruity between boxing and the gay lifestyle, homosexuality was not a taboo subject or something that couldn't be discussed with some degree of wit and intelligence in the gym. That said, talk of 'queers, poofs, faggots, shit stabbers, bum bandits' and the like usually contained very little of either. One afternoon in the gym, Clinton suggested that amassing a gay following could be a great marketing angle for a fighter. 'I reckon if you pretended you were gay, you'd get a massive following,' he said, to which Terry quipped, 'Yeah, into the nearest fucking toilets.'

Fighters were inclined to call each other 'poof' or 'faggot' as a form of barracking as much as they would use 'girl' or 'pussy'. Effeminacy equalled weakness (for in the eyes of the male fighter, women are the weaker sex) and, in a fairly unsophisticated way, to a fighter homosexuality equalled effeminacy. To be called a woman or a queer was thus one and the same; they were mutually inclusive insults.

I always felt that as a boxer, your manhood was fairly clear cut. People could question your intelligence, your motivation for fighting or your moral or ethical beliefs but who could doubt your manliness, your bravery, your balls? These were the things that were commonly held up as the benchmarks of masculinity; so whether you preferred a male or female partner was actually irrelevant.

On 24 March 1962 the welterweight Benny 'Kid' Paret died at the hands of Emile Griffith following a third grudge match at Madison Square Garden. Paret had goaded Griffith at their weigh-in, calling him a *maricón* or faggot, reputedly because he worked for a New York milliner. In the twelfth round Griffith smashed Paret repeatedly in the head with eighteen unanswered blows until the referee made him stop. The Cuban fighter slumped to the canvas. Ten days later he was dead. Did that provocation make a difference? Griffith maintained that, like any other fighter, he was simply following his trainer's instructions. He set out to win the fight which he did albeit with tragic consequences.

chapter 22

I was starting to think and act like a professional now. I soon found I had a greater economy of movement, better punching technique and less anxiety, all of which had the net effect of increasing my stamina. Improved fitness helped. I was meant to be on a diet but I still managed to squeeze in the odd Mars bar or seven. I was pleasantly surprised that, unless you had a genetic problem with weight, dieting where boxing was concerned usually meant eating less, not eating differently.

My weight was steady at 89.5kg (14 stone 1lb). The six-pack was coming on and I had noticed an overall increase in muscle definition. The regime now consisted of twelve rounds of shadow boxing, the wobbly board, ten minutes on the running machine and six rounds of sparring, three with Scott, three with Danny. 'More haste, less speed,' said Howard when I worked the heavy bag. I wanted to be so fast that sometimes I'd lose sight of the technical side of my work. 'Try and do a few things well, not loads of things badly.' Howard never gave me more than a handful of instructions or concepts to deal with at any one time. The big man was big on patience. 'Keep it nice and simple,' he'd often say.

I was now capable of putting together more complex combinations of punches and had progressed from just throwing jabs and straight rights to a varied repertoire of shots. Although my technique was far from perfect, my left hook, which I had struggled with initially, was improving steadily.

After training, Scott told me about his new job on the door at Jongleurs, a comedy club in Leicester.

'It takes a lot of bottle to be a stand-up comedian,' he said. 'But then it takes a lot of bottle to do this job, doesn't it? To quote Shannon Briggs,' he added, referring to the American heavyweight, 'everything else is a walk in the park compared to boxing.'

As my confidence grew over the months, I began to think more about what possibilities lay ahead of me. Yes, it did take a lot of bottle to be a fighter and if I could summon all that courage, willpower, dedication and commitment to be a fighter, surely I could be anything I wanted to be, do anything I wanted to do. A lot of guys who got into boxing 'found' themselves. For some, it gave them a purpose, a reason to get up in the morning. For others, it helped build self-confidence. Cynics liked to misinterpret the confidence of the fighter as arrogance. The more time I spent around fighters the more I realised their arrogance wasn't just a form of macho posturing, a peacock-like ruffling of feathers and a show of strength. Fighters actually saw themselves as harder, tougher and more durable, both physically and mentally, than 'normal people'. After all, if you weren't arrogant enough to think you were fitter than the average guy, faster than him, harder than him, why box? Fighters have a superhuman belief in themselves, a feeling of invincibility, a belief that somehow it's always the other guy who winds up in the coma or the morgue, not them. No one could force you to get into that ring. If you were smart, you were selfish. You did it for yourself, to satisfy your own hopes, dreams and fantasies. Hope is one of the fundamentals that drives a fighter on. Without hope, a fighter, much less an ordinary man, has little to live for.

'I don't want to wind up on some building site somewhere getting up at six o'clock in the morning,' said Scott. 'To be a world champion is my dream and every time I get into that ring I'm chasing that dream.' Scott's idol is Mike Tyson.

It was a slow process, making the metamorphosis from writer to fighter, but suddenly I felt alive to the task. When I stepped through those ropes into the ring I felt an incredible sense of purpose. Nothing made you more aware of life and your tenuous hold on it than living on the edge. Boxing put me on the edge.

Nevertheless, I was still concerned about the risk of personal injury. Although I had encountered no serious damage, my body had to adjust rapidly to the pressures of life as a professional fighter. The will was there but having spent the last few years as a couch potato I was feeling the heat. Busted hands, creaking joints, niggling aches, pains and muscle strains were a constant reminder of my failings as a boxer. Tom Wolfe said of the writer George Plimpton, who once played five downs as a quarterback for the Detroit Lions for the book *Paper Lion*, that '... his performance reinforced the myth that professional athletes are superior to ordinary men.' I wanted to dispel the myth.

streets of towering brownstone factories. 'The lot of 'em.' Thanks to a less than enthusiastic promoter, Scott had fought three times only in two and a half years. Now aged thirty-two he'd returned to camp to train with Howard for the next seven weeks for what would probably be his swan song – a crack at regaining his British heavyweight crown from Julius Francis for the princely sum of £10,000. Having gone from earning £300,000 to ten grand it was no surprise to hear that he now regarded boxing as nothing more than a dangerous hobby.

'Listen, this is a hard game, mate,' said Scott, glancing at his Rolex watch and then at me as if to punctuate the statement. I sat in the back seat stroking the leather upholstery and nodded sagely. 'People get killed doing this. You've got to take it seriously.'

The first and last time I had seen Scott in action was at the Peacock. He had trained there on and off. In fact, he trained in a lot of places on and off. There probably wasn't a gym in the country he hadn't trained in. He'd had more trainers than Lillywhites, more coaches than National Express. He seemed to have a problem with consistency. Nevertheless, he took his training very seriously, especially sparring. The sparring sessions between him and Terry were not much short of the real thing.

'A real fight is not like sparring,' said Scott. 'It's just not the same thing. All this play fighting you do in the gym doesn't prepare you for a fight.'

Scott advised me that I had to harness all the hatred, anger and resentment I had inside and channel it into my opponent's face. He said I needed the 'killer instinct'. He thought one advantage Danny and I had was that we were black. Black fighters were better than white fighters said Scott because black people had more to be pissed off about than whites. But the visceral rage I once possessed as an angry young man in the East End had evolved into something wholly different. Maturity meant I could articulate my feelings with words not weapons. I began to fear that, no matter how angry I thought I was at society, my predicament or even my ex-girlfriend, I didn't have the pent-up aggression, the hunger to make a go of boxing the way that those around me did. This was obviously a weakness on my part, a dysfunction in my attitude, and I sought to overcome it, often with little success.

For the next seven weeks, throughout May and June, Howard would take Scott, myself and usually one or two other fighters to the local track for interval training, specifically fifteen fifteens: 15 seconds of jogging followed by a 15-second sprint repeated non-stop over 10 to 12 laps of the track, a distance of 4,000 to 4,800 metres. We did these routines on alternate days for about four weeks leading up to a fighter's bout. The idea behind interval training was to improve explosive power. A fight never operated at one pace. In the course of a round, a fighter may be on the defensive, slipping, feinting and blocking or catching a breather. Within a split second he'd go on the offensive BANG! and explode with a flurry of punches. By mixing jogging and sprinting you could train the body to shift rapidly from a slow heart rate to a high one without shocking the system. I hated the track. Sprinting was not my forte; neither was waking up at the crack of dawn and the track meant an early start. The earliest I could possibly wake up was 7.30 a.m. I'd spend the next hour contemplating the day ahead, the meaning of life etc. and then spend a further hour in bed reading, trying to stave off the inevitable. I'd brush my teeth, wash my face and put on roadwork clothes – running shoes, lightweight track pants or shorts (depending on the weather), T-shirt, hooded sweat top, windcheater and woolly hat.

After the track, Howard would go to the gym and I would usually return home for breakfast, which these days consisted of cereal, orange juice, scrambled egg on toast, a cup of tea and a banana. I would then chill for three or four hours – the minimum recovery time – sleeping, reading or perhaps writing before heading off for the gym.

I was trying desperately to keep to a roadwork schedule. As a cardiovascular or fat-burning exercise, running took some beating. I had always had the impression that it was an essential part of a fighter's training regime. Nevertheless, I had a bit of a problem with running. I found it arduous, mind-numbingly boring, strenuous on the joints, uncomfortable and – have I already said boring? Jim Fixx, the keep-fit freak who 'invented' jogging reckoned that the advantage of running at the crack of dawn was that the air was clean and free of pollution. Then of course the streets were quiet and there were no meddling pedestrians getting in your way. Still, what did Jim know anyway? He dropped dead from a heart attack in Central Park at the tender age of forty-seven, while out jogging. My theory was that it probably suited those who worked full-time to run before the daily grind and others, such as Scott Welch, did it partly out of habit and also 'because it's hard, it toughens you up'.

On a few occasions I did 45-minute runs with Scott along the canal from the gym to Meadowhall shopping centre. For a big fella he was amazingly quick on his feet and I'd find it difficult keeping up with him. Scott was obsessed with running, contrary to Howard's philosophy that running should be over relatively short distances and not too long in duration. I usually ran in the late evening, after 10.30. The way I figured it was I'd be fighting in the evening so apart from suiting my work pattern (I'd write into the early hours of the morning and generally got up at midday), running at night helped adjust my body clock. Of all the aspects of my training, I found running to be the hardest physical part, even harder than sparring. In the gym you had competition – sparring partners raining blows on you, Howard barking orders. There was always some form of opposition, something to bounce off. But on the road you were on your own. There was no one watching over you, ordering you around. How tempting it was in the middle of a run to stop and walk, buy a drink or a Mars bar. Self-motivation in the first place was bad enough. I found it too easy to skip runs, convince myself I had an injury or find some excuse (like the rain) to stop me from hitting the road. But for all the stress of running, the impact on the knees, the cold, the wet, the uncomfortable sweat, when I did get into it, running could be therapeutic. Late at night with only my thoughts for company, I had an opportunity to get lost in my head, disappear into flights of fancy or resolve things that had been on my mind. Often when running through the woods, I'd give myself pep talks on how I was going to win the fight. I'd visualise my opponent in the shadows, throw a combination and then POW! he's down for the count. I'm the winner.

chapter 23

Lunch had evidently taken its toll on Danny. He lasted one round in sparring later that afternoon.

'Where's your skirt . . . where's your skirt, bitch,' scowled Terry as he battered Danny with a furious combination of punches. 'You fucking girl. Danny, you're a girl . . . a pussy.' Terry continued to pummel Danny into the ropes until the younger man could offer no defence and made the fatal mistake of turning away. He took two looping right hands to the back of the head and crumpled into a tangled heap at the foot of the ropes, yelping, 'You fucking bastard,' as he went down. The master had taken his pupil to school.

I was standing at the side of the ring. Howard was shaking his head. Nicki was forcing back a laugh. The other bystanders at ringside looked disparagingly at Danny and went back to their workouts. A lot of people in the gym secretly relished seeing Danny get a good hiding, me included.

Terry beckoned me for a drink. I picked up his water bottle and as he approached squeezed it so a stream of water cascaded into his gaping mouth.

'How was that?' he whispered. Danny was still doubled up on the other side of the ring in agony.

'Impressive,' I said, 'very impressive.'

'D'you think he was ready for the finish?'

'Definitely.'

Terry grinned. He always sought a second opinion on his performance in sparring, usually from Howard and occasionally from me when I was ringside. Apart from very minor details, I never found fault in his boxing. Even someone with his talent had insecurities about his boxing ability. I guess in return for him giving me an easy ride Terry knew he could always count on me to boost his ego.

'Danny's new nickname is Picasso,' Terry announced to the gym, ''cos he's always on the fucking canvas.' For a change, Danny didn't have a smart answer. He was having to eat a lot of crow lately. Clinton had dropped him three times with body shots that week and now Terry, who had acted as a teacher to Danny, had suddenly got in on the act.

Terry and Danny had a strange, strained relationship. Danny looked up to Terry as a mentor, an idol even. Most of his moves came straight out of the Terry Dunstan school of boxing. He had fast hands like Terry and was able to throw punches from unpredictable angles with speed, just like Terry. He had good lateral movement and footwork which allowed him to move from one part of the ring to another effortlessly. He even came out with the same inane cries, 'Oooh, baby' and 'Hurt me', in sparring. He was lithe, agile, tall, had good reach and was the perfect pretender to Terry's crown; in some ways too perfect. Apart from experience and power, Danny had all of Terry's attributes and more. His potential was unquestionable. Crucially he had something that Terry didn't have – youth.

'Two years' time, two more years and I'll take 'im,' Danny would say conspiratorially when Terry got heavy with him. Time waits for no man in boxing. Terry knew that Danny, hungry to succeed and even hungrier to impress Howard, was always testing his virility and stamina. A boxing ring is a cruel place to be an old man. Terry told me that he thought his young protégé had been pushing his luck lately and deserved a beating. It was a matter of respect.

'What's he expect?' said Terry as Danny made his excuses to Howard and anyone who'd listen. 'He thinks he can take my head off? Nah . . . he's fucking having a laugh. He can't expect to go in there, trying to knock everyone out and not get hurt.'

Danny was flash, he had a lot of mouth. Respect is a key word in boxing. Terry and Clinton were basically keeping Danny in his place, letting him know where he figured in the gym hierarchy. By asserting his power over Danny, Terry was also galvanising his reputation in the gym as someone not to be messed with.

When I first arrived on the scene, Terry and Danny were thick as thieves. Terry would take him to one side and show him the kind of tricks and moves only seasoned professionals knew. When they sparred together, which was often, it was hard but good-natured. But things had changed. Gradually new faces were coming into the gym and Terry, as the grandee, was feeling the pressure. A recent recruit for example was Kelly Oliver, a four-time ABA champion and a future prospect for a British title. Kelly was a personable professional who travelled from Lincoln to Sheffield daily to train and got on well with everyone in the gym. As a cruiserweight he was a direct threat to Terry in a gym that had a fairly even distribution of weight divisions. The first time the two sparred together Terry bloodied Kelly with some fierce right hands, which set the precedent for a lot of hard sparring between the two in the future. Justin didn't mix it with Terry; Scott Lansdowne provided a challenge in terms of weight and power but lacked the experience and technique to be a serious threat; and apart from the weighty fists of Scott Welch in the early summer, while he prepared for his British title shot, Terry had the run of things among the gym's big hitters.

Naturally, I was in a league of my own and thus posed no threat whatsoever. The first time I sparred with Terry, Howard had gone off on an adventure somewhere and left the two of us alone in the gym.

'You fancy working me over?' asked Terry.

'Sure, why not? But I've got no training kit. I've left it in Howard's car. I got no gloves, no gumshield, no . . .'

'Don't worry. I'm not gonna go heavy on you. Here, use these.'

Terry threw a battered pair of 16oz sparring gloves at me and I gloved-up without bandages.

As soon as the timer hit zero, Terry rushed me but didn't throw a punch. He stuck his guard up and I threw a flurry of unconvincing body shots.

'What the fuck was that?' he yelled. 'Come on. I'm a punch bag, bring it on.' I was throwing shots but he was slipping the bulk of them. Every time I managed to connect with a clean blow he responded with an immediate counter to the temple or the body. 'Come on, give it to me, fucking hurt me,' he said, backing himself into a corner. As he propped himself up against the ring post I worked his body stepping from side to side trying to catch him with kidney punches. 'Head and body, head and body. Go upstairs,' he said, his dark eyes peering through his red head guard. 'Fucking hurt me.' My punches were lame. I knew he could blast me out in seconds if he went on the offensive. I feared retaliation.

'I can't hurt you, Tel. You're my mate,' I said with a hint of sarcasm.

'Fuck that shit, bring it on.'

The first round had gone on for at least six minutes. Occasionally the buzzer didn't sound on the timer and you'd lose yourself. We went into the second round in the same vein as the first – me throwing most of the shots, Terry doing the 'rope-a-dope' technique and blocking and slipping. The second lasted about five minutes. By the third round I was knackered.

'Come on, ten more,' implored Terry. As he leant against the ropes, I pummelled away, grinding to a halt. 'Eight, nine, ten. How do you feel?' said Terry.

'Out of it,' I gasped.

'See, it's not easy when you have to do all the work, is it?'

The more I trained, the harder it seemed to get. Maybe all those late nights in the eighties, those halcyon days, maybe it had all caught up with me. My latest affliction was an abscess in the mouth, the result of having a tooth cracked in sparring. I went to see a local dentist who said he'd 'whip it out' for me. Having a tooth out would put me out of action for at least a week. He prescribed some antibiotics and suggested I come back in seven days. I never did. Howard kept telling me my motorisation was kicking in.

'I'm very pleased with you, kid,' he said. 'You'll be bang on. By August you'll be ready for regular hard sparring.'

Howard's running machine had just received its worldwide patent. Apart from a vertical pet scratching post mounted on a treadmill, there was nothing on the market like his invention.

'If I have that machine made and you get a second-round knockout, this'll be a good year for me!' I felt honoured that Howard took me so seriously. There were times when I felt like the gym's runt, the second-string novice with whom anyone could take liberties. Knowing that Howard took personal satisfaction in what we were doing was important to me. I enjoyed his praise and actively sought it out, just as his other lads in the gym did. There were times when I looked at Howard and he reminded me of my dad. He even smelled like my father at times – a steely aroma of sheet metal, oil, Swarfega and Old Spice.

I trusted Howard as I would my own father. So that evening when it came to discussing who would manage me I let him know I wanted Lorna to do it.

'You what?'

'Only kidding, Howard.'

'She can't manage you, anyway. She ain't got a fucking manager's licence. I have.'

'Bollocks,' said Lorna. 'I thought you were going to leave that to Dennis Hobson, anyway.'

'What for? What's it got to do with Dennis Hobson?' I said.

'Well, I thought as he runs the club you might . . . well, I don't know. Howard, are you going to manage him?'

Howard looked me up and down and paused.

'Yeah, I may as well be the one to take his thirty-five per cent of three hundred quid.'

'As much as that?' I said.

By the end of June, I weighed 13 stone 12lb. But what had happened to my smooth skin? Once succulent flesh, firm and still glistening in the twilight of youth, had given way to tight, hard reptilian scales. My back now had a catalogue of scars from rope burns and old bruises to skipping rope lashes and scratches. I was becoming hard-bodied, tough. I was muscular and, dare I say it, leaner and meaner than ever before, weighing in most days at a dry weight ideal for cruiserweight. I was, however, destined for the light-heavyweight division.

Scott Welch failed in his bid to recapture the British heavyweight crown following a mediocre performance at the London Arena. Who cared anyway? These days a British heavyweight title didn't count for much. The average Joe in the street couldn't put a name or a face to the champion. Every now and again someone like Cooper or Bruno would come along with a 'Yeah, yeah, yeah, he's a good boy, he's a good boy' or 'Know what I mean, 'arry?' and capture the public's imagination. But neither Julius Francis nor Scott had that sort of appeal. They weren't showmen, just workaday fighters trying to earn a crust.

The post-mortem into the fight ran for days. The telephone at the Raineys' buzzed constantly with analysis and comment from friends and professionals who had seen the fight. The consensus was that while the fight was a lacklustre affair, Scott had done enough work to have been at least two rounds ahead come the final bell. Howard would run the tape of the fight over and over and just sit in his corner of the sofa meditating on every move.

'He'll be like this for days,' said Lorna, thrusting another cup of tea into my hands. 'He'll sit there for ages watching the fight. He has a lot of concern for his boys, know what I mean?' He seemed to be in another world. 'Howard. HOWARD! D'you wanna cup of tea, love?' A grunt indicated 'yes' and Lorna went back into the kitchen.

I arrived typically late for my medical examination with Dr Singh at the Harold Street surgery on 5 July. Nevertheless as soon as I walked through the door the doctor left to attend to a heart-attack case.

'I've got an appointment for a medical,' I said to one of the receptionists, handing her my medical form from the Board. She flicked through it and gave me a small container.

'I need a urine sample from you, love.' I went off and produced the sample. My urine looked fluorescent yellow. I even saw a couple of floaters in there. In the name of Christendom . . . floaters! This didn't look right. What now, an ulcer, kidney failure, liver damage? I knew those bloody body shots would catch up with me sooner or later.

The two receptionists were nattering, not in strictest confidence, about the patients when I got back from the WC. The reception area was crowded with people – a couple of grubby-faced tinkers, a small group of Somalians, an old man, a crazy ragga in a string vest and two women in their thirties one of whom had a deep tan, extensions and massive tits.

'Why mek me appointment fe one a'clock if me nah 'ave it now?' said the ragga to one of the receptionists in a heavy patois. The receptionist tried to explain the reason for the delay and advised the youth to take up his grievance with Dr Singh. He kissed his teeth and went back to lying on a bench in the waiting area.

After a nearly two-hour wait, Dr Singh returned and apologised to everyone. He was a funny little character. He came from Guyana, my parents' country, and did most of the boxing shows and fighters' medical examinations in South Yorkshire. The woman with the tan and tits got up and went into his surgery. She was at least six foot tall and muscular. Two minutes later she re-emerged, beckoned her friend and left. I noticed on the way out she had big hands and a heavy jaw line – maybe Dr Singh did sex changes on the side.

The other patients traipsed in and out until it was just the ragga and me left. I overheard Dr Singh say something to the ragga about having the clap. They didn't stand on ceremony here. Dr Singh gave the young ragga a prescription, a couple of condoms and sent him packing. Now it was my turn.

'You could write a book about this place,' said the doctor as I explained the purpose of my visit. 'We had one guy in here, a Jamaican, spoke broad patois. The last doctor he had, a white man, went and referred him to a psychiatrist because he couldn't believe what he was saying. His accent was so broad he thought he was talking nonsense, gibberish.'

The good doctor whizzed through a list of questions on the BBB of C's medical examination form covering every conceivable medical condition bar bubonic plague and malaria.

'Have you ever suffered from headaches, blackouts or fits, visual disturbances, bowel disorders, haemorrhoids, any kidney or bladder problems, diabetes, renal colic, venereal diseases? You don't suffer from anything like that, do you?' said the good doctor as more of a statement than a question.

'No I don't,' I replied.

'No' was then scrawled next to a dozen or so questions. The doctor measured my height and weight and took my pulse, all of which seemed to be in order. Most of the other questions he answered with 'normal' apart from genitalia which he described with some prescience (he never set eyes on them) as 'healthy'.

'Am I going to make it then, Doc?' I said.

'I think you'll live,' he replied. He signed the form, which was now complete apart from the HIV, brain scan and eye-test results. I gave him two crumpled-up tenners and a fiver in assorted change. He gave me a receipt and two onion bhajis from a brown paper bag and I left.

Howard and Lorna had a lot of love for one another but when the shit hit the fan, as it occasionally did, I didn't feel comfortable being in the middle of their domestics. Firstly, all that screaming and shouting reminded me too much of growing up in my parents' war-torn household. Secondly, I had enough crap in my own life without getting caught up in someone else's mess. I had to accept that family feuds came with the territory. As Lorna had told me when I first arrived, the Raineys weren't 'going to put on any airs and graces' for my benefit. I'd made the decision to live with them. The best I could do during turbulent times was be impartial, at least on the outside. My private loyalties lay with Howard. He was my trainer, my guru. I had to trust this man with my health, my life even. I had a lot of respect for Lorna, but she wasn't going to be in the corner for my fight.

Sensing a storm brewing in the living room, I retired to my room, my own private Idaho. While I lost myself in the pages of Norman Mailer's *The Fight* and dreamed of being Muhammad Ali, Lorna raged, castigating Howard and her two sons for being thoughtless and insensitive to her needs. 'Does anybody care about me?' she screamed 'Nobody asked me what I wanted to eat . . .'

'Still what is genius but balance on the edge of the impossible,' said

Mailer referring to the 'rope-a-dope' technique Ali used to sucker the formidable Foreman into defeat. While boxing had given me a greater sense of self-confidence, I wasn't arrogant enough, just yet, to call myself a genius. But here I was, having never fought either as an amateur or a professional, having never previously engaged in any form of full-contact sport or martial art, having only a modicum of fistic skills gleaned during a misspent youth of playground fights and bar-room brawls, here I was being schooled by probably the best trainer in the country and even at nearly thirty-two I was supposedly a prospect.

According to Lorna, Howard had told her, 'It's a shame that David only wants to have the one fight. What a waste.' Howard had told me time and time again over the weeks spanning June and July 1999 that I had a lot of potential, enough in fact to make a career out of boxing! One day he had the audacity to say, 'Stuff the writing. Be a boxer,' as he watched me shadow box in the gym. I'd been hitting the heavy bag with greater power and timing of late. I could feel the *chi* energy running through my body out of my fist and into the bag every time I threw a stiff jab or crunching right hook. 'You're ready to go up to the next level now, mate,' said Howard. 'Good work.'

Howard had been jacking me up with the idea that I should carry on boxing after my debut. 'You could get twenty fights in until you're thirty-five and win the Central Area title,' he said. The Central Area title, that old chestnut. Carry on at thirty-two! I couldn't – could I?

I had reached a point in my training where it was obvious to those around me that I had the necessary balls, desire and raw talent to make it into the ring for that all-important fight. Trouble was, my rapid progress was beginning to convince a number of people, not least Howard, who had great faith in me not only as a boxer but as a writer and a friend, that there was more to me than just one fight. Distant voices were saying, 'Go on, have another and another and . . .' I was slowly, reluctantly becoming aware of my own capabilities. I was starting to believe the hype. So I was faced with a dilemma – fight or flight after my debut. I had said I would have just the one. That was what I set out to do. But perhaps to get through the one fight, I did have to start looking beyond it.

chapter 24

Royal Hallamshire Hospital, Department of G.U. Medicine, 30 July 1999. I was about to take a giant leap towards becoming a fighter. Since the mid eighties, professional boxers have had to be screened for HIV and AIDS as part of the licensing procedure, so I made an appointment at the local hospital and saw a consultant, Dr Fraser, regarding an AIDS test. Dr Fraser talked me through the whys and wherefores of the test and the implications of a positive result.

'Some people aren't comfortable knowing or finding out that they have a disease which will ultimately kill them.' Thanks Doc. I told her the reason why I was having the test and that I'd be comfortable with knowing the outcome, whatever that may be. Dr Fraser offered me the option of going for the full monty and being tested for herpes, syphilis, gonorrhoea, that sort of thing. I said, 'Sure, why not?' What's a little STD among friends?

The doctor took me into a small room and gave me a going over on the examination bench, gently handling my shrivelled penis as if it were a Fabergé egg. I looked down at it as the rubber-gloved doctor poked and prodded, thinking how small and insignificant it seemed. I wondered how many the good doctor had handled in her career. A hundred? Five hundred? A thousand? Imagine that, a thousand penises passing through your hands! I wondered what she thought when she saw a particularly large one, whether it would cause her to raise an eyebrow of appreciation or whether she just stoically went about her business regardless of size. A friend of a friend who works in a similar department in Middlesex Hospital, London, said that the nurses awarded points and gave fictitious prizes to the patients with the largest members.

Most of us go through life without ever having to face judgement, real judgement that determines liberty, life, ultimate success or abject failure. We are continually put through selection processes such as exams, job interviews, mortgage applications and club memberships, but how often are we judged on the sum of our intellectual, mental, physical and spiritual merits? Everything in boxing was a test. There were tests of courage, will, fitness, health, determination; eye tests, brain scans, medical examinations, AIDS tests, hepatitis B – I have never felt so scrutinised in all my life.

Dr Fraser had said the test results would be ready in five days but it took nearly two weeks for me to summon up the courage to go back to the hospital. A lot was riding on this. A positive HIV result would have meant a much shorter book for one thing. It would also have meant a much shorter life. Deep down I believed I was in the clear but there was doubt. The eighties and nineties were punctuated by endless scare stories concerning the spread of AIDS and, having led an intermittently promiscuous life, I was worried about falling victim to the big disease with a little name.

After my separation from Lara I'd started playing the field once again, for old times' sake. It was a vacuous attempt to galvanise my manhood and overcome the emptiness of singledom. I did try while in training to refrain from elicit or casual sex. I wanted to embrace the underlying Zen philosophy of boxing as a pure, Spartan discipline, you know, get right into the Western martial art thing. To that end I had abandoned a life of fornication – well, sort of.

For research purposes I owed it to myself to experiment with the effects of libido on my training and performance in the ring, so to speak. In the course of a year I'd met a few women who had unwittingly become guinea pigs in my bedroom laboratory – sex was definitely better with two than as a lone pastime – but the jury was still out on whether sex was a help or a hindrance when it came to boxing.

Howard told me repeatedly that sex took the vim out of the legs. 'Take it easy on the shagging,' he'd say whenever I had a break from training or a weekend away. Empirical evidence suggested this was true to an extent; you needed your legs to stand up and fight. But he did agree with my assertion that the endorphins produced through sexual activity had a therapeutic effect on the body, which I often found cured niggling aches, pains and, most importantly, bachelor's balls. There was, however, a widely held belief that the satisfaction that came from ejaculation dampened a fighter's aggression and made him soft. From personal experience, I'd say there was some truth in that. If you were making love, did you really want to make war?

'I used to shag two days before a fight,' Justin would brag. 'Don't make owt difference to your performance, man.' Terry said he abstained three weeks before a fight, five weeks if a title was at stake. Most of the other guys tended to sit on the fence. The consensus was, if it was there to be had, it was there to be taken. Just don't go out of your way to get laid.

Having an AIDS test was probably the single most daunting health issue I'd ever faced. Yet I'd never had a blood transfusion, I didn't do intravenous drugs, I'd never had gay sex and the last time I'd had unprotected sex was when Luca was conceived after the 1996 Notting Hill Carnival. Theoretically, I was low risk, but I was still worried about the results.

Around half a dozen guys were in the waiting room when I arrived. The whitewashed walls and coffee table were covered with posters and leaflets on syphilis, HIV, hepatitis B, gonorrhoea, NSU, herpes, genital warts – you get the picture.

A procession of bodies sauntered in and out of the waiting room with envelopes, rattling paper bags, tubes of cream, dry mouths and watery eyes. I tried to look cool, unaffected by the wait, but I could feel my palms sweating and my heart racing. I flicked through an *Independent on Sunday* supplement, boring, and the *Sun*, inane. I noticed a magazine called *Positive* with a fresh-faced boy on the cover. I couldn't look at it. The name said it all. Over the past few days, every time I'd seen that word in a newspaper or a book or heard it on TV it freaked me. My damned paranoia was cancerous. What the hell was I worrying about?

Forty-five minutes passed and I was the last but one. Jesus Christ, they'd left us till last because they had bad news. Were they worried I was going to throw a wobbly or something? I had noticed that Dr Fraser's name was not on the list of consultants that day. It was a set-up.

'David Matthews, please.' The consultant gave me a compassionate look. She was cute. I got up and felt my knees buckle slightly. Muscle cramp? My palms were sweating even more and my heart was pounding. Stay cool, everything's going to be just fine. No it's not. I remembered the scene in *Kids* when Chloe Sevigny got a positive HIV result and fell apart. I'm dead.

'Take a seat, David.' I do believe in God, honest.

'Right. I understand you've come for some results.'

'That's right.' My throat was dry. Just get it over and done with.

'OK.' The consultant produced a sheet of paper from a file with my name at the top. I was about to have a heart attack.

'I can tell you that your HIV test was negative.'

'Ha . . . yes . . .' I leaned back in my seat, smug. I shifted round to get a look at the results. There was a list of coded entries with the words 'not detected' next to each one.

'And you're also clear for all other sexually transmitted diseases,' the consultant added with a wry smile.

I had a clean bill of health. The consultant agreed to send me a letter confirming the result of the test for my licence application. I'd just overcome not only a major professional obstacle, but a personal one as well.

As soon as I arrived at the gym that afternoon Howard and the boys were on me. They knew that I had gone for my results and had been winding me up about it ever since I took the test.

'Will we be able to drink out of thy water bottle now, then?' asked Clinton.

'Eh?' I replied, coolly.

'How did thy AIDS test go?'

'Oh that,' I said. 'Oh it was . . . er . . .'

'Fucking get on with it,' said Howard.

'It was negative. Do you really think I'd be standing here right now if I was HIV positive?'

Every fighter I'd met had reservations about taking an AIDS test. A boxing licence had to be renewed each year, so it was an annually necessary evil. A bad result could ruin a fighter's career. Howard told me that one of Colin McMillan's opponents once tested HIV positive immediately after a fight and was so devastated he went on a nihilistic crime spree culminating in him attempting to smuggle six kilos of heroin into the US. Two years later, while the fighter was languishing in jail, it transpired that there had been some sort of mix-up and the test result was in fact negative.

chapter 25

The car pulled away and Luca's face got smaller and smaller and smaller. She waved, I waved, and then she was gone. I stood outside White City tube station, masking my tears from passing travellers, rubbed my eyes and then headed for Victoria and the four-hour coach ride back to Sheffield.

'Everything would be all right if you just gave me more attention,' Lara had said before dropping me off. The talk that weekend, once again, had been of reconciliation.

'That's the answer to the world's problems,' I replied. I wasn't going to let sentimentality cloud my thinking any more. In just over five hours, on 9 August, Lara and I would both be thirty-two. We shared the same birthday, a starsign and a beautiful daughter, and that was it. Time had moved on.

A few weeks earlier we had attempted a reconciliation. Lara had arranged a five-day break at her parents' holiday home, an old chapel in the sleepy village of Hunstanton in Norfolk. We, or more accurately Lara, had started to interpret an improvement in our platonic relationship as a sign that the old flame was still burning. My heart wasn't really into getting back together but I believed, naïvely, that it was the best thing for Luca. Within an hour of Lara and Luca meeting me at King's Lynn railway station the old petty differences began to resurface. A couple of days later she took me back to King's Lynn and our relationship was officially over, again.

Luca and I spent precious little time together. I was fearful that whatever bond I had with my daughter would in time get weaker and weaker as we saw each other less and less. Not all estranged fathers disappear without trace. For those of us who maintain contact and want to see our children there is always the reality of feeling powerless, fearing the more interest you show, the more the child's mother might have on you. I tried on numerous occasions to swallow my pride, eat humble pie and just play along with Lara so I could see more of Luca.

For my thirty-second birthday, Howard gave me double rations in the gym. I hadn't trained for nearly two weeks having previously torn a muscle in my left shoulder during sparring. I'd tried everything from Olbas oil to one of Howard's many electric massagers to alleviate the problem. I felt guilty when I didn't train, not least because it resulted in weight gain; I had now crept back up to 14 stone 2lb. I hated the idea of time slipping by while I wasn't learning something or honing my skills. I suppose I had become a gym junkie insofar as I'd suffer withdrawal symptoms whenever I didn't train. Even though there were many days when I walked into the gym dreading the thought of training, especially sparring, the moment I had to sit on the sidelines and watch the other lads work I felt envious.

Shaun Stokes came into the gym and said he was making a comeback. He wanted to live the life again.

'I haven't got time for four or five fights,' he told Howard. 'I want to get straight in there with someone decent. If I lose then I'll retire. Simple as that. I haven't got time to be hanging around, not at twenty-nine.'

Howard and Dennis were trying, diplomatically, to convince Shaun he needed a few warm-ups before he could get the title shot he yearned for. Somehow I got the impression they'd rather he stayed retired.

'I've been around, I know all the dodges,' Shaun told me. 'Even though I've been eating pizzas and curries and drinking beer, I've been running every night. I can keep up with Clinton on the track. I'm as fit as he is. I know I am.' Shaun, of course, was deluding himself.

'If Dennis wanted to get me on that Prince show, I'm sure he could. He's a bastard.' Dennis was co-promoting a show with Naseem Hamed's Prince Promotions at the Hillsborough Leisure Centre, Sheffield in six weeks' time. Clinton was top of the bill, defending his Commonwealth title for the first time in his hometown against a Trinidadian called John Lennox Lewis. Scott Lansdowne was also set for his second professional appearance. Shaun was desperate to get in on the act.

'I could make ten stone ten in six weeks, easy. Even if I didn't have to get on the scales. I've had it before, with Ross Hale. I took the fight and they [the promoters] knew I weren't ten-ten, so they told me to take a walk around Bristol, just stay out of the way at the weigh-in.'

Fighters live in a dream world. Nothing in boxing is ever what it seems. The fight game is all smoke and mirrors. Promoters, managers, agents and trainers are all part of the illusion. To protect himself a fighter has to be a consummate liar, inside and outside the ring. One of the greatest skills a fighter has is the art of deception. What is the feint if not a con trick of movement? Or the right-hand lead or throwing a hook off the jab? A guy can win a fight before a punch is even thrown by intimidating an opponent, even when he himself is scared witless. Fighters feign injury, fake tiredness and pretend to buckle at the knees in order to sucker an opponent into a false sense of security. But a fighter always saves the biggest lie for himself, the one that deludes him into thinking he can go on when he's way past his best.

On 11 August 1999, I witnessed my first total solar eclipse. It was also the first time I'd ever seen stars. Justin and I were into the fourth and final round of what had been a gruelling sparring session. I was pulling back from a clinch when I dropped my guard momentarily and for some unknown reason, glanced away. At least, that's what I think happened. In that lapse of concentration, Justin caught me with a swooping right hand over the top of my gloves – PHWACK! The blow turned me 90 degrees jolting me upright. I heard a dull thud and a whirr like the sound of an afterburner firing on a jet engine, and for a few seconds my vision became blurred, an opaque, glassy film seeping over my retina.

I scanned the periphery of the gym taking in shapes, faces, the ropes, the ceiling, the floor (somebody stop that floor from moving). I saw everything in black and white, like a bad dream. I was trapped, suspended in monochrome animation. The eclipse! I'm blind, I'm blind! I should never have gone out that morning and stared at the eclipse, even if it was through a bloody cloudscape. The shot came. I didn't see it coming.

The best shots, the body blows that can drop a 200lb man like a sack of potatoes, the eardrum-splitting left hook, the killer right-hand KO, all the best shots are the ones you never see coming. There's no time to think, to counter, to react. It's just BAM! Kelly Oliver, who was shadow boxing in the adjacent ring cried, 'WOO!', acknowledging the ferocity of the blow.

'Sorry, Dave. You all right, you all right, mate?' My senses were out of synch, my balance and coordination melted away. I muttered something to Justin about being all right but I wasn't. I was still in a daze. Only my ego kept me on my feet. Tiny white specks flashed in front of me. I felt as though I was looking at the world through a puddle. This was a trip, like acid or mescaline, or like drowning – no awareness of time or place and an acute feeling of mortality. But unlike drowning, having my brain temporarily shifted in its cranium wasn't wholly unpleasant and that was the strange thing. In fact, it had a mildly narcotic buzz to it.

About ten seconds passed and I began to compose myself. Justin seemed to have cooled down the pace having sensed I was still groggy from the blow. I tried to do the macho thing and went for him, not so much with a physical resolve but a mental one.

'Come on, Justin. Is that all you got? Fucking give it to me . . . you know you want to. You wanna knock me out. You've been dying to ever since I got up here. Come on, you just tried to have me over when I wasn't looking, you dirty bastard. Come on, just imagine I'm Terry Dunstan, or better still Danny . . .'

They'd finally got to me. I had succumbed to all that macho bullshit I once derided. Even though I'd nearly been knocked out on my feet I was goading, taunting, using that old psychology on Justin, just like Terry did on Danny or Scott. I'd tried for months to avoid the baiting game, but it was no use. They'd drawn me in.

From round one I had set out to have a brawl. Pound for pound Justin was one of the hardest punchers in the gym. He was also the one guy who, when put under pressure, would react with near authentic brutality. He hit hard and seldom pulled his punches so I knew when I sparred with him he was throwing his best shots. Justin became the benchmark for my threshold of pain. Howard said he could turn pro tomorrow and have ten straight wins on the trot. I reasoned that if I could handle him, I could handle my eventual opponent.

For the next three days I was convinced that I had a detached retina. My right eye kept twitching and occasionally I'd see tiny black flakes in front of me. My jaw ached. My back ached. My hands ached from punching bags, pads and faces. My shoulder was killing me. Getting pummelled wasn't such an attractive proposition any more. This week I'd had more fat lips than a pack of gorillas with collagen implants. While sparring with one of the amateurs, an even greener novice than I was, he managed to chin me repeatedly with his jab and I couldn't counter. Howard looked on bemused. I felt stupid. I got frustrated in the end and resorted to roughhousing him. I nearly broke his jaw with my elbow.

Becoming an athlete was a joke. As an overweight, unhealthy slob, I didn't give a toss about my condition and I felt fine, well at least mentally; but since turning into a health freak, I'd realised what bad shape I was in. I noticed bulging veins appearing on my temples, for instance – a sign of fitness according to Lorna, but I swore they were indicative of a cerebral haematoma. I'd totally underestimated the extent of my hypochondria. I had become hypersensitive to every twitch, sneeze, cough, ache, spot and blemish. I was neurotic about my health and weight and everything I ate or drank. I'd bite into a burger or a bar of chocolate and have immediate pangs of guilt. Guilt was what it all boiled down to really, that and fear. I was allowing two of the most negative, most self-destructive emotions to get the better of me.

After a week of soul-searching, I went fishing with Howard, one of the lads from the gym, his two sons and Justin. The countryside, the fresh air and running water provided succour for my mild depression. 'I had my doubts about you at first,' said Justin as he set up a rod and line for me. I knew as much about fishing as I did about boxing. 'But after that spar we had, I've changed me mind. I think you'll do all right. In fact, I think you'll win.' Earning respect in the gym was crucial to a fighter's survival. If you didn't fit in, you were out. It had taken a beating, and five months of hard graft, but finally I was in.

'I saw stars about three or four times when you hit me,' said Justin. He told me that word had got round the gym that I wasn't a mug after all. 'I hope you don't think I was taking a liberty, but I had to give it to you [a good hiding] otherwise you'd have knocked me out.' Apart from paid sparring partners (who were little more than human punch bags) the gentlemen's agreement in boxing was that you didn't 'take liberties' in the gym. We all paid our £6-a-week subs regardless of status and trained together, in a very loose sense, as brothers-in-arms. Occasionally things got out of hand, especially when a new face arrived on the scene and guys were keen to test him. But knocking people out or maiming them wasn't the point of sparring. Sparring was fundamentally an exercise designed to authenticate a real fight without the intention of knocking out your opponent. Even in a fight proper a true pro had concern for his adversary. Grudge matches aside, fighters entered the ring with mutual respect. Despite the apparent brutality of boxing, only the most twisted pro, and the fans, wanted to see a fighter get seriously injured. As one old pro had told me, 'We fight to win, we don't fight to kill.'

Death in the prize ring is always a possibility. Since the Marquess of

Queensberry introduced his rules in 1884, some 500 fighters around the world have died in the ring or as a result of boxing. But, like dying in a plane crash, dying in the ring is a freak accident, something that happens to other people. You have to look at it that way, otherwise how could you box?

On an excursion to a gym in Bradford one evening, I met Jim Moor, an amateur coach in his early fifties. A genial man, Jim had been a pro between 1968 and 1978. He had once killed a man in the ring. It was in 1972 during his eighteenth professional fight.

'I fought a guy called Dave Pickney,' he said. 'I stopped him in the fifth round. They took Pickney to the dressing room and he collapsed. After that fight I was never the same. But I still had another fifty-eight contests.' Jim was matter-of-fact about the incident. 'If you're worried about being killed in the ring, you shouldn't be in there in the first place,' he said, repeating a sentiment I'd often heard from fighters.

'One punch is all it takes, one punch can end your life,' my old buddy Tyrone had told me. Whenever I trained with him he spoke of pro fighters being 'licensed to kill' and his fists being 'weapons, killing machines'.

I once asked Jackie Bowers if he had ever thought about quitting boxing because of Bradley Stone's death. 'Sure, after what happened to Bradley I wondered whether it was worth it or not. Then I look at the lads in the gym and think, "What else can they do?" If it wasn't for them, if I didn't have so many boys coming in saying they wanted to box, I'd probably give up. But they keep me going. As long as they're there to want to do it, so am I.'

My state of mind worsened. All the optimism of a few months ago had disappeared. I felt vulnerable and exposed. My fear of fighting heightened my general fears – my daughter's wellbeing, my health, financial security, the future, everything! Nothing fitted any more or made sense. I had no control over what was happening around me. I'd gone from a state of independence to near total reliance on other people. What I ate was largely determined by someone else, my clothes were washed and ironed by someone else. It had become apparent that I was a long way off target and that I'd never get a fight by the end of the summer. I felt it all slipping away. I'd go mad before I made it as a pro. I lived in a sweat box at the top of the stairs, hemmed in, isolated from the outside world. I'd been in Nicaraguan prison cells bigger than this.

'Why don't I go the whole hog and put bars on the windows?' Lorna said when I started moaning. 'No one's keeping you here, you know. You can go any time you want, mate.'

With those long, hot days and nights during the Indian summer, I'd wake up in the morning dripping with perspiration and nauseous from the heat, even with the window wide open. I felt burnt out. I now weighed 13 stone 5lb and was convinced I was weaker for it. I'd been eating like a sparrow in the mornings for the past couple of weeks, skipping lunch and having just a main meal in the evenings in order to bring my weight down.

Sheffield was a dump. I was fed up with the local riffraff, the tinfoil wielding junkies, the joyriders, the spotty-faced oiks hanging around the streets, the prepubescent slags. The Steel City had given me mettle fatigue. The house was a mess. Everywhere I turned there were clothes strewn around, ashtrays laden with week-old fag butts, empty sweet wrappers and cigarette packets, half-drunk cups of tea, dog hairs, toys . . . I had to get out. This was driving me mad! Trouble was I couldn't afford to leave. I was living in Hotel California, but there was no way I'd cope being in the house in the build-up to the fight. I'd have to find some way of renting a place for a couple of weeks before the fight – get some space, some peace and quiet. Lorna was forever shouting at the kids, ranting and raving. The telephone rang constantly, but could I get reception on my One2One? Oh no! Every five minutes there were urchins knocking at the door for Simon and Scott, that fucking chopper overhead . . . Then there was music and shouting coming from the Springwood pub, the neighbours screaming and bashing each other up. All this and I'm cooped up in an eight by six microwave. Aaaaaaaaargghhhh!!!!!!!

When you live in a poor neighbourhood, you come to appreciate that privacy is a bourgeois concept. You learn to put up with the rubbish, the potholes, the cracks in the pavement, the dirt, the smashed-up bus shelters, the people screaming, shouting, fornicating, blaring music they think you want to hear but you don't really, and the coppers chasing joyriders. I'm not a communist but I believe the poor exist for the benefit of the rich. Poverty breeds wealth. For all those poor maggots to exist out there on the streets of S2, someone has to get rich. So it was for boxing. This was the relationship between poverty and boxing. For every 100 fighters, one manager or promoter had to get fat. Boxing was another one of those con tricks in life that ennobled poverty, elevated it way beyond the reality. For fighters to exist, there had to be a relationship between visible wealth and poverty. The poor need something to aspire to in order to fight for a living. They also need access to the resources and infrastructure to make it happen. Perhaps this is why so many fighters come out of the poorer areas of the richest nations in the world and very few come from the poorest of the poor. There is nothing noble about being poor.

Lara called to say the mystic forces of feng shui had told her that she lived in a flat that was not supportive to women. The gods had therefore determined it was time for her to move.

'I saw a house in Coventry that I'm interested in buying,' she told me. She explained that Daddy was going to put up the bread so she could buy the place, rent out her flat in London, go into semi-retirement and become a feng shui consultant. Simple.

'Well, that's great.' I could hardly contain myself. 'So when am I going to get to see Luca if you're in Coventry?'

'You travel to London now from Sheffield. You could just as easily get to Coventry. In fact, it's nearer to Sheffield than London.'

'Yeah, but by the end of the year I'll be back in London,' I said with my fingers crossed. We bickered and bickered over the issue until we once again reached deadlock. If this Chinese astrology crap was so effective, why didn't Lara feng shui her life instead of worrying about in which direction her furniture was pointing. We were back to square one, i.e. not talking.

I spent a week with my mother in London, doing the Lennox Lewis bit – eating soul food and being pampered. I needed to catch up on work and earn some more money to pay off the increasing debt I was running into. My shoulder was still grieving me. In the back of my mind I worried that I might have sustained a permanent injury or a problem that would either prohibit me from reaching my goal or put me in serious jeopardy for the fight.

I was surprised at how little the professional fighters socialised with each other. Terry and Danny had fallen out over a botched business deal and apart from Clinton and Shaun Stokes, who were old friends, only a few of the amateurs fraternised with each other outside the gym. Perhaps I had overestimated the scale of unity in the gym. Then again, for the professionals, the gym was a place of work, not play. 'Look after number one' was the pervasive attitude. Fighters came and went so there was little reason to feel attached to your peers. Howard commanded the most loyalty of anyone in the gym. Most of the pros wouldn't even watch each other fight at a show unless they happened to be on the same card. I once asked Terry if he was going to watch

Clinton box one weekend. 'What do I want to watch him for?' he said and changed the subject. Danny articulated the same attitude. The others usually had some excuse or other.

My life had become consumed by boxing and the sacrifices such a life brought with it. I was prepared to do almost anything to get a fight, just to end the frustration and waiting. Frustration makes a man desperate. I understood how desperate men are drawn to a desperate business like boxing and, accordingly, often act in desperation. Yes, I would fight tomorrow given the chance without giving a rat's arse about the outcome. But what sort of attitude was that? Fighters were trained to win. I felt like an absolute loser. I'd been on this mission for an eternity and it was costing me blood, sweat, tears, not to mention money. Why did I get involved in this in the first place? I now understood the frustration that fighters went through playing the waiting game. The longer I waited the more acutely aware I became of my own inadequacies as a boxer, and as a person. I'd trained in Sheffield for five months and before that, what had I done? What did I expect? A British title? A Lonsdale belt? Despite the college diplomas, the university degree, by-lines, teaching posts and publishing contracts, I'd been taken in by the dream factory that is professional boxing just like all the other mugs I'd met. I had my head up my backside just like Shaun Stokes, Scott Welch or Terry Dunstan. Boxing was a farce.

If there had been an easy way out at this point, I would've taken it. I hated myself for stooping so low that I had to get my head busted open to make a living. What was I trying to prove, after all? Where was this taking me? I was so consumed with anxiety and self-doubt that I even worried that I was worrying too much. I had to get out of this vicious circle before I went crazy.

One thing that did help me deal with my stress was hypnotherapy. I'd been in Sheffield for a couple of months when Howard introduced me to Paul Dorking, a hypnotherapist who occasionally worked with some of the boys in the camp. Paul had managed to get Lorna to quit smoking, albeit for just one month, and had also helped cure Old Man Dennis of his gambling addiction.

Some of the boys thought hypnotherapy was too whacko even by Howard's unorthodox standards but it isn't uncommon for fighters in the modern era to use hypnosis. Mike Tyson has dabbled with hypnotherapy, as has Nigel Benn. Former WBO middleweight and super-middleweight champion Steve Collins not only used hypnosis, but successfully nobbled Chris Eubank in two world title fights by claiming he would fight him in a trance which would make him immune to fear and pain.

I found that the effects of hypnosis were not always immediate and out of four or five sessions I encountered a trance state just twice. But going under was not the only aim of hypnotherapy. Through a series of exercises and techniques, I learnt to increase my self-belief and self-confidence and to overcome some of my more irrational fears, even ones unconnected with boxing such as a phobia about rats and mice. Hypnosis was like taking vitamins – you didn't realise the benefit of it until you stopped using it.

Reconciling the duality of fighting and writing was proving difficult. In some ways the two disciplines were incongruous. Here I was trying to write about boxing by slowly destroying the thing that gave me the creative power to write in the first place: my brain. My brain was the centre of my universe, the progenitor of my thoughts, emotions and creativity. It was quite simply my most valuable organ. By choosing to box I had made my head and thus my brain a primary target for destruction. Had I become some sort of nihilist?

I was in the habit of staying up until two or three in the morning banging away at a keyboard, staring at a radioactive computer screen, frustrating myself. When I trained in the late afternoons or early evenings, I could humour my insomnia by simply lying in bed until lunchtime. But early sparring sessions and the track deprived me of quality sleep. My head was so full of crap at the end of the day that even with the rigours of training, I very seldom managed more than seven hours of solid sleep. For a professional athlete this was pitiful. Howard had been on at me all week about my late writing getting in the way of training.

'You finished whatever it is you're doing?' he warned. 'Because next week you're really gonna have to work. I don't want you running 'cos you'll be too knackered after what I've got in store for you.'

Lorna had also pulled me up about working late.

'Howard respects what you're doing,' she said, handing me the obligatory cup of tea. 'He's got a lot of admiration for you, we all have. But he doesn't care about your book. He doesn't see you as a journalist any more. He sees you as a fighter and getting you through that fight is his main concern.'

There was a time when I had looked like a journalist. I used to take my laptop into the bar at the club and write. I'd take notes in the gym and made sure I was always armed with a dictaphone. I made a point of letting everyone know what I was doing. But all that had changed. Now I was one of the boys. While acceptance from the camp didn't ease the pain of training, it did give a greater sense of freedom and belonging. I felt more comfortable with my position in the gym hierarchy, having climbed a few notches. As an insider, as a fighter, I enjoyed a personal relationship with the gym. The gym was my space, my territory, my home.

I had some sharp moves. These days I took it for granted that I could step inside an opponent's guard, drop six inches, stick an uppercut right under his chin, twist my back foot, come up twelve inches and with that extra leverage make his head snap back like a nodding dog. I could throw a left hook blindside on a fighter and make his head wobble like jelly. Bobbing, weaving, ducking, rolling, feinting, showing a left then throwing a right, stepping off and turning opponents were par for the course. I was also developing my thousand-yard stare and working on other subtle modes of intimidation like the occasional low blow or accidental head butt.

I was desperate to drop one of my sparring partners, for no other reason than to appease my bulging ego. Dave from Swinton, a twenty-two-year-old aspiring amateur, was one of the lads I got closest to knocking out. One afternoon I leathered him with so many big right hands, my knuckles swelled like ping-pong balls.

'Oi! Fucking take it easy,' hollered Howard from across the gym.

'What? What have I done?' I said, playing the cheeky schoolboy. Dave was puffing. The shots had clearly taken the steam out of him. I felt a little guilty once Howard had mentioned it, rather sarcastically, three or four times throughout the sparring session.

'Ooh, you can be a right bully when you want to,' said Howard on the way home.

'I couldn't help it, Howard. I've had enough of taking shit. I want to start opening up on these guys. Besides, it wasn't that bad, was it?'

'It wasn't. It was good technique,' he said with a wry smile, one which suggested maybe now he really had a fighter on his hands.

The next day Howard took me on the pads. He rarely did pads on account of having a bad wrist, so it was an honour of sorts. Howard was a master on pads. Using the pads was an ideal way of working on combinations, speed and stamina. It was gruelling. We went through an endless drill of combinations – double jab, straight right, left hook;

left hook, straight right, left hook; right uppercut, left hook, straight right, left hook . . .

'I'm not gonna tell you again. Elbows in. Come on, let's go. Fucking turn those shots.' Howard kept chiding me for not placing my shots correctly, not turning my fists, poor footwork . . . 'Elbows in and fucking turn those shots. What the hell was that? Come on. Right uppercut, left hook, straight right.'

As my punches connected with increasing venom they sent out a cracking sound like an overhead railway cable arcing. Thwack! CRACK-CRACK! 'That's better. Stick it in there . . . fucking mean it. Come on!' We'd pause momentarily for Howard to berate me and twist my body round into a better stance. I felt like a shop-window dummy as he bent my arms, contorted my shoulders and kicked my feet out into an array of Action Man type poses. Then I'd throw combinations from these positions. Every minor improvement I thought I made was quickly followed by another litany of criticism and abuse. It was a case of one step forward, two steps back. Howard had told me he was going to put me under more pressure and I was going to hate him for it. He was right. He was grimacing, snarling at me, like some deranged colour sergeant. 'Feet. Look at where your feet are. Turn your back foot. Come on, get your guard up. Come on, move it!'

After twenty minutes I wanted to give up, just stop there and then and quit. Maybe I'd go to the bar and order myself a nice cool pint of Guinness, kick my feet up and watch MTV on the big screen. I couldn't give up, could I? That option was far too ridiculous to consider seriously. I'd have to grin and bear it. Come the end of the session on the pads, I was punching somewhere near to a force of deadly intent. I felt like I wanted to smash Howard's hands off. There was only a handful of people in the gym at the time – Terry, Mark Brooks, his girlfriend – but I felt I'd endured a minor public humiliation. That was part of the art of being a trainer, knowing which buttons to push.

'Speed and power now. I want you on that bag over there and really fucking give it to it,' said Howard, lighting up another Sovereign. 'Combinations. Boom, boom, boom, BING! Fucking give it some, then walk away.'

'What does your missus think of your physique these days?' asked Terry as I stripped off in the changing room after the day's session. I could see him scrutinising me out of the corner of his eye. 'Does she say, "Ooh Dave! I *lurve* your *bodeee*"?' I told him that *women* loved my body. I put the emphasis on the plural because by missus Terry had meant Lara and I wanted to reassure him that that was yesterday's news. I had told him on numerous occasions that I had nothing to do with Lara save for making contact with her to see Luca – and, of course, arguing – but he could never get to grips with the fact that I wasn't in a steady relationship.

All fighters had a 'missus', 'bird', 'sort', 'her indoors' or 'old lady', and more often than not a few 'bits on the side' as well. One of the reasons why Lennox Lewis had not warmed to boxing's macho men was because he didn't fit the stereotype. He didn't have a string of glamorous wives or a bevy of conspicuous beauties in tow like Holyfield, Tyson and De La Hoya. Like Lennox, I elected to stay footloose and fancy free because I didn't want the complication of developing a relationship while I concentrated on boxing and completing my mission. This is probably why I got on with Sass Brown who lived 3,000 miles away in Montreal. We had met in the Metro Hotel after the Holyfield–Lewis fight and conducted most of our affair via email . . . very Y2K.

Anyway, back to my body. Yes, if I may say so myself, I was in great shape. After six months I had developed not just a good physique, but a fighter's physique. My weight had stabilised at 13½ stone, just a pound under the cruiserweight limit, but Howard thought I still had a stone to go. 'Look at that fucking derby and that fat arse,' he'd say grabbing my stomach.

I now made a point of parading round the gym showboating like the other fighters. They regularly commented on my physique, saying, 'Aye, you've really come on, Dave,' or, 'You're looking in great shape, pal.' The boost to the ego was incredible.

With the keys to the city firmly in my grasp, I could cavort around the ring half-naked, camping it up like Terry Dunstan. I could stop and pose in front of the mirror and spout declarations of self-love like, 'I'm just too gooood,' like Danny Daley. And when the mothers showed up in the evenings to watch their kids do kick-boxing, I could flex my pecs and wiggle my hips and know every one of 'em would die for a piece of my ripe black ass. In the beginning, all this posing was a sideswipe at the macho body culture, a self-mocking attempt at a few cheap laughs, but I'd reached a point when it was no longer post-ironic or self-parody. I was fitter, stronger and tougher than the average guy on the street. I had power. I was superhuman. I *had* to love myself, I created myself. After a while you had to believe your own hype; the moment you started staring at the cracks, it was all over.

Any, and I mean any, opportunity I had to admire my naked or semi-naked form in a mirror I took with narcissistic relish. Often in the gym, as soon as I warmed up and the sweat began to pour, I'd strip off to the waist, not so much to cool down but so I could fleetingly catch a look at myself in the mirror. This was absurd. I knew it was. I'd seen them all do it. When they weren't looking at themselves they were looking at each other, openly scrutinising every contour, muscle, ripple of the body. But this wasn't the kind of furtive eyeballing I'd seen in sports centres or weight-training gyms. In a boxing gym, people seemed very honest about their opinions of themselves and others. If you were having an endearing love affair with yourself based on some vainglorious ego trip, the whole gym knew about it. You'd parade, strut, stop to pose in front of the mirror flexing your muscles or pull up your top to reveal the anatomical trophy – the six-pack. 'Damn, it hurts being this good,' I'd say to myself and anyone who'd listen.

I realised that one of the best ways to overcome the depression and insecurity I had developed as a fighter, was to turn the whole shooting match on its head. You were 'simply the best', not only a great fighter with an Adonis physique, you were also an unstoppable sex machine. Your ego could almost suffocate you in purely self-congratulatory flights of fancy. Oh the hubris! It was how you looked. One oft repeated saying in the fight game is that boxing revolves around style. Fighters talk about 'winning in style' and place a great deal of importance on the aesthetics of the sport. It is important not just to win, but to win in style.

You have to look the part and act the part. Outcomes and results are relative. Many a fighter will swear blind that he was robbed of a decision and excuse a black mark on his record as a temporary glitch. Even when a fighter is knocked out cold, he'll find some excuse to redefine the context of his defeat. 'I walked on to the punch,' he'll say, or, 'I just ran out of steam.' It's always what he did, not the efficacy of his opponent's power or technique.

Weeks passed and the seemingly eternal grind of training trundled on. Despite all my efforts at ego-boosting, this period was like purgatory. I knew I had turned into the home straight, that soon all this would come to some sort of conclusion. But unlike in the beginning when the novelty factor was high and I absorbed new knowledge at a rate of knots, now life was constant repetition, drilling, working out, doing the same thing over and over again.

'You'll do light-heavy easy. In fact, you might even make super-middleweight.' Howard's latest brainwave was that I could make 12 stone and fight at super-middle. Like everyone else in the gym, I thought I was nearing my plateau as far as weight and physique were concerned. I'd reached the benchmark of 13 stone and I still needed to lose another seven pounds to make light-heavy. I anticipated a tough time shedding those last few pounds. I looked in great shape. I felt pretty good, too. My physique, combined with the rounds I was clocking up in sparring, meant I was asked in the gym by all and sundry on an almost daily basis, 'When are you fighting?' The consensus was I looked ready. Was I ready? Howard didn't think so.

He taught me subtle manoeuvres, such as turning an opponent, switching my stance to southpaw or stepping off during those endless sparring sessions, which were all designed to meet that one universal credo in boxing: protect yourself at all times. In many respects, Howard's style of boxing was predominantly defensive – a lot of head and foot movement, blocking (either by parrying a punch with the glove or blocking with the forearm) and maintaining a solid guard, something I didn't always do. A bad habit I'd picked up from admiring the likes of Sugar Ray Leonard and Muhammad Ali on TV was to drop my hands when I moved round the ring. I did this partly because I usually overestimated the speed of my reactions and underestimated the speed of my opponent's, but also because several rounds of being beaten about the head, body, arms and shoulders tends to weaken your resolve when it comes to holding two sweat-soaked 14oz gloves up to your chin. How many times had I heard Howard yell 'Keep your fucking guard up' during sparring? The best advice on defence that he ever gave me, however, had to be, 'Don't get caught stationary because you'll get your fucking head taken off.' I just wish I had paid more attention.

chapter 26

Scott Lansdowne had an appointment with fear. Trouble was, he didn't want to show up. He didn't want to go to the Hillsborough Leisure Centre, he didn't want to get in the ring in front of a thousand people, and he certainly didn't want to fight some geezer called Luke Simpkin.

Scott had been staying with Howard and Lorna for a few days in the run-up to his fight on the Clinton Woods undercard. Howard and Lorna had wanted to keep a close eye on him precisely because of the problem he'd had with nerves before his debut. Now things were looking shaky. Paul the hypnotherapist had worked with him extensively to help him overcome his pre-fight collywobbles. And then, of course, there was me ...

'Just think of it this way, Scott,' I said, trying to ease the tension round the dinner table. 'This is your moment. All those people, the crowds, the adulation, the TV. It's what it's all about isn't it?'

'Yeah, I suppose so.' Scott didn't seem too convinced by the pep talk. Neither was I.

'Lorna, can I have a word?' Scott got up from the dinner table and headed for the kitchen.

'Sure, love.' Lorna followed him into the kitchen, looked over her shoulder, snarled at me and closed the door behind them.

Howard and I sat there shrugging our shoulders at each other. A couple of minutes later Lorna and Scott emerged from the kitchen.

'Can you make the lads a cup of tea please, Dave?' said Lorna.

'Sure.'

Scott looked bemused. He gave a forced smile and disappeared through the living room and upstairs.

'What d'you go and say that for?' whispered Lorna.

'What?' I said.

'That crap about being on TV. He's feeling bad enough as it is without having that dumped on him.'

'Uh? I was only trying to boost his morale.'

'Scott went into the kitchen earlier and got some water from the fridge . . . he was shaking like a bloody leaf. We're trying to take his mind off the fight and you're putting it on him.'

'Sorry, I . . .' Scott suddenly appeared in the living room and joined us at the dinner table.

'Well, what's it gonna be then, Captain?' asked Howard. 'We having this fight or what?'

Scott was scratching his head, rubbing his jaw, humming and hawing.

'Howard, I . . . you know me, Howard . . . I mean . . . I don't want to let anybody down . . . I mean . . . Christ . . . it's . . .'

'Terry was a bag of nerves, weren't he, Howard, before his thirteenth fight.' Lorna was trying to humour Scott with small talk. I thought we weren't supposed to talk about the fight? 'You know, superstitious and all that. Ooh, what was he like, Howard? He still won though, didn't he, Howard?'

'What, Lorn?' Howard was loading up his toolbox of equipment for the fight – bandages, adrenaline, cotton wool, ice pack . . .

'Listen, Scott, I know what it's like,' said Howard, rummaging through his box of tricks. 'I've been there meself. When I first started out I used to go into the toilets and start coughing my guts up before a fight, I were that racked with fear. People used to say, "You all right, son?" and I'd just nod and get on with it.

'I know what the problem is – 'cos you do the doors you're worried that if you don't beat this fella you'll lose respect.' Scott gave a lacklustre nod. Howard had a theory that Scott would feel inadequate as a bouncer if he lost a fight – his peers and enemies alike would have something over him. But there had to be more to it than that, surely? Despite the fear, the nerves and the anxiety, a professional boxer who didn't want to fight was like a rock climber being scared of heights or a claustrophobic pot holer. In boxing you had to feel the fear and do it anyway. Fear was part of the deal. You did it in part because you wanted to feel scared.

Fighters are a product of what social anthropologists call 'the rollercoaster phenomenon', the pursuit of controlled danger that had the underlying possibility that something untoward could happen. I accepted that I had to take a beating. That was the trade-off – you hit me, I hit you. I just didn't like the 'you hit me' part of the deal. Sugar

Ray Robinson had 202 fights in his career and regained five world titles. He'd had 175 fights before he lost his first one, and yet he said he didn't even *like* boxing. At the other end of the spectrum, Justin said out of almost sixty fights he never enjoyed a single one; and he could have a proper tear-up. When I asked him why he did it, why he still did it, he had no explanation. 'Just one of those things, I suppose,' he said. 'I started as a kid and it just became a routine, summat you do, like. You can't stop, you don't know how to stop. But I can honestly say out of all those fights I had, I did not enjoy a single one. I used to shit mesen every time I was in that dressing room.'

I got anxious whenever I thought too deeply about my own fight. At shows I'd look at the ring, the officials, the crowd and think: one day I'll face all that. I'd feel a knot somewhere in the pit of my stomach. Sometimes when I anticipated sparring with Terry or Justin or Danny my palms would become sweaty and I'd feel a wave of anxiety come over me. Boxing was great when you were kicking the crap out of someone but when it was your head that was the speedball . . . oh boy! As soon as I feared boxing, which was often, I hated it.

Every boxer experienced some degree of fear or nerves before a fight, but they all agreed that the fear subsided once they stepped through the ropes and the bell went. Scott's problem was dealing with the fear sufficiently so he could get to that stage.

'Go on, son, go to work,' cooed Lorna, clasping Scott's hands. 'You'll be all right.'

'Come on, let's go or we'll be late,' said Howard.

Scott grabbed two training bags which were on the dining-room floor. I took one from him and we traipsed outside behind Howard and Simon who was coming to the fight as a reward for being a good boy for a change.

'You're coming with me, aren't you Dave?' said Scott, putting the bags in his car boot.

'Sure.'

I got in the passenger side and Scott went to get in but realised he'd forgotten his mobile and went back into the house. I heard Lorna say, 'You all right, love?' as he passed her on the doorstep.

'Psst . . . psst . . . psst.'

I turned round to see Lorna standing in the driveway mouthing something. 'Dave, Dave . . .' she whispered conspiratorially, 'whatever you do, don't let him talk about the fight . . .' I raised my eyebrows at Lorna to get her to shut up because at that moment Scott had stepped out of the backdoor and was right behind her. 'Oh, er . . . ha . . . good luck, Scottie.' Jesus, she was so conspicuous at times.

Scott started the ignition and the radio came on instantly. He turned the radio off and did a three-point turn.

'I can't do it, Dave. I just can't do it.' Thirty seconds into the journey, with Howard and Lorna out of earshot, Scott made his confessional. 'I'm worried that it would come to . . . this means a lot to my family. They honestly don't think that there's much else I can do with my life.'

'What's the worst that can happen if you don't fight?' I said.

'Ah, Dave. If I don't fight tonight, my father would be devastated. A lot of people are expecting me to go through with this and I don't want to let them down. But I don't feel my heart is in it. If it was I would've said something to Dennis about getting me more fights, but I haven't, have I? My father would be really disappointed in me, Dave. The pressure I've been under, I really think it would come to me having to get out of the house.'

'That bad?' I interjected.

'That bad. I don't think he'd ever forgive me. He'd never let me live it down if I didn't fight.'

Everyone had their own reasons for boxing. It was the nature of my investigation to try to discover what these reasons were, what motivated men to fight for a living. I knew there were universal driving forces, such as self-respect, discipline, physical fitness and, of course, money, behind every professional, and I liked to believe that fighters were fighters regardless of colour or creed. However, Scott's motivation for being a boxer illustrated a fundamental difference between black and white fighters when it came to desire.

Most white fighters start boxing at a very young age, often eight or nine, and usually do so with the encouragement of their families. Boxing is something that their brothers did, fathers did and their fathers before them did. Among white working-class communities (and perhaps the upper classes in the military and public school), boxing is seen as a rite of passage and participation is generally more important than talent or professional pretensions.

Black fighters, on the other hand, tend to start much later in life, in the teens at the earliest, and usually independent of any family support or interest. As a consequence of this, there is very little tradition of boxing among black families in Britain. For a black youth, the impetus and the desire to become a fighter are self-generated – he boxes because *he* wants to and as such he has a high level of self-confidence and self-awareness. A black amateur will almost certainly have aspirations to turning professional, so his mindset from the beginning of his career is more goal-centred. This sort of self-motivated attitude combined with a host of social factors explains in part why black fighters often fare better than white fighters at the highest level.

Scott seemed to want to box to suit others and not himself. Once that bell went it would be him in there and no one else. To fight in a ring for anyone other than yourself is madness. But what could I do? If I counselled him towards not fighting, I'd have Howard and Lorna on my case for talking him out of something he may well regret in the future. On the other hand, I felt uncomfortable about trying to deceive Scott. I had a lot of time for him. He was a decent guy. He was sensitive, vulnerable, honest about his feelings, more so than the others in the gym. He was the closest to a new man I'd met in boxing. I knew the right thing was to agree with him and go with how he felt, tell him not to box. But honesty isn't always the best policy. Anyway, Scott was way too smart to be hoodwinked with cod psychology and ego massaging.

'So come on, Dave. You're a smart geezer. I know you wouldn't bullshit me. What would you do in my position?'

'Well, I . . .'

'You wouldn't fight, would you?

'If I were in your position . . .? I don't know about that, Scott. I've got a different agenda. I'm out to have one fight and one fight only. After that I'm gone. I'll do whatever I have to. I can afford to feel gung-ho about it.'

Scott was grinning at my attempted diplomacy.

'Look, I've got to be honest with you, Scott, there's a selfish side of me, and I think a lot of people around you want to see you box to satisfy wholly personal reasons. I'd be lying if I didn't admit I'd like to see you go out there tonight and knock this guy out in a blaze of glory and all that. But you've got to do this for you, to satisfy *your* feelings.'

Scott was listening intently as we followed Howard in Titanic. We reached a roundabout at the end of Prince of Wales Road, two minutes' drive from the Rainey house. Howard took the second exit on the left. Scott shifted gear, speeding up as though he were about to miss the turn-off, but we continued right behind Titanic.

'OK, let's look at the pros and cons,' I said. 'What happens if you don't fight tonight? Would you be able to go back to the gym?' I knew the answer already. Was I subconsciously emotionally blackmailing him?

'Dave, I love the training, I love the gym. But if I bottled out tonight I'd never be able to show me face there again. I'd be letting Howard down and as for Dennis . . .'

I told Scott that he'd be missed at the gym; his departure would be a loss to the team, even the sport. There just weren't enough Scott Lansdownes around in boxing.

Scott's fear was the same as all our fears, the ghosts and spirits that walked through the walls of your mind. Insecurity, self-doubt, feelings of inadequacy, debt, sexual hang-ups, these were the demons haunting you, waiting to throw you into a flaming pit of failure.

Eventually we made it to the venue. I got out of the car and met Howard pacing up and down the car park talking to a rather disgruntled Dennis Hobson accompanied by his sidekick, Tosser. It was the first time I'd ever seen Howard agitated.

'What's the score, then?' said Howard.

'I don't know. He's on the phone right now,' I said.

'We've got to get him inside. They want him on.'

Scott was sitting in the car punching numbers into his mobile. The promoters wanted him on within half-an-hour. He still didn't want to box. He got out and Howard took him to one side. Then Dennis took him to one side. Scott punched some more numbers into his mobile, wedged it between his shoulder and ear, opened his boot and took out the two training bags. All the while he was saying 'Hmm . . . yeah . . . hmm . . . I know . . .' into the mobile and nodding his head. I grabbed one of the bags.

'Paul's sorting him out,' said Howard. 'Let's go. They're waiting.'

From the car park through the reception up a flight of stairs along a corridor and into the dressing room – a converted weights room – Scott stayed 'online' getting therapy on the telephone. A skinny guy in a tuxedo wearing bucket headphones came into the dressing room.

'Right, have we got him?' Heads nod. 'OK. Get him gloved up. He's on next.'

Scott was still on the telephone as he slipped out of his clothes and into his shorts and boots. He sat down and Howard went to work quickly on his hands applying the necessary two-inch gauze bandages and regulation tape. Within moments of his gloves being laced, the skinny tuxedo man reappeared informing us it was time.

Howard, Dennis, two of Scott's friends and I accompanied him down a flight of winding stairs to the arena entrance. Cheesy dance music blared over the PA as we came out of the shadows to an appreciable applause. Simpkin was already in the ring pacing about as Scott stepped between the ropes and took small paces in a circle tight into his corner. He kept his head bowed making sure not to make eye contact with his opponent. The two fighters walked to the centre of the ring. The referee gave his instructions. The bell went.

It all seemed to happen so quickly that Scott had little time to dwell on the situation. Scott smashed Simpkin's nose in the second round with a right hook that caused a gash about one and a half inches long across and down the bridge. Blood poured from the wound, covering Simpkin's face and chest as Scott kept pounding away. He looked like a victim in a slasher movie. The sight of blood got my juices flowing.

'Go on, Scott, go on baby!' I was at ringside screaming like a madman. 'You got him . . . serve him up, Scott . . . open him up, my son!'

Claret was flowing with abandon but despite my blood lust, I thought the referee should have stopped the fight there and then. Simpkin was clearly in agony every time Scott clocked him on the nose. Apart from an overhand right in the last round which momentarily wobbled Scott, Simpkin never recovered from the busted nose. Scott won the fight on points, 39–38.

We followed Scott out of the ring up the winding stairs that led to the dressing room. He was beaming, screaming, 'Yes, yes!' We reached the dressing room and he gave me a big hug with the added attraction of a small peck on the cheek.

'Thanks for your support, Dave.'

'Well done, Scott. You were great.'

I tried not to be trite but these are the moments sporting clichés are made of. As he pulled away noticed my shirt was stained with blood. It didn't matter. I felt such an overwhelming sense of relief, excitement and triumph that even I, as anal as I am about smudges and stains, marks and creases on my clothes, could ignore such a thing.

'So you still thinking of giving up, then?' said Howard as he and Scott embraced.

'No, no.' Scott was shaking his head emphatically and laughing.

'So we'll be seeing you in the gym in a couple of weeks, then?' added Howard.

'Yeah,' said Scott, nodding, still beaming, still embracing Howard, still a fighter.

chapter 27

The day after Scott's fight, Howard told me I would not be fighting until at least the end of the year. How could I survive that long? Financially I was nearing rock bottom. My plastic was on meltdown, I needed the IMF to reschedule my overdraft and soon my cheques would be bouncing like a kangaroo in rubber-soled shoes.

'If any trainer in the country is going to do the right thing for you, it's going to be Howard,' said Lorna as we discussed my future late into the night.

'It'd be better for you to write your book and win your fight than write your book and lose, wouldn't it?' interjected Howard. He had a point. But I hardly cared about the result and that was dangerous. I just wanted a fight, any fight. Certainly, deep down I wanted to win. But the mental and physical demands of writing and fighting were such that I was prepared to do anything, to fight anyone, anywhere, to reach the end.

The longer I spent training, the more discord I felt within myself. I felt as though I was neither fish nor fowl. Was I still a writer first and a fighter second? I had spent so long lost in boxing that I wasn't really sure. I had to accept that for my transformation to be complete, for me to authenticate the life of a fighter, I would have to put my literary pretensions to one side. If I was not prepared to give myself over to boxing 120 per cent, as Lorna had said in the beginning, I was nothing but a dilettante, a white-collar boxer.

'Don't worry about giving us any board for the next couple of weeks,' said Howard. 'I had a good night last night so we're all right for money. If I had it all the time, you wouldn't pay a penny. You're like family now.'

Over the months, my relationship with the Raineys had gradually shifted from professional to personal. They were indeed like a second family to me. We had developed a mutual, personal investment in each other and as such, they were as aware of my personal problems as I was of theirs. The moratorium on paying board soon changed to a 'no rent policy' after Howard and Lorna decided they could no longer accept my money. I felt uncomfortable about receiving the generosity of people who plainly struggled to make ends meet on a daily basis. How many times had I heard a knock at the door followed by Lorna pulling the curtains, whispering, 'Ssh! It's the money man, I haven't got any money. Tell him I'm not here.' I thought I was taking a liberty living rent-free, but despite my protestations, Howard and Lorna insisted I stop paying them rent.

There were times when their concern for me caused embarrassment, like the time I went missing for forty-eight hours in London. I had travelled to the capital at the weekend as usual but decided to stay on for a couple of days *incommunicado* in my Ladbroke Grove retreat, trying desperately to meet an editorial deadline. Unbeknownst to me, less than half a mile away two commuter trains collided on a stretch of track killing twenty-six people in what has become known as the Paddington rail disaster. Hearing the news, Lorna put two and two together and came out with 5.3. She broke into my briefcase, found a clutch of telephone numbers and started a frantic manhunt involving my mother, my agent, my publisher, Lara and the Metropolitan Police Missing Persons Bureau. When I finally resurfaced, having switched on my mobile and retrieved ten fraught voicemail messages, I learnt that Howard was beside himself with worry and most of the guys in the gym thought I had been crushed to death in a train carriage thanks to Lorna's anxiety. It was an embarrassing episode but it demonstrated the Raineys' depth of feeling towards me.

So there I was – family. Intimacy was not without its problems. Howard based his development of me as a fighter, not only on technical issues, but also on genuine concern for my health and welfare. He was very protective towards his 'boys' and, like any trainer worth his salt, he sought to shield us from unnecessary danger for as long as he could. Clever matchmaking was the key. Howard wanted the odds as much in my favour as humanly possible, without me having to fight an absolute stiff. Rather than line me up with what is called in the trade a 'body', he wanted me to reach a level where I'd be good enough to fight a half-decent pro. At times I felt as though the goalposts were continually shifting; the more improvement I made in the gym, the greater the expectation for me to perform. As the ante increased, any slip-ups on my part were viewed with greater concern. But my conceit meant I had totally underestimated what it took to reach that level. How could I have thought that I could just walk in off the streets and six months later win a professional fight? I had to resign myself now to the long haul.

I had become party to so many personal and intimate details about the people with whom I lived and worked that it had become practically impossible to separate my professional and personal obligations. For example, one of Howard's former contenders once held a knife to the throat of another fighter from the gym, outside the house. The row had concerned a 'business deal' that had collapsed. The ex-contender had wound up a few thousand pounds out of pocket and on the hit list of a heavy mob from London. What followed were accusations and counter-accusations, threats, cars containing shadowy (and supposedly armed) figures turning up at the gym and the house, and various characters lurking around on the lookout for one person or another. I naturally kept a safe distance from all this but there were times when my assistance or opinion was sought concerning such matters and I had to tread very carefully. This was one of the greatest risks of participatory journalism – the level of influence the journalist has on his subjects.

An example of cause and effect was introducing the joys of the internet to Lorna. It all started as a harmless giggle. I made the mistake of showing the Raineys a twenty-three-second clip of the infamous Pamela Anderson and Tommy Lee video, which a friend had sent me via the internet. Lorna was curious about how this material was transmitted so I showed her how to send emails and download information from websites. She started gradually, got into a variety of chat rooms and, as time went by, began to develop a mild obsession. Before long, there were two telephone lines in the house.

Now Lorna had a bit of a history when it came to telephones. Several years ago she had run up a substantial debt with British Telecom, using premium-rate chatlines. She had been hooked on that '0898, make new friends on the telephone' crap. Lorna loved telephones. She'd call Howard on his mobile at least six times a day (at 50p a minute) to tell him stuff she'd repeat when he got in from work. She had companies on the go that gave her special codes allowing her to make cheap long-distance telephone calls. Of course, she never paid them. Periodically, she'd run up a telephone bill she couldn't pay and BT would cut off the line. Then she'd switch to the second line and BT would cut that off, too. However, by this stage she would've done a deal with them to reconnect the first line; and on it would go. One day on our way to the gym Howard bemoaned the telephone bills he was having to pay.

'I don't know how she does it,' he said. 'Two hundred and fifty bloody pounds a time it's costing me.'

'She wants to get out more,' I said. 'That's a bit much to fork out every quarter.'

'A quarter . . . that's every month!'

In the early days she struck up a friendship with a 200lb frustrated housewife from Malta called 'JoJo' via a chat room called Living Chat. The relationship progressed to daily phone calls and eventually Lorna even went to stay with JoJo at her home in Malta. JoJo used to come on to me over the telephone and tried to get me into having cybersex with her. Apparently, she was addicted to cybersex. But Living Chat and fat housewives soon lost their appeal. It was then that Lorna got sucked into the virtual world of Gor. Now that shit costs *money*.

Gor was a kind of BDSM version of Dungeons and Dragons based on the pulp fiction of American sociology professor, John Norman. The internet was littered with sites dedicated to this tripe. At best Gor was a harmless, if not ridiculous, way for sad techno-geeks in Hallowe'en outfits to get their kicks; at worst it was the recruiting office of a bunch of far-right freaks holed up in a disused army bunker in Wyoming.

Gor had a language and secret code all of its own. It was like the Masons for computer nerds. Disciples had names like Sabre, Dark Lord and Takanitin. Lorna had been variously known as Melassandra, Melassandra Ubara GC and Melassandra Virgo. She had been a free woman, then a slave. Sometimes her Gor buddies would come over for dinner or a ritual sacrifice or something. 'I was in the tavern the other evening and Knight Wolf tried to put a collar on Nona and make her his kajera. He was drunk on paga, stumbling all over the place. You should have been there.' Oh how they laughed!

These people had real lives, real families and real jobs. They were in construction, one was a nurse, another a designer for British Aerospace involved in projects of national security. The thick end of the wedge was that some of these loons were into locking each other in cages, wife swapping and God knows what else. Jesus, what had the world come to? Talk about an identity crisis. Howard thought they were all nuts. He was right.

With hindsight it was easy to feel that moving in with the Raineys was a bad move. Having got so close to the subject, I had now become the subject; it was harder to distance myself from Howard and Lorna. In some ways, I felt I would have been better served by having fallen in with a mercenary trainer, someone who didn't give a rat's arse about his fighters and was strictly in the fight game for money. I would have been under those lights and in that ring months ago.

Howard's concern for his fighters' wellbeing meant he was inclined to take a frustratingly long time over schooling. In truth, in the time I had been at the gym, I had seen seasoned pros come and train for months without ever getting a fight. Scott Lansdowne made his pro debut in December 1998 and didn't fight again until autumn 1999.

Howard had his way of doing things and I had to respect that. Compared with many other trainers, he seemed slow and meticulous but I had become accustomed to his methodology. After all, I was placing my life in his hands so I had learnt to trust his judgement unconditionally. Men who had numerous amateur and professional bouts under their belts were taken back to school by him. You needed the patience of a saint to be a fighter in Howard's eyes. You had to bide your time, wait your turn and be stoical. Bad habits had to be unlearnt. New techniques had to be developed. What Howard lacked in gruelling attention to fitness – an obsession many trainers had at the expense of teaching anything about boxing – he made up for with his huge repertoire of technique, skills, subtle moves and tricks of the trade.

'It's Lara calling back at five o'clock. I can't actually believe you're letting me down at the eleventh hour for my [feng shui] course. It's a hundred pounds a day for this course. Now I have to miss it just because you've got work that you think is more important . . . and plus Luca. We need to talk . . . seriously. Bye.'

More post-relationship fallout. It was a year since Lara and I split, but I was inexorably linked to her because of Luca. It was as though we were still in a relationship, only all the good bits had been siphoned away leaving a residue of bitterness and resentment. What about my dreams, my aspirations? Maybe I'd been really naïve thinking that I could find more to life than this. Perhaps I didn't deserve a greater sense of achievement or self-worth. Maybe being an automaton, a slave to conspicuous consumption was my destiny. I should pay off those endless bills, overdrafts, loans and credit-card bills and shut the fuck up. Maybe boxing was just about money. Maybe everything was about money. Perhaps somewhere along the line, my enthusiasm and blind ambition to do something out of the humdrum of everyday existence had turned to biting cynicism. Maybe I too had sold out and was just in this for the money.

Maybe maybe maybe – life is full of maybes, and then you're dead. I was aware that as far as the outside world was concerned, I was a nobody and it was to this outside world that I had something to prove. Why? Why feel the need to prove anything to anybody? And then, in a moment of nothingness, it dawned on me. Boxing wasn't about money, religion, catharsis or sex-appeal. Boxing had to do with the individual proving something to himself, and that something was everything and nothing, so personal it probably hurt too much to reveal. I'd taken this route through boxing because I wanted to be the guinea pig, to understand how a fighter thinks, feels, lives and grieves by becoming the thing itself. I couldn't speak for anyone else. I couldn't get inside someone else's mind. I had a tough enough time psychoanalysing myself.

Boxing was a dream and fighters sought to make that dream come true. Was it a sport in the legitimate sense of the word, gruesome entertainment or a combination of the two? I still wasn't quite sure how to define boxing. I had learnt, though, that being a fighter meant being hungry and not accepting the shit that everyday life threw up in your face living in the slow lane stacking shelves in Tesco or frying burgers at McDonald's. Sure there were other easier, safer things to do than fight for a living, things that in the short term could make you moderately more money for a whole lot less effort. But could they give you that life less ordinary, that sense of achievement, that feeling of self-respect we all crave?

chapter 28

A faint buzzer signalled the start of the round. As I went to touch Justin's gloves, he caught me with a cheeky right hook.

'There's nowt in the rules against that,' he said. 'Watch that. I'm gonna catch you in a minute with something. You keep making a mistake.'

'What's that?'

'You'll see.' BOOM! Right hand to the side of the head. 'There. See what I mean?' Justin gestured a blocking movement over his ears with his hands.

We got into the spar and I kept my hands up copying Justin's 'peek-a-boo' high guard. It was getting harder for him to get through with straight shots and in the second round he caught me with a stiff right uppercut under the nose. I felt a slight flush around my nasal passage and assumed it was just mucous. I was slightly startled when I looked down momentarily and saw blood dripping from my nose.

'Don't worry about that,' said Justin. 'Come on. Get thy hands up.'

'Justin, knock him out,' shouted Terry from across the ring. 'He's ready to go.'

Claret was flowing like bubbly at Ascot. I could feel my legs going. I felt weak and staggered back to the ropes where I sought refuge propping myself and then crouching down on to the second rope. I absorbed some more punishment as Justin waded in with hooks to the body and stinging overhand blows. I thought he'd punch himself out but he was relentless. I stood up and tried to punch my way out but my knees felt spongy. For a sickening moment I felt like going down, just hitting the canvas to get some respite but my pride kept me up. I looked up at the timer – thirty seconds, twenty seconds, ten seconds.

'Time! That'll do yer.' Justin gave me a hard two-fisted thump on the gloves.

'Fucking good spar that,' he said as I crawled out of the ring. 'You caught me with a good shot as I were leaning back, then followed up with a left hook. I saw fucking stars.'

'Over 'ere,' cried Howard.

'You got to stop mollycoddling him, Howard.' Terry was grinning his stupid face off. So he'd been British and European champion and fought for a world title. Big fucking deal. He still got his arse kicked though, didn't he? 'I don't know how the fuck you think he's gonna get a licence looking like that,' he continued. 'The Board won't have it, mate.'

'Yes they will,' said Howard

'You must know something we don't then, Howard.'

'I do.'

I walked over to Howard. He was holding a dirty yellow towel that looked like it was used for oil changes on diesel engines.

'I hope that's clean,' I said. Howard smeared the towel under my nose, briskly wiping a large clump of congealed blood away. 'Nsssssshhhh!' I blew my nose.

'Don't do that! Your brains'll come out. Blowing's the last thing you want to do.'

'Break his nose back into shape, Howard,' said Terry, laughing. He was droning on and on. I looked him straight in the face. At times he was my worst nightmare.

'Jesus. Don't you ever shut up?' He looked dumbstruck, picked up his towel and headed for the changing room.

Hell, my nose wasn't really broken was it? I held on to it and jiggled it slightly. There was a bit of movement, but not much. Most of it still seemed intact. A broken nose was an occupational hazard; 90 per cent of professional fighters wound up with some form of nasal trauma, most commonly a flat nose. Thankfully, I wasn't in need of rhinoplasty.

Howard looked at me and went slightly pale. Given his grey complexion this was saying something. He gave me a genial slap round the face and said, 'I worry about you as if you were me own lad. I know I shouldn't give a fuck, but I do.'

I tried not to let the barracking in the gym get to me. You had to put a brave face on. But at times those ghosts would appear. Someone, usually Terry, would have a snide dig at me and replant a seed of doubt. Although I had to view his criticism during and after sparring for what it was, a piss-take, it raised doubts that had been lingering under the surface for some time. Was Howard really mollycoddling me?

'It'll get a lot harder before it gets any easier,' said Howard, taking my sweat-soaked gloves off. 'But it'll be worth it. Another couple of weeks of this and it'll level out.' Jesus. 'You've turned that corner and from now on this is what you want – hard sparring. Nothing fucking crazy mind you, but hard work that'll test you. Well done, son.'

'That's what you want, Dave,' said Justin, joining the post-spar conversation. 'Plenty of hard sparring. Not so's we're trying to knock each other out, but hard pressure sparring at a good pace.'

Boxing hurt. No, boxing *really* hurt. I didn't want to be a boxer, I never did. What was I thinking of? Why had I come to Sheffield? Why was I doing this? Maybe I was mad. Was boxing the manifestation of my insanity? Some lunatics walk into McDonald's with an AK47 assault rifle screaming 'I don't give a fuck'. I chose boxing. I was certain I was mad. No, it was hubris . . . and madness. I wanted to give up desperately, curl up in a ball somewhere and forget this ever happened but pride, the dog, kept forcing me on.

'There's no point you sparring with the likes of Terry or Danny,' continued Justin. 'No offence but we're too old for all that slipping and sliding . . . too slow. I think you'll piss that fight,' he added as we settled down on mats to start our groundwork. 'The kid that you fight'll be my standard.'

'I fucking hope not,' I said.

'But if you leave your guard open like you did just now, and give a pro that opportunity, he'll take your head clean off.'

I finished training and went into the bar for a lime cordial. I needed to sit down and get my head straight.

'The usual please, Vicky.'

'Why can't you have something different for a change?' Vicky gave her usual scowl. She always got in a flap about fixing up my drink. What difference was there between serving a lime cordial and a pint of lager? Was unscrewing a bottle top too much for her lard ass?

'All right. I'll have a pint of Guinness then,' I said.

'We haven't got any Guinness.'

'What's that, Scotch mist?' I looked down at a gleaming Guinness pump on the bar.

'There's no barrel,' said Vicky.

'OK. I'll have a bottle instead.'

'We haven't got any bottles. Why would we sell bottles when we've got draft?'

There should have been a sign over the bar saying: YOU DON'T

HAVE TO BE A FUCKING IDIOT TO WORK HERE, BUT IT HELPS.

'But you haven't.'

'Haven't what?'

'What about Beamish or Murphy's?'

'We haven't got any stout.'

'Shall I come in and start again?'

'What?'

'I think I'll stick with the lime cordial.'

'I think you'd better.'

The word was the bar was going to close down. I wasn't surprised with this kind of service. There had been arguments and recriminations among the Hobson clan regarding the running of the club and, apart from occasional karaoke nights, the odd strip show and private functions, the bar was a dead loss.

The following day I blew my nose and gooey red pus along with maroon flakes of dried blood came out. My nose felt sore. I noticed a red blotch on my scalp that looked like dirty, smudged lipstick. I ached, so I ran a hot bath and took a soak. This was one of my few luxuries. Peace and quiet in the bath with a good book away from the bedlam of the Rainey family.

I no longer gave a monkey's cuss about the training. I just wanted to fight. I could feel all that suppressed rage of my youth returning. I was the angry young man of yesteryear, denied new trainers, a holiday, love. I was pissed off. This life was bullshit and someone had to pay for it. I knew from the moment that Justin gave me a black eye and a busted lip I was improving as a fighter.

'Who did that to you?' Lorna had asked, her face squinting down at me as I lay in bed lost in the pages of some American pulp fiction.

'Oh it was Justin, sparring,' I replied casually.

'I'm going to have words with that boy, the bully. You've got a right gladiator's wound there.'

Black eyes are funny things. They make people stare at you, like you've got the pox or chronic acne. This particular shiner wasn't swollen or cut, just a bit black and blue, red and purple. I didn't care about getting marked up any more. It was part of being a fighter.

Lorna, her mother, Simon and I were in the town when we ran into Johnny Nelson. Johnny was smooth. For someone who had lost his first three professional fights when he started out, he wasn't doing too badly. He had an office above a herbal remedy shop from which he ran

217

some kind of recruitment agency. He drove a BMW, had sponsorship deals, modelled and, most importantly, was a world champion. He was everything Terry wasn't, which was why Terry despised him.

'Hey, I remember you,' said Johnny. 'I met you late-night shopping with Howard, at Asda.'

'That's right,' I said. 'I won't say what you were buying if you don't say what I was buying.' Johnny laughed, showing off a perfect set of teeth. He looked a bit fleshy and probably weighed 14½ stone at the time, but when he dropped down to 13-8, his fighting weight, he looked ripped. Man, Johnny was smooth all right.

'What weight you fighting at?' he asked, scanning me up and down. 'Light-heavy?' Naturally he assumed I was a fighter. Sporting a black eye, who could blame him. To Johnny and the rest of the world, even before I got into boxing, I was the stereotype of the black man – a testament to brawn over brains; a strapping six-foot-two menace to society; big, black, muscular. That's what people saw because that's all they were capable of seeing. Somewhere else on the list of stereotypes was mugger, rapist, doorman and drug dealer. All black people had to fight for a living somehow.

'What do you weigh?'

'About thirteen three, thirteen four,' I said. I really weighed 13-7. I'd learnt from Howard always to lie about my weight.

'When you fighting?' What was Johnny, a policeman? So many questions. I glanced over at Lorna.

'Christmas,' she said.

Even I was confused these days when some stranger innocently inquired if I was a professional boxer or when my next fight was. Was I a professional fighter? Well bar the final paperwork, the granting of a licence, I suppose I was. But I still didn't see it. I knew that struggling to maintain my soft-focus identity as a thinking man not a fighting man ran contrary to the cut and thrust of boxing but somehow I still refused to submit 100 per cent to boxing. I wrestled with my conscience about why this was. Initially, I wanted to believe I was playing a role, like a method actor becoming absorbed in a part. One day this performance would be over and I'd move on (hopefully not in a wheelchair) to my next engagement. But this was not a play. I was not in character. Yet I had come to the conclusion that the problem was one of identity, my own identity. My insecurities as a man, a black man, were coming to the surface. I had spent a lifetime struggling against the stereotypes that society had created for me but by choosing to become a boxer I was playing into that most insidious of racial stereotypes, the black man as a violent brute. As a journalist I sought respect, and I suppose acceptance, from my peers, friends and family for my creative ability. As a boxer, to those outside the fight game, I was nothing more than a fucking animal.

'I'm actually a journalist. I'm writing a book on boxing and I'm training with Howard to have one pro fight.'

'That's deep,' said Johnny. 'That's really deep.' He found the concept amusing. 'I remember when Claude Abrams was slagging off Naz in *Boxing News* [Abrams was the editor], saying he had no power and that, Naz got him up to the gym and took him to school. Man, he dealt with him in style.'

The times when I gave in to boxing and neared that 100 per cent, I felt everything else slip. For days I would be unable to write and then suddenly as if awoken in the middle of a nightmare I'd snap back to reality and disappear inside my room for days, slaving over my PC trying to make some sense of what I was doing while having panic attacks about not being able to cut it. The pressure I put on myself was unbearable at times as were my growing mood swings, which were beginning to worry me. I had never had a problem with depression, but now the thought of pinching a couple of Lorna's Prozac entered my mind. I felt as though I had gone to the edge and back on a number of occasions. It was all becoming too much, too much, too much.

With little prospect of a fight in the near future, I had become disheartened. The past couple of weeks had been a struggle, what with the shoulder injury, a few good hidings and on-going personal problems. I was experiencing physical and emotional breakdown. The physical and psychological demands of fighting and the mental and emotional demands of writing were pulling me in two different directions. At times the temptation to just pack it in and disappear was immense.

The situation wasn't helped by the fact that I'd encountered that fancy psychological barrier called a writer's block. During various stages of my life I've had builder's bum, athlete's foot and bachelor's balls. But this was the first time I'd had writer's block. I'd arrived. For weeks I'd stare at my PC screen late into the night, with no ideas or direction. I'd play the stupid little games that Bill Gates gives away with his crummy software; you know, solitaire, minesweeper and hearts, that frustrating card game you play with three imaginary friends and never win. I'd become more physical than cerebral. I couldn't think straight. I couldn't write coherently. I gave up trying and started grunting my notes into a dictaphone.

This route I'd taken into boxing had changed my life dramatically. Damn, it was my life. Boxing had become an obsession, affecting my career and my personal life. It bled into everything and at times like this, moments of melancholy when nothing seemed to go right, I thought I would go insane from the mental and physical pressure it brought down on me.

chapter 29

It had to happen eventually. A momentary lapse of concentration and the World Champion Shadow Boxer nailed me with a straight right, bang on the chin. The blow was delivered with such force, speed and accuracy it caught me completely by surprise. I didn't even feel the punch. I must have blacked out for a split second, as I had no recollection of how I landed on my backside. I simply felt a sharp jolt on my coccyx and found myself sitting on the grubby carpet of the ring dumbfounded, my legs bent and arms by my side as though I was preparing for a yoga class. I shook my head in disbelief.

'Sorry, Dave. Are you all right?' asked Ben. 'Are you all right, pal?'

'Yeah, what the fuck happened?' I tried a forced laugh to shake off my embarrassment. It didn't work.

'What d'you fucking think happened?' shouted Howard. 'You're not concentrating. You're leaning too far back on that back leg.'

I got up slowly. My legs felt heavy and my head felt light. The peripheral vision from my left eye was fuzzy and I had trouble focusing. I felt like I'd just been thrown from a fairground ride and everybody else was still on board going round and round laughing and giggling at me. My eyes met those of an Asian youth who had been sitting at ringside watching the sparring. He looked at me vacantly. His eyes betrayed nothing. I continued scanning the gym to find a measure of reaction to the knockdown. There was none. The handful of people in the gym were just going about their business as usual.

'You sure you're all right, Dave?' Ben repeated.

'Yeah, yeah, yeah. Let's carry on.'

I weighed almost 14 stone. Ben Coward was around 11½ stone. How could a little punk like him put me on my backside? I'd taken way harder punches from Terry, Justin, Scott and Danny. I felt humiliated. My pride had had a hole punched right through it. I was mortified. For the rest of the round, groggy as I was, I tried to take Ben's head off, swinging madly, hoping somehow I could redeem myself by knocking him down – better still knocking him out. I was raging inside, raging at myself. I kept rushing him but the knockdown had taken the wind out of my sails. I was too slow and too predictable. Ben sensed I wanted to nail him desperately so he simply bobbed and weaved, ducked and dived and slipped every punch I threw until Howard called time. We touched gloves and Ben climbed out of the ring and went straight over to Howard.

'It were only a flash knockdown, Howard,' I heard Ben mutter. He sounded contrite. 'You turned away from me as I threw the punch,' Ben said, walking towards me. 'What were you doing?'

'Oh, I don't know,' I said. 'For a split second I was somewhere else. I just lost my concentration. I don't know what happened.'

'What are we going to do with you?' said Howard, frowning. 'I don't understand you. You can do all the complicated things, easy, and make a mess of the simple things.'

Would I, could I, recover from this dent to my ego? My pride was in pieces. I'd never been floored before. No one had ever had me over. Was my chin suspect? Did I have a glass jaw? I tried to convince myself that it was just a flash knockdown. Fighters far greater than I had hit the deck, many several times in their careers. In his preparation for the Rumble in the Jungle Ali was floored four, maybe five times by his sparring partner Roy Williams and went on to batter George Foreman senseless. Nobody made a big deal of me landing on my backside so why had I taken it to heart? It was a flash knockdown for Chrissake. Why was I harbouring this feeling of resentment? I could reason that I simply lost my balance and Ben got lucky. I dared not talk to anybody about it for fear of exposing myself as some sort of bottle job, so I spent the next few days suppressing my feelings and got all introspective and sunk within myself. I felt as if I was failing on all counts.

Like many of the fighters who trained at the gym, Ben knew that boxing offered just a slim chance of success. In the meantime, it was a case of not giving up the day job.

'I'm waiting to hear about a civil engineering job in London. Seven hundred pounds a week it pays,' he said. 'It's a couple of months' work which means I'll miss Dennis's show [in December].' It presented a dilemma – fight for £700 a night or flight for £700 a week. 'I've got to give boxing a bash. If I stay at home watching telly and eating pizza I'll never know if I'd have been good enough. But I'm skint and boxing don't pay the bills.'

Later, when the dust settled on my paranoia, I realised the knockdown had taught me a valuable lesson – not to underestimate any fighter, no matter what size, age or level of experience. I also learnt the value and importance of concentration. I knew I had to, as Tyrone would say, 'keep my eyes on the prize' and stay focused at all times. A moment's lapse in concentration could prove disastrous, fatal even.

Mental preparation was another thing I came to understand. How could I, having travelled for some five hours, arrive in Sheffield, hit M&S, stuff my face with a triple sandwich, a banana and yoghurt, head straight for the gym and spar on a full stomach, still stressed from half a day's travelling? With hindsight it was a stupid thing to do. The physical and emotional demands of boxing are such that it is foolish to expect to train hard and spar if you are not fully *compos mentis*. The travelling wore me out. Just as it took time for me to make the switch from the cerebral demands of writing to the physical demands of boxing, I had to switch from that catatonic state that long-distance travel engulfs you in to the strain of a two-hour gym session.

Howard tried his best to be true to his word and make sure that I'd hate him in the forthcoming weeks. After six, sometimes eight, rounds of sparring he'd get me to work the heavy bag, then one of the lighter full length bags, then the ground-to-floor speedball. This was followed by a succession of pyramids, i.e. fifteen squat jumps, fifteen squat thrusts and fifteen burpees followed by ten reps of the same, then five. I'd go through the same combination for press-ups, triceps press-ups and bounce press-ups, and the same combination for knee-to-chest sit-ups, alternate knee-to-chest sit-ups and pikes. In between the exercises would be a series of excruciating leg stretches and callisthenics with light weights.

Each training session offered little in terms of variety and soon the monotony added to my frustration and increasing ennui. I'd taken on the life of a fighter in the hope that I'd escape the robotics of being a desk jockey but I'd just exchanged one daily grind for another.

Although the temptation to bale out had been unbearable at times, pride, that same dubious virtue that keeps men fighting in the ring, kept me battling out of it. I'd lose too much face and professional credibility if I didn't go through with it. I had to get to the end.

In Titanic on the way home Howard gave me the customarily brief post-mortem of the day's performance. 'Think Muhammad Ali . . . not

Rocky Marciano. You're not going to be a fighter, so don't go acting like one.' There was the fundamental difference between fighters and boxers. All boxers could fight, but not all fighters could box. Maybe it was splitting hairs but the way I saw it 'fighter' and 'boxer', terms that could be interchangeable, in certain contexts were labels that defined a style, or even a philosophy, of fighting. A fighter could be seen as someone who used natural power and aggression and marshalled it within a simple style of boxing. A boxer, on the other hand, relied on technique and strategy. The Ali–Marciano example was a good one. They were two fighters with fundamentally different but very effective styles.

Howard had been berating me lately for 'getting into tear-ups' and 'standing and having it'. 'What's the point in getting in the ring and getting bashed up during sparring?' he remonstrated. 'There's plenty of time for that come the fight. In sparring you're supposed to be learning from each other, not trying to bash the hell out of one another.' Howard's motto was it's better to give than receive. He certainly saw boxing as 'the noble art of self-defence' and emphasised techniques that avoided scrappy confrontations and taking too many blows. 'Remember the human body is not designed to receive punches, especially to the head,' he kept reminding me.

Somewhere along the line I'd lost the plot and started getting into stand-up battles in sparring. The result, as I've already mentioned, was a succession of black eyes, wobbly jaws, busted and bloody noses, welts, stiff necks, sore ribs, swollen fists and sundry bruises, aches and pains. Howard had been trying to teach me to box, but something inside me kept wanting to stand and trade blows like I was Jack fucking Broughton in a nineteenth-century boxing booth. I suppose I was hell bent on proving I could 'have it' (whatever 'it' was) and take as good as I could give. During some sparring sessions I'd just shut up shop and say, 'Come on, fucking give it to me!' What was I on? That dubious machismo, I suppose. I'd seen others, including Terry, 'give it the large one' in the ring and as one of the senior members of the gym (in terms of age, obviously not experience) I wanted to demonstrate my manliness to all those young pups and pretenders who thought they could slap this hack around.

'We've got to think about getting you through six twos safely,' continued Howard.

'And winning,' I hastened to add, sensing his priorities had changed from success to survival.

'Of course, of course,' said Howard. 'Sometimes I think you're there, that we've cracked it, and then something happens and you're all over the place.'

I told Howard that I had a lot on my mind of late. I always tried to be as honest as I could about my state of mind and my feelings towards my training, but I was also conscious of the relationship we now had. I felt slightly overprotected by Howard. We had become quite close. Sometimes I felt guilty about this, insofar as I worried that I was muscling in on Terry or Danny's territory. They'd known Howard a lot longer than I had and in many respects they deserved his attention more. One day, in the not too distant future I hoped, I'd be gone but they'd still be around. I had a lot of respect for Howard, both professionally and personally. The relationship between a fighter and a trainer was pivotal to the fighter's success. As Carlie Carew had told me many moons ago, 'a trainer can win or lose a fight for a boxer.' A bad personal relationship spelled trouble on the professional front.

That night I went to bed early, nursing a scorching headache. I slept for an unbroken and uncharacteristic twelve hours. Cautiously, I took the following day off. My head still didn't seem right and I didn't want to take any chances.

When I returned to the gym no one said anything about the knockdown. I was still hung up about it and anticipated a barracking from the rest of the boys, especially Terry. When I mentioned the incident to Clinton he simply shrugged his shoulders and said casually, 'These things happen.' I was relieved that nothing more was said about it. Experience had taught me that perhaps I had overstated the impact of what had happened.

To help me overcome my anxiety, Howard put me in the ring again with Ben. We did six rounds of very light sparring and Ben helped me with my movement, jabbing, working off the back foot. 'That's better,' said Howard encouragingly. 'That's what I want.' Working with him again after the knockdown earlier in the week helped to restore my confidence, which had taken a battering of late.

chapter 30

I took the flash knockdown as an omen and decided that being fit wouldn't be enough. I needed to be superfit to keep my head above water. I became more disciplined with my running and made sure I got a good thirty to forty minutes (four to five miles) on the road every evening. The younger fighters in the gym could get away with youthful energy and the old pros had experience on their side. I had neither, so I had to condition myself better and work harder than the others in the gym. In the beginning I had trained twice a day but now I was doing a comparable amount of training to the other fighters, i.e. one session a day. To compensate for my lack of experience, I needed to do more than this. Once again in this life, it was a matter of having to prove myself better than those around me just to be on an equal footing.

Even after a week of regular roadwork, the benefits were clear. I looked leaner and more toned. The guys in the gym continued to remark that I was looking in great shape. To me the aesthetics of training were important. For all the physical torment, pain and anguish I'd put myself through over the past year I wanted to have something corporeal to show for it. I was near to having the body I had always dreamed of. That sounds vacuous because it is, but that's the nature of boxing. The flip side of all that insecurity, that daily self-doubt, 'can I do it?' constantly ringing in your ears, was a heightened self-perception and a blown-up ego. But the pendular relationship between self-doubt and self-love, between a fragile id and a supercharged ego, a tough exterior and a vulnerable inner self, means fighters have a schizophrenia that makes them arrogant beyond belief one minute and as humble as proverbial pie the next.

As the chill of autumn began to bite I decided to switch from doing my roadwork at night to mid-mornings. Running down Sheffield streets, sweating my arse off and panting like a greyhound with an elastic band round his balls, I'd get a range of reactions from passers-by. Usually folk gave me a pitying smile as if to say, 'Poor bugger. Look what he has to do of a morning.' Sometimes I got derisory looks and once a junky who could clearly see me heading in his direction walked straight into my path. I literally ran over the hapless fool, barging him to the ground, and kept on running. I looked over my shoulder to see him in a crumpled heap and nearly ran into some railings at the side of the road.

I felt my training on the whole was going well although anxiety about sparring still came in waves. If all was well in my world I took sparring with a pinch of salt but when I had personal problems (which was more often than not) my anxiety would resurface and start monkeying with me psychologically. At times I felt so depressed, so moribund, I thought I would step into the ring and never come out alive. Such fatalism was not healthy. An abnormal degree of fear put you at even greater risk of injury. A boxing ring was not a place for the fainthearted. My anxiety had been subsiding steadily in recent weeks until one afternoon, Dean, a twenty-two-year-old amateur welterweight who was desperate to turn pro, told me about his minor neurological crisis just as I was about to spar with Big Dave.

'I got this right bad headache after sparring with Big Dave,' he said. 'Last week he caught me with a shot just here,' he pointed to his left temple, 'and it stunned me. It weren't right hard. I didn't have blurred vision or owt like that. But he's fifteen and a half stone or summat and I'm around ten. The weight makes a lot of difference, dunnit? Afterwards I got this headache and it wouldn't go away. Me mum and dad said, "Right, we're taking you to hospital." I had one of them X-rays, in that thing that goes round and round like.'

'What, you mean you had an MRI scan?' I ventured.

'Yeah, that were it. Anyway, the doctor said I had severe bruising on the inside of me head. I've been told not to spar for the next three weeks and to tell the hospital if the headaches come back. I suppose that's what happens when you spar with someone the size of Big Dave.'

Big Dave was a six foot seven, nineteen-year-old amateur with an infinite reach and a right hand like a jackhammer. He was something of a chimera – he had a long angular face, jet black hair, a big nose (of which he was highly self-conscious), a deceptively skinny upper body with square shoulders, rangy arms and massive legs. He could easily, would easily, carry another two stone. Howard said Big Dave would be world heavyweight champion one day, if he kept his head together.

Big Dave and Dean were two out of nearly twenty regular sparring partners I had, around half of whom were pros and half amateurs. It was common for most of the fighters in the gym to spar with each other regardless of size, weight, age or ability and by mixing in this way we were able to take advantage of each fighter's different attributes. For instance, the smaller, lighter boxers were faster and harder to hit. Sparring with them helped me improve hand speed, footwork and head movement. Fighters of my own weight gave me a comparable measure of power and speed and thus were ideal for hard competitive sparring. Heavier fighters, who were perhaps slower but harder hitting, presented a larger target for me to practise my combinations on while also disciplining my defence against potentially concussive blows.

Even though I was so much older than Big Dave, at least half the time we sparred together he gave me more of a caning than I gave him. His combination of youth and build meant his ego often got the better of him in the ring. He was aware that a lot of guys in the gym resented him because of his size. One time he wound up brawling with Justin and the pair had to be dragged off each other. He was at that age when young men get caught up in trying to prove themselves a little too much. I sparred with Big Dave on a regular basis and generally hated every minute of it. Even though we were adversaries in the ring, outside it I couldn't help but feel compassion for him. 'I fucking hate my old man, he's a bastard,' he once confided. Like so many fighters I had met, Dave was another guy who had an unresolved beef with his dad and was trying to find catharsis in boxing.

'Given the chance he'd have no problem with knocking you out,' whispered Richard, a lanky, pale-faced guy in his mid-thirties who was one of the amateur coaches. I had just finished sparring with Big Dave and was leaning against a punch bag trying to catch my breath. 'You have to look out for number one.' I made some comment about having an off-day and told him, rather disingenuously, that Big Dave was still only a kid and I had nothing to prove by trying to blast him out. 'Forget about what anybody else has to deal with,' said Richard. 'If he's old enough to get in that ring, then he's old enough to take the consequences. Don't matter whether they're fifteen or fifty. It's every man for himself.'

It was every man for himself which was precisely why I would fight my battles my way. I knew that Richard didn't like Big Dave or one or two other amateurs in the club. He felt they undermined his authority because they sought more advice from Howard than from him. The Richards of this world loved it went you beat one of their enemies down for them. What did he think I was, a fucking mercenary? When it came to boxing, I took my cues solely from Howard.

As a professional trainer, Howard, according to British Boxing Board of Control and Amateur Boxing Association rules, was not supposed to coach amateur boxers and could not represent them as a second during an amateur contest. In reality, promising amateurs who trained alongside professionals in the gym always came under the *de facto* tutelage of a professional coach. This was the nature of boxing, the nature of the farm system. Those amateurs whose flirtation with boxing would never amount to more than a few plastic trophies were generally left to the devices of the amateur coaches like Richard and Tim Rowland, well-meaning but limited fellows who could take a guy only so far in terms of technique, fitness and application. They were inclined to feel insecure when the amateurs started getting close to the pros.

The Don Valley Sports Academy, like all gyms where professionals and amateurs trained together, had a well-established farm system. Around half of the amateurs in the gym had aspirations to become professionals one day and those who showed promise naturally caught Howard's eye. By watching him and the pros, they would learn skills and techniques that would prepare them for a career in the professional ranks. Having made the transition from the amateur to professional school of boxing, a young fighter would be morally obligated to pledge his allegiance to Howard (and of course Dennis) and turn pro under their aegis.

I had no interest in becoming a career fighter. For me it was a case of get in and get straight out. My agenda was journalistic. The only thing driving me on was the will to finish. I had lost interest in the result. I didn't care whether I eventually won or lost. I was like a journeyman without a track record. Get in, get out, pass go, collect £400, end of story. This was my attitude. This is what I had become.

I coughed up some blood later that night before I went to bed. It wasn't much, but enough to remind me of the risks I was taking as a boxer. I thought about Dean and his bruised brain and how absurd it was to participate in a sport where internal bleeding, headaches, minor brain damage and the like were everyday occurrences. I'd previously considered the risks as short-term – black eyes, busted noses, fat lips – but since the knockdown I had become more aware of the potential for greater harm. The risks were twofold – the high-impact short-term injury of the kind that killed Bradley Stone and the long-term mental and physical deterioration characterised by punch drunkenness. Of course, in extreme cases, serious neurological damage can occur, such as that typified by Muhammad Ali's Parkinson's disease. The public focus was always on the immediate injuries that occurred in competition but the long-term damage was really done in sparring. Even allowing for holidays and breaks between fights, based on an average of four to eight rounds of regular sparring five days a week, an active pro could easily notch up over a thousand rounds in a year. Most fighters managed to navigate their way through boxing without any major medical catastrophes. Statistics (man's second best friend) point to boxing as being a relatively safe, injury-free sport compared to rugby, motor racing and even football. That said, flying is statistically the safest form of travel until you're killed in a plane crash.

I lay in my little bedroom on my single bed and looked at the picture of Luca gazing down at me. I wanted to be such a great father, better than mine was to me. I wanted Luca to have not only financial security, but emotional and spiritual security too. I wanted her to have these things so that in thirty years' time she wouldn't be messed up like I am and doing this crazy shit in order to pay the bills.

I cried myself to sleep that night. How many times had I done this, secretly? Ten, twenty, a hundred? At times like this I could feel my resolve buckling under the pressure – self-inflicted though it was. I had lost my way in the world. I wanted out, the sooner the better. Every time I stepped into the ring, I took a huge risk. Dean sparred with Big Dave and wound up with brain damage. Justin had recently been in hospital and had an operation on a hole in his heart. He had been training, sparring all this time with a bloody hole in his heart! It could have killed him at any moment. And within days of the operation, he's back in the gym. Justin had a hole in his heart and I had a hole in my fucking head.

Getting busted up again? Why was I back in the gym the following day? Because I thought I was a macho man, I suppose. Boxing is a game for macho men. Take Justin for example. Instead of staying at home convalescing after his heart op he vented his spleen on the heavy bag. In further defiance of his condition he had (against Howard's advice) also resumed sparring and sent his work mate Billy to the hospital.

'That bastard reckons I've cracked his ribs,' he said lunging at the bag with a fearsome right hand. 'He came down here and told Howard he had to go t'hospital 'cos of me. The fucking liar. Has thou ever had broken ribs?'

'I can't say I have,' I replied.

'When I broke two of me ribs at work, I couldn't breathe, man.'

Justin was incredulous. He hated any suggestion that he was unduly rough in sparring even though he was generally very heavy handed. As far as he was concerned this was a slight against his character, another vicious rumour that needed to cease immediately.

Justin got wound up really easily. Only a couple of weeks earlier he had gone on at me for days after I jokingly called him a bully for knocking one of his mates out of the ring. 'I won't spar with thou 'cos thou says I'm a fucking gym bully,' he kept saying. I had to reassure him for a week that he was a cool geezer. It all started when he sparred with this guy, an ex-bodybuilder and bouncer who dabbled with steroids, and a bit of cockfighting and dog fighting. The pair had been body sparring when Justin caught his mate with a sweet right hand over the top of his guard (his favourite punch), straight on the chin, which doubled him up and sent him crashing through the ropes colliding into the back wall of the gym. He missed the concrete edge of an adjoining partition by inches. It was a spectacular knockdown, which owed more to the guy's lack of balance than Justin's brute force. He took it in good part and was philosophical about being bowled over. I made an innocent wisecrack about Justin being a bully for hitting him square in the face when they were supposed to be body sparring. He didn't even have a gumshield in. The story that eventually got around was that Justin had KO'd him.

Another time Danny said to him in poor jest, 'See, me, I don't like white people.' Justin tried to take it as a joke but after a day or two the comment had got to him.

'Here, Dave, you're Danny's mate. What's with this "I don't like white people" crap?' he said, cornering me in the changing rooms.

'You've known him longer than I have,' I said. 'I'm sure he doesn't mean anything by it.'

'He's been right winding me up lately. If he fucking wants it, I'll give it to him. What do you think? What's his problem? I'm gonna have words with Howard about him.'

I was surprised when Justin claimed he was going to 'fill in' Danny. He had got it into his head that he was the subject of ridicule and criticism. He was sensitive to these things, a tad too sensitive I told him. He was the kind of guy who knew how to hold a grudge. Justin was at that age – early thirties, hurtling towards a mid-life crisis over which he had no control. He thought the world was against him. He saw himself as a kind of vulnerable older male in a pride of lions, waiting to be picked off by one of the young bucks.

"Ere Richard, has thou ever had bruised ribs?' Justin was now seeking second and third opinions. The fourth and fifth would be along shortly.

'No, but I had a couple cave in once,' said Richard, a promising sixteen-year-old amateur.

'Could you breathe?' Justin probed further.

'Breathe? I couldn't walk!' laughed Richard.

To let Justin work his obvious annoyance out of his system I suggested we do a few rounds of sparring.

When I was on top of my game, sparring well and making all the right moves, inevitably somebody other than me was getting hurt, not just physically but emotionally as well. And I still had the capacity to feel guilty about that. I'd see it in their eyes as they shook hands at the end of a hard spar; or when they left the gym and gave me a parting glance that betrayed their innermost sense of loss, failure or sometimes resentment. I could see their anxiety sometimes. I was a novice, but I had learnt fast. It would be potentially embarrassing for one of the pros, even a decent amateur to take a pasting from me, the writer. In a strange way, I had the power to make or break the will of some of these guys.

This evening, for example, I sparred four rounds with Mark Brooks and three with a thirty-year-old former amateur called Brian, whom I hadn't seen in the gym for a couple of months.

'Have a move around with these two,' said Howard. 'Nothing heavy . . . just keep sticking that jab out and move off the back foot.' The instructions were simple. Now that I'd reached trained mutt stage and could respond to directions, the boxing equivalent of fetch, sit and heel, I could get into the ring with an agenda, a strategy if you like, and work to that. It made life easier, taking orders, as I knew what was expected of me.

I went to work with Mark first, bobbing and weaving, dancing around the ring remembering Howard's other instruction to 'hit and not be hit'. Brian and I took it in turns to spar with Mark for the first four rounds. We then did a round with each other and as I had an obvious height, reach and weight advantage (of around three stone) it was easy for me to pick off the more experienced, but smaller Brian.

'That's some jab you've got there,' said Brian at the end of the round. 'I couldn't seem to get through it.' I reacted modestly to his analysis of our first encounter. I could see a bruise the size of a golf ball developing over his right eye. I did that. I was quite proud of my handiwork at first. I'd stuck him steadily with a stiff jab, trying not to turn the shots too often so as to reduce their power. 'Remember, hit at, not through,' repeated Howard and I thought I had done just that.

The sparring with Mark was fairly uneventful and quite pedestrian. He was marked down as a spare for an amateur show in two days' time, so the pattern with him was not to go mad, keep it nice and steady and just move around blocking and slipping shots with neither of us getting too heavily involved. Brian, however, had other things on his mind. From the off of our second round he came at me with more venom, trying to rush me with looping right hands over the top of my guard. I parried most of them away, took a few on the gloves and, of course, one or two on the chin. He switched to the body and I kept jabbing him out of range, slipping what he threw and countering with stiffer jabs to the head. It's easy to tell when someone is trying to stick it on you. They simply hit you harder. I could see this was Brian's game plan. 'Hit the bugger harder and slow him down so I can get under that jab,' he must've been thinking. One thing being bowled over by an 11 stone middleweight taught me was don't underestimate anybody. I reacted in kind to Brian's aggression and turned more of my jabs and threw in a few right crosses for good measure. By the time the third round had come, I was warmed to the task. 'BING!' He walked straight on to a peach of a right hand after I'd teed him off with the jab. 'POW' a crunching uppercut jolted him upright for a double left jab, straight right combination, then jab, jab, jab. His head snapped back repeatedly. I was teeing off on this guy. It felt good. Too good. It was like the fleeting past experiences I'd had in the gym when I'd caught a seasoned pro with a good shot or battled my way out of trouble.

'Oi, fucking slow it down with them right hands,' yelled Howard. I knew he was talking to me.

'What?' I said, once again going into my 'who me, ref?' routine. I could see a patch of blood now over Brian's left eye. I didn't do that, did I?

'Right, time. That's enough of that,' bellowed Howard. Brian and I looked at each other incredulously. He had that battle-weary expression which said 'yeah, this is hard but that's the way I like it'. He was up for a beating as long as he could load up on me. He had, after all, for a good half of the round tried to take my head off with big right-hand swings. If some guy's going to try to knock me out, he can have a taste of what I've got in store, too. As Scott Welch had told me months earlier, 'Don't get into all this play sparring. Boxing isn't a joke. You've got to treat everyone you spar with as the enemy. You've got to think that they're trying to deprive you of everything you've got.'

For a couple of months I'd gone through a phase where I wanted to prove, to myself more than anyone else, that I could mix it, that I wasn't some fancy Dan who simply boxed by numbers. But as Howard pointed out, I'd got involved in too many tear-ups, messy, hard spars, that didn't suit my rangy physique or emerging style of boxing. Having satisfied myself that I could run with the best of them, I reverted to my boxing and concentrated more on working off the back foot as opposed to steaming in and leaving my chin out to dry.

By this stage I had around 300 rounds of sparring under my belt, 900 minutes. Was I coming up to scratch? I thought so.

'There's no substitute for experience,' said Howard, giving me the post-mortem on the way home from the gym. He slipped a tape into the cassette player – Harry Black's Greatest Hits. 'Happy music' Howard called it. An orchestra of banjos playing at 168bpm blared out of Titanic's tinny speakers. The music sounded how I felt – insane. 'You've got to learn the skills and techniques . . . ,' lectured Howard, '. . . gain the experience in ten months that it takes most fighters three or four years to learn. You can't rush these things.' I sat in the passenger seat in stony silence. I knew I was being set up for bad news.

Howard and I had a sit down. The news was I would not be fighting until March at the earliest. I could not believe it.

'If you go out before then, you'll mug yourself off,' he said. 'I think we've turned the corner now but I had my doubts. About six weeks ago I thought, "What the fuck is going on here?" You were all over the place. I was starting seriously to worry about it. Sometimes I think what the fuck have I taken on here. But we've gone this far and we have to see it through to the end.'

It was the first serious talk we'd had in a long time; and it was the first time Howard admitted that he was concerned about the effects my performance in the ring could have on his reputation. He repeated what he had said to me on several previous occasions. 'You want a happy ending, don't you? People always remember a winner, not a loser. If you got out there before you're ready and mug yourself off, people are going to say, "Who was that idiot?". Whereas if you go in there and look the part, win or lose, you've got your self-respect intact.

You want to be authentic. If you give a good account of yourself, people'll say, "Who's that fella? Not bad was he? What do you mean he's never had a fight before!" Come March, maybe February, you'll fight and win. Before that, well, I just don't want you to make an arse of yourself.'

I felt as though I was in a no-win situation. The ante was being continually upped, the goalposts were forever shifting. In boxing parlance, I had been ticking over for the past eight months; I was on an endless conveyor belt of running, skipping, sparring, bags and pads. Day in day out, I gritted my teeth through scores of press-ups, pull-ups and burpees. I devised my own groundwork routine of fifteen different abdominal exercises and was now doing 450 to 500 reps a day. I had a washboard stomach, rippling biceps, lats, abs and pecs to die for, but where the hell had it got me? What was the point? The harder I tried the harder it got – two steps forward, one step back. As I improved, the commitment and performance expected of me in the gym increased. As this happened, the expectation of the eventual fight's outcome grew. I felt positive that many other trainers would have taken a chance and already lined up an opponent for me. I knew I always had the option of going elsewhere, but how could I? Howard wasn't just my trainer, manager and landlord. He ferried me to and from the gym on a daily basis, bought me breakfast in the café when I was stony broke, took me to boxing shows and football matches (well, Sheffield United) and along with Lorna kept me going through some tough times. They let me live with them rent-free. How much more indebted could I be to him? But the closer I got to Howard, the further I seemed to get from my goal. The sense of overprotection was looming again. If I had kept a healthy distance from them, maybe Howard would've taken a more mercenary attitude and just slung me in there sooner rather than later. I was hoping that this wouldn't turn into a battle of wills, that my desire to get the job done at all costs wouldn't run contrary to Howard's desire to get the best out of me.

The morning after our talk there was a knock at my door. It was Lorna.

'Are you all right?' she said.

'Hang on a second, I'm not dressed.' I pulled myself away from my computer. Every morning I tried to recapture those thoughts I'd slept on overnight in words on the screen. I had tried to explain to Howard the night before that one of the problems I faced writing about my experiences as a fighter was that I was constantly navel gazing, analysing every detail of my actions and reactions, thoughts and feelings. When I was on an up, this was fine as it served to maintain my wellbeing, but when I was down, writing about my depression reinforced the melancholy. Sometimes I could sink into bouts of near clinical depression. I don't think I ever got truly suicidal although I did once buy a packet of 100 aspirin with the view to an overdose. After I took the first two, however, I felt fine.

'Howard asked me this morning if you were happy ... after last night's conversation.' What was Lorna, some sort of Dave Matthews avatar now? 'I said, "Of course he's not. I know David." He seemed to think you took it well.'

I hummed and hawed and made a passing comment about being pissed off at having to wait to conclude this odyssey.

'Howard's only got your best interests at heart, love.'

'Hmmm,' I said.

'I've got to go to Howard's mum's now. I told him I'd talk to you about it. We'll have a chat later, eh?'

'Yeah.'

What was this, good cop, bad cop? What had happened to all that early praise, all that puff about me being good enough to win a Central Area title in two years, being a natural? Later, I talked to Howard about what that meant, being a natural.

'People talk about fighters being naturals but what's natural about clenching your fist and punching someone? What's natural about being hit right here?' Howard motioned his meaty fist against his forehead. 'People box ...', he paused for thought, 'we have boxing so that some of that violence and mayhem that's on the street can be put into a gym, into a ring and off the street. If we didn't have boxing, there'd just be more fighting in the streets.'

The air stank of burnt wood and fireworks on the streets of Manor, Darnall and Attercliffe. Kids begged 'penny for the guy' in shop doorways, then bought cider, fags and dope with the proceeds. October had faded into November and my ambitions were put on ice while Howard concentrated on developing the careers of Terry, Clinton, Scott, Kelly Oliver and Carl Greaves.

Thirteen is a lucky number in Chinese astrology. Perhaps Don King was a follower of oriental mysticism because he again chose the 13th, this time of November, for the Holyfield–Lewis rematch. Eight months had passed since the first fight and I had just about come to terms with the two hundred smackers I had blown on a seat in the gods at Madison Square Garden. My credit cards were still reeling from the cost of the airfare, accommodation, shopping and sundry expenses I had incurred while in New York. This time around I saved myself a few grand and watched the fight for nothing at a mate's house in Walthamstow. King Don, ticket touts, British Airways, Footlocker and a host of other money grabbers weren't going to make a sucker out of me again. Lewis won on points and became Britain's first undisputed heavyweight champion for 102 years.

As the biting cold of the northern winter sank its gnarled teeth into the guys at the gym, the atmosphere became more and more downbeat. The amateur club was in disarray due to a civil war over coaching methods between John Naylor on one side and Richard and Tim on the other. Many of the young amateurs had abandoned the gym, attendance was down and with the bar now inoperative a rumour was going around that the gym would soon close due to financial difficulties. 'Young Dennis is saying he can't afford to run the gym,' Howard told me. 'Apparently he's the only one putting money into the place. Old Man Dennis wants out of it.'

Apart from a small hardcore of pros and diehard keep-fit fanatics, the Don Valley Sports Academy had become an empty, soulless place to train. A gym needs bodies, sweating, heaving, energetic bodies to give it lifeblood and an inspiring atmosphere. Howard was being kept in the dark and had become disheartened with the uncertainty of the gym's future and the internal politics that surrounded it. For all his efforts, which included putting in a fifty-hour week, running the gym and paying for training equipment out of his own pocket, he was paid a measly £100 a week. Howard earned peanuts considering the work he did.

Despite a growing disenchantment which had prompted him to speak in recent weeks about getting out of boxing sooner rather than later, Howard was in his element training fighters. His passion for the academic side of boxing, as opposed to the business side or politics of it, genuinely far outweighed his interest in money, fame or self-aggrandisement. His humbleness also made him a soft touch for those who would exploit him cheaply, and as a consequence he was caught in a trap – because of his loyalty to his fighters, he wouldn't go to another gym unless they went with him. But Howard was too proud to work in another trainer's gym in Sheffield, where he'd have to be second fiddle. As he couldn't afford to buy or rent his own place, he was stuck in Don

Valley. And so was I. Unless Howard found an alternative training ground, if the gym were to close in the immediate future, I was finished. I had come too far to find another trainer. Coming to Sheffield was a shit or bust move. But it was not only circumstance that made me realise that I needed Howard in order to achieve my goal. Just as he had shown faith in me and given me a chance to prove myself as a fighter, against the odds, the very least I owed him was my loyalty.

I'd hitched a ride to Grantham in Leicestershire with Howard and Simon to watch Carl Greaves make the first defence of his British Masters super-featherweight title against the journeyman of journeymen, Peter Buckley. Buckley had had well over a hundred fights, losing more than 75 per cent of them, usually on points. Buckley had the honour of being statistically one of the worst fighters in the country.

In the cramped dressing room at the Grantham Mere Leisure Centre, Carl was on the edge. During the course of the evening I popped in and out of the dressing room. Each time I returned he'd ask what the crowd was like, what the vibe at ringside was, etc. etc. I continually reassured him that everything was cool, but eventually I slipped up. 'It's been kicking off all night,' I informed him, rather unwisely. 'The bar had to close because some fella got whacked over the head with a beer barrel. Then ten geezers kicked the shit out of some guy at ringside.'

'*Fucking* hell,' said Carl, momentarily losing his cool. 'That's all I fucking need. I told 'em not to come here and cause any trouble. Wankers!'

A large number of Carl's supporters, who were Nottingham Forest fans, were having a running battle with rival Derby County supporters who had their own local hero fighting on the bill.

I left the dressing room to get an update on the situation outside. Security had managed to bring about a cease-fire between the warring factions. (The fighting did eventually end when a number of police officers from the local constabulary stormed the leisure centre.)

As promoter John Ashton was fully occupied with the problems outside the ring, I was able to join Carl's corner team to view proceedings from much closer.

During the first round I had become so transfixed by the action I had lost track of time as Carl boxed Buckley's head off, winning practically every round. He retained his title on points and extended his record to fifteen wins and two defeats.

As our posse wound its way through the throng of well-wishers, family and friends Carl got the full local hero treatment. The back-slapping, grabbing, kissing, handshakes and head rubbing he got after the fight threatened to do more damage to him than the punches he'd taken during it.

In this way, every fight, every venue and every dressing room I went to was yet another ascent on the learning curve. The different atmospheres and environments I subjected myself to were part of the conditioning process that would prepare me for my day of reckoning.

Terry Dunstan had blown off the cobwebs with a one-round technical knockout against a journeyman in a recent warm-up in London, and was about to face the durable Mancunian Carl Thompson for the vacant British cruiserweight title. Both fighters had previously held the title. Thompson, thirty-five, who had controversially lost his WBO world title to Johnny Nelson after a debatable refereeing decision, was fighting to regain what he saw as rightfully his. For both men, success meant being back in the money. Failure would mean the scrap heap.

After a few days at the house while preparing for the Thompson fight, Terry unceremoniously packed his bags and returned to the flat he shared with Nicki near the city centre. Howard wasn't happy with him being out of his reach before a big fight but nevertheless Terry travelled to London two days later to complete his training at the St Pancras Gym with seventy-three-year-old Arthur Urry, one of Howard's buddies from way back and the man who kept Terry ticking over when he was in the capital. With less than a week to go before the fight, Howard gave Terry express instructions not to spar and to take it easy in training while in London. He did not follow those instructions. The following week at the Bushfield Leisure Centre in Peterborough with fifty seconds of the twelfth round remaining, Carl Thompson knocked out Terry Dunstan to regain the British cruiserweight title. Terry had won the first six rounds of a non-stop battle with superior boxing skills, but Thompson's sheer brute strength began to tell in the latter part of the fight. In the eleventh Terry was caught on the chin by a sweeping right that sent him staggering along the ropes before hitting the floor. He took a six count and survived the round. But the *coup de grâce* came when a booming overhand right from Thompson sent him tumbling to the canvas, falling flat on his face and out for the count. Terry had lost the second fight of his professional career but this point was academic. As *Boxing News* reported after the fight, 'Terry Dunstan's big-time career was in ruins . . .' There it was in black and white. It was official. The dream was over.

chapter 31

With a couple of weeks to go before Christmas, Howard got some bad news. Progress on his running machine seemed to have stalled. Prospective investors had come and gone but so far there were no takers. Apparently, there were also problems with the wording of the running machine's patent application. After months of re-designing, new drawings, writing letters, filling in forms, sending faxes and making telephone calls, it looked as though Howard would have to start the whole arduous patent process all over again. Being an inventor was hard work, unless you were 'Big' Ned Rawlins. 'I've got five directors on board,' boomed Ned down the telephone receiver, 'we've formed a company and are awaiting the funds.' The 'funds' were something in the region of a paltry £20 billion. Raising such funds was a remarkable achievement for someone who only moments earlier confessed to have 51 pence to his name. Remarkable.

Lorna had been trying to hustle Frank Maloney once again into promoting my fight. A couple of calls earlier in the day had solicited no response but she was finally assured by his PA that if she called back at 3.30 that afternoon, Frank would be on hand to talk business. Three-thirty came and there was no Maloney. Lorna called again. Still no Maloney. Lorna got in a flap. Still no Maloney. His PA finally told Lorna that he was unable to take her call because he had in fact been in a meeting with Dennis Hobson at the appointed time. Now she was really in a flap. I told her to forget it.

'No, it's out of order,' she said, flicking through her phone book. 'I can't believe he was in a meeting with Dennis all that time. I promised Maloney first refusal on this. He hasn't got the common courtesy to get back to me and he's in a meeting with that scumbag Dennis Hobson. No, man. That's not the way to do business.'

I couldn't care less. I had a sore throat and had put in only three days' training that week. I thought I had glandular fever or tonsillitis. I felt as though I'd had an ice pick stuck in my neck. If I could've cut my head off, put it in a box and come back for it when it had got itself together, I would've done so. Physical fitness did not make you immune to life's little ball aches. In fact, it seemed the more finely tuned my body became, the more susceptible it became to odd glitches and ailments.

The Grosvenor Hotel, Sheffield, 9 December, was the time and place for Dennis Hobson's Christmas show. He put on a dinner show around this time every year. It was a sort of tradition. Clinton had long outgrown these affairs so Shaun Stokes topped the bill with Scott Lansdowne as chief support and a couple of club fighters bringing up the rear. I went for a walk with Scott a couple of hours before his fight against Geoff 'The Bounty' Hunter. He was less nervous than in his last outing and beat Hunter comfortably on points over six rounds.

For fifty quid you got three fights, flock wallpaper, Uriah Rennie (Britain's only black Premier League referee) and cream of mushroom soup, pan-fried breast of chicken with a tomato, herb, garlic, mushroom and onion sauce, seasoned vegetables and potatoes, sherried fruit trifle with cream, freshly brewed coffee and chocolate mints. Black tie was optional. John Ashton was there, squeezed into a tight, navy blue three-piece Burton suit. He looked like the broad-shouldered head of security for a provincial department store. He was much taken with Vicky's tits, which were hanging out of a tight little black number like a couple of sun-dried haggises. Seeing a promoter behaving like this, perhaps having had one too many, at a show was a rarity. Admittedly this wasn't his gig, and he was among friends, but nevertheless I'd never seen Frank Warren pinching bottoms in the aisles of the York Hall or Maloney creating his very own pavement pizza outside the Elephant and Castle Leisure Centre.

Justin, Bill and I were drinking at the bar, Bill and Justin on pints of lager, me on orange juice.

'So when's thou fighting then, Dave?' asked Bill. I went into the usual whine about having no idea, no say in the matter and no money. I must have really pushed the money side of it because Justin suggested to Bill he fix me up with a job at the factory where they worked welding industrial crushers.

'Aye, I might be able to get you a job on our firm, Dave. It'd only be labouring like, minimum wage, fucking shit work.'

I said I was that desperate I might have to take him up on the offer.

It had been a while since I had done any freelance work and as I was well behind schedule with the book, my publisher was keeping a firm grip on the purse strings, but labouring, in a factory? Nah. My days of manual labour were long gone. That said, I really was desperate, so much so I had been on Dennis's case about getting me a fight, any fight, asap. It was no good trying to talk to John Ashton about it that night. Anyway, I hardly knew him although he had tried to get chummy earlier on. I put it down to the drink.

All fighters seemed to get a raw deal, which was par for the course in the unholy trinity of fighter–manager–promoter, but better the devil you know. If I was going to get ripped off (which was a given in professional boxing), I might as well keep it in the family. The Maloney thing looked like a crock of shit, Frank Warren was a waste of time, then there was Dave Lewis who had quit Frank Warren to promote for Golden Fist (Terry's new promotional team). But why did I need to sell myself to a promoter? They should be beating a path to my door! Why did I need to jump into bed with Dennis and give him all that free publicity? As Lorna pointed out, despite the publicity I could potentially generate for the gym, I hadn't received any sponsorship from them. I had to pay my subs like everyone else. No, to hell with that. I had to go on the offensive. I was a promoter's dream. I was the man!

First thing on the Monday morning following Dennis's show, Lorna, who by now had become my *de facto* agent, called Frank Maloney to find out whether his interest in promoting me amounted to just shooting the breeze or if there was some substance to it.

'Have you had a chance to read that material I sent you, Frank?' she said. I could just make out a high-pitched squawk on the other end of the line. 'So you haven't had a chance then . . . not interested? OK, Frank. Take care. Speak to you soon, love.' Frank Maloney was out of the picture. So what if he managed Lennox Lewis. So I wouldn't get on the undercard of Lennox's first defence. So what?

Three days before Christmas I scaled 12 stone 10lb, the lightest I'd been for ten years. Weight loss was a curious business. Having reached 13 stone a couple of months earlier it was a struggle to get under that weight until one day I finally broke through to 12 stone 13lb. From then on I seemed able to shift anywhere between two and four pounds either side of 13 stone. By drinking plenty of water during a training session I could easily lose a couple of pounds and it was surprising how radically different my body shape could look not just from day to day but from morning to evening.

Justin kept telling Howard that if I lost any more weight I'd 'look like a Biafran'. I was not only muscular but sinewy, taut, hard-bodied. I now took my six-pack for granted. No, I loved my six-pack. I had a stomach like corrugated iron. I was obsessed with my 500 repetitions of stomach exercises every day – crunches, side-crunches, knee-to-chest, alternate knee-to-chest, pikes, alternate pikes, leg raises, scissors . . . Depending on how hard Howard wanted to push me on any given day, my training regime now consisted of anywhere between four (very hard) to ten (moderate) rounds of sparring; four to six rounds on the heavy bag; groundwork (as above); callisthenics; stretching exercises; skipping; and a pyramid circuit of the usual agonising floor exercises.

I came down with a bug that kept several people from the gym out of action. I had also sprained my right hand (again) so as a consequence I had not sparred for two weeks. I still didn't feel up for sparring when I got to the gym. I deliberately left my gumshield indoors so I could wriggle out of it, but as luck would have it, Tim had some for sale. Howard insisted I do a few rounds with Tim's son, Spencer, a twenty-three-year-old fireman who boxed for the amateur club. When I finally stepped into the ring with Spencer, I felt that pissed off at having to spar that I gave him a right good caning. Howard cried out the obligatory 'Oi' when things started to get heavy in the third round, after Spencer looked close to dropping. We did one more round and Spencer climbed out of the ring with a bloody nose.

'That was a good spar,' said Tim before following a disconcerted-looking Spencer into the changing room.

'I had to pull you up earlier, 'cos his old man was looking a bit worried,' Howard said later. He explained he had to placate Tim because it wasn't good form for him not to demonstrate clemency when a guy was under severe pressure. Ninety per cent of the guys I sparred with (Spencer included) had far more boxing experience than I had, so being the dominator was a rarity. Exerting power was a buzz, the submission of an opponent a moment to savour.

I chose not to moralise about boxing any more. Any ethical sensitivity I had ever possessed for the sport was long gone, destroyed by the indiscriminate virtue of the ring and the harsh environment in which I existed. I had developed a wholly libertarian view of boxing – if men chose to fight, chose to maim and be maimed, chose to die, then so be it, let it be their right. Did we not live in a society where the rights of the individual were rapidly surpassing those of the collective? As far as I was concerned there were far more noble causes to champion than the abolition of boxing. As a consequence, I no longer had any truck with the well-intentioned but nonetheless misguided opinions of the BMA and boxing's miscellaneous detractors.

It pained me that my interest in boxing had become purely mechanical. Given the lofty ideals I had set out with perhaps I had betrayed myself. But to me boxing had become simply a means to an end. I did it because I had a job to do, a task to complete. In a tangential way, through the writing of a book, boxing was how I made my living. To that end I was no different from any other man who fought for money and shed blood in order to put food on the table. I rarely read a newspaper now, apart from skimming through them occasionally for boxing stories. I had little contact with the outside world so I had little interest in it. All I watched on TV was boxing and sometimes football. I was unconcerned about famine in Africa, European monetary union or gun crime in the US. I learnt that by simplifying my outlook on life, I could survive – no more 'paralysis by analysis'. My ignorance had become a defence mechanism. I was no longer a journalist. My transition from a thinking machine to a fighting machine was almost complete.

Part Three

Looking for a fight

chapter 32

After spending an awkward Christmas Day with Lara and Luca ('it would be nice for Luca's sake'), I took off on Boxing Day for a new millennium experience in Montreal. This was my last opportunity to indulge myself in pleasures of the palate and the flesh. Soon I would be back in the gym sparring, back to the taste of fear with the bitterness of blood on my lips.

I returned to Sheffield on 3 January with a greater appreciation for the north. During the past week I had endured six-inch snow drifts and temperatures of –37 degrees in Montreal (apparently this was mild by Canadian standards) so the sleet and driving rain of an English winter were almost a welcome relief.

Howard had told me that in terms of fitness, I had a ten-day window before I would start experiencing any loss of fitness. While in Montreal I had maintained my five-mile running regime so by the time I got back into training I was still around 12 stone 10lb and fighting fit.

The New Year brought with it the same old financial problems. No sooner had I mentioned the depressing cost of Christmas, credit-card bills and January being the most popular month for suicides than Justin pipes up, 'Billy's fixed you up with a job on our firm.' My jaw hit the floor.

'You what?'

'Aye, Dave. I'll give you his number and you can sort it out yasen,' said Justin.

'But I thought he was joking, you know, you'd both had a drink.'

'You can't back out now, Dave. Billy's gone out on a limb for ya. Here's the number.'

I couldn't believe it. They'd got me a job. What was I going to do? Bill was the gaffer at the factory, which was based in the outskirts of Sheffield. I had to ring him and let him know I couldn't take the job.

'The money's right crap but the work's piss easy,' said Bill. 'You'll not have owt to do apart from a bit of sweeping up and driving a forklift truck. You can drive a forklift, can't you?'

'Yeah, sure. No problem.' What was I doing? I was talking myself into a filthy low-paid job in a fucking steel works. And the hours!

'I'll get you on, Dave. It's five twelve-hour shifts Monday to Friday. On the night shift, six while six.' Christ Almighty! Six in the evening till six in the morning.

'Is that gonna affect your training?'

'Well, it kind of makes it awkward, Bill, you know.' Here was my excuse – the hours, my training.

'I'll be down the gym tomorrow, Dave. We'll sort if out then. I gotta go now, mate. Bye.'

'Yeah, but Bill . . .' The phone went dead.

'Yeah, it'll be good for ya,' said Howard, rummaging through his locker, 'lumpin' all that steel about. It'll toughen you up.' He seemed more concerned about his latest invention than this latest twist in my career path. He was currently into a sort of ski simulator, fashioned out of two fabricated steel tracks, a metal support frame and roller-skates.

'So d'you think I should take it, then? I mean, it might not hurt to give it a go. After all, I could do with paying a few debts.'

'A bit of money in a man's pocket gives him self-respect,' said Howard. 'Besides, it'd stop you from poncing off me.' Howard walked by me and gave me a dead leg . . . for a laugh. ''Bout time you paid your fucking way. Do some real work, some man's work for a change.'

Bill arranged for me to start the following Monday. I was hoping that something might come up in the meantime, like Armageddon, to save me from my return to manual labour. I tried to kid myself that a full-time factory job combined with my training would provide me with an excellent insight into what the average low-paid professional fighter had to endure. In reality, I had taken the job because I was desperately broke. How desperate? Well, the job paid £3.62 an hour which was tuppence more than the hourly national minimum wage. The company, in its largesse, had added tuppence to the hourly minimum wage rate, just so they could say they paid more than the minimum wage. What a public relations coup!

❖   ❖   ❖

'You're not going to be able to cope with working and training, David. It's too much. And what about your book?' Lorna had been protesting all week about me taking the labouring job. I could still hear her voice ringing in my ears as I set off for the gym. I had my first day on the job to contend with that evening and I was still smarting from a blazing row I'd had with Lara the day before. Because I still lived in Sheffield, had gone 'swanning off' to Canada (i.e. I was having sex with another woman) and was not in the slightest bit interested in a reconciliation, Lara castigated me. I was, of course, a 'useless father' among other things. I had wound up rising to the bait and it went downhill from there.

Perhaps it was inevitable that living the life of a second-rate fighter would lead me to a third-rate job. Until now I'd concentrated mainly on the mechanics of boxing. Partly through lack of foresight and in part due to the emotional and physical changes I'd gone through, I hadn't concerned myself with the financial ramifications of what I had taken on. I had assumed that, given the time I had set myself to achieve my goal, the money I earned as a freelance journalist and with my publishing deal would last the duration. My schedule was, of course, all out of whack. I was at least three months away from getting a fight and as for the book . . .

So here I was working as a broom-jockey, getting my hands dirty, busting my balls for £3.62 an hour. What can I say about sweeping the floor of a sprawling factory, surrounded by overhead cranes, acetylene bottles, forklift trucks, drills, metal shavings, dust, grime, filth? It was shit. The fellas I worked with thought I was an absolute fruitcake. 'You're the most educated man on the firm,' said Gary the drill operator. 'You've got degrees and all, and you've got the worst job of the lot.' He thought it was a scream that someone like me could *want* to work in a factory.

Now I had come full circle. Having fled the incarceration of wage slavery as a gumshoe reporter I was back to being a wage slave for a company that made 32 ton Tonka toys. I was broke, miserable, discontent, my personal life was a mess, a kerfuffle of loose ends and unresolved matters with people I either cared too much about or couldn't care less for.

Trapped in the quagmire of twelve-hour shifts, I was just like the other guys on the factory floor, just like millions of ordinary folk, running in the rat race in order to stand still. In the short time I worked at the factory, I truly appreciated for the first time in years what a miserable, woeful existence many people endure. There was no love in emptying bins, sweeping up metal shavings and dirt, changing gas bottles or humping tempered steel around with back-breaking regularity.

The only respite from the tedium came at break times or when I skived in a quiet corner somewhere and wrote, read porno mags or caught forty winks. Manual labour? Slave labour more like. What a waste of time and energy it is. As long as the working classes had an eye on the rich, as long as there was *Hello!*, bingo, the lottery and 'Who Wants to be a Millionaire', there would be fighters. Boxing thrives on the desires of young men who can see across the tracks but cannot reach the promised land on the other side. It fuels the burning ambitions of those who can smell success but cannot taste it.

I wished even more that I could turn my back completely on boxing and rid myself of all the baggage it carried with it but I had dug myself a hole and I couldn't get out. I was in too deep. If anyone had bothered to ask me where I was going, all I could've said was, 'I'll tell you when I get there'. I felt as though nobody appreciated what I was going through, or if they did they could not or would not reach out. I was locked inside my own thoughts, unable to articulate my frustration without sounding completely bonkers. All right, with hindsight (oh you beautiful thing, you) perhaps I had bitten off more than I could chew. But here I was. Maybe this depression was what you had to experience to be a pro. Maybe you had to be stripped of your dignity, pride and privacy, be cut down to your base self to have that desperate hunger you see in the eyes of a fighter.

Somewhere out there was an unknown opponent, a man with hopes and dreams, fears and resignation, and loved ones, perhaps mouths to feed, just like me. Neither of us knew we were on a trajectory towards each other, paths laid by fate which would soon cross with potentially lethal consequences.

'Ten weeks – eight to ten weeks – and we'll have you out,' said Howard as he took off my sweaty gloves after another hard sparring session with Scott. I couldn't believe what I was hearing. We were talking in weeks now. Finally, there was a light at the end of the tunnel. Howard said he was putting the feelers out for a light-heavyweight opponent. 'I'll get a couple o' lads to go down to the cemetery and dig someone up for ya,' he joked.

I had never leaned heavily on Howard to put me in the ring even when the frustration of waiting ate at me like a cancer. Lorna would occasionally whisper in his ear, remind him of the pressure I was under and try to influence him. 'I know how you feel, Dave. I've been there myself,' said Howard when I told him the frustration was driving me over the edge. 'But I've learnt that there are certain things you have to wait for . . . patiently. Twelve months from now you'll look back at this time and wonder what all the fuss was about. Trust me.' Hmm . . .

Men in boxing dealt with a curious mixture of emotions – guilt, resentment, anger, rage, love, honour, respect – but overriding them all was trust. The whole concept of boxing hinged on trust, personal and professional. Without it, discipline was lost. Without discipline anarchy reigned, which was intolerable even in the brutal freewheeling world of boxing. I trusted Howard. He trusted me. I knew this because he gave me a shot when all others showed me the door.

I make no bones about the fact that for most of my life I have been a useless bum. As a natural cynic I have never tried too hard at anything I've turned my hand to and for many years I have never had any real sense of direction or purpose. I've had tough times when all I had in my pockets were holes. There were occasions when waking up in the morning was like staring down the barrel of a loaded gun, and wrapping a rope around my neck seemed like the only way out. But deep down I always knew that things weren't that bad. I would always bail myself out of trouble somehow, and come up smelling of roses. I've always been one of those people who could get away with it.

But I have never proved myself. Some time ago I made a contract with my soul to do something with my life, to mean something, to make a change. Don't ask me why. All I know is that one of my greatest fears is to go out to pasture as a consummate underachiever. Better to have tried and failed and all that. I have a dear old friend who was educated at public school, has a minor aristocratic genealogy and a stately mien. And what is he? He's a bum, that's what, a junky bum. But does he care? Of course not. He's not the son of poor immigrants, a product of oppression, a descendant of slaves. He can trace his ancestors back to the Domesday Book. But I can't. He has nothing to prove but I guess I do.

Lorna was right. I couldn't cope with working and training. After two weeks on the job, I quit. The routine was insufferable. I would start work at 6 p.m. then finish at 6 a.m. Thankfully one of my workmates lived near me so I'd get a lift home in the morning. I'd get in, fix myself a light breakfast (or was it dinner?) and fall into bed by 6.45 a.m.

Around one o'clock in the afternoon, I'd get up (having struggled to sleep through daylight), wash, get changed and have lunch (or was it breakfast?). I'd leave the house at two, get to the gym at three, train (badly) until five, grab a sandwich (if I had time) and start work again at six. My schedule was so tight I barely found the time to fart. I had no idea when the day began and when it ended. My new working arrangement also brought conflict with Lara because it meant I was unable to be in London on Saturdays. This meant Lara couldn't do her part-time shop job or her feng shui. As a consequence, she was reluctant to let me see Luca on Sundays only, so we reached an impasse over access which led to a total breakdown in communication.

chapter 33

On 1 February 2000, I finally signed a management contract with Howard. I still had no promoter, no date for a fight and no opponent but at least I had a manager. Lorna had arranged my brain scan and an eye test for later in the week, and crucially she had made an appointment for me to see the Central Area Council of the Board at the end of the month to submit my licence application. At last I felt as though I was making real progress.

'Sorry we haven't got any champagne, love. How about a cup of tea?' Lorna was in her element, being a busy-bee, making arrangements and fussing about. Howard just sat there, laid back as usual.

'Come on, Howard, make an effort,' said Lorna dishing out the teas.

'Er . . . what?'

'Well this is a big moment for the boy.'

'Is it?' I said.

The contract was a standard agreement approved by the British Boxing Board of Control. Under the Board's rules, the agreement was conditional upon me gaining a boxer's licence within sixty days and Howard holding a manager's licence. As well as being a licensed trainer, Howard also held a manager's licence. Everything in boxing is licensed. Even an MC has to be licensed.

The maximum period of any one contract between a boxer and his manager is three years. There is no minimum period. We agreed that the contract should be for a year. Howard signed, I signed, Lorna and Jane, the nextdoor neighbour, signed as witnesses to the signing. I didn't bother reading the contract.

'You know you've just signed your life away there, boy,' said Lorna, rubbing her hands. 'You haven't even read the terms.'

'I trust you guys implicitly,' I said.

The telephone rang. It was Paul Dorking the hypnotist.

'Hi Paul. I just signed a contract with Howard to manage me . . . Yeah . . . He gets eighty-five per cent of everything and I get a whole fifteen per cent. Can you believe it! I get fifteen per cent. What a result!'

This was of course a joke. In reality, Howard was entitled to 35 per cent of my purse – 10 per cent as my trainer and 25 per cent as my manager although under his £1000+ rule, he stood to earn sweet Fanny Adams.

Originally, I had wanted to make a song and dance about my fight. I had a fantasy that coachloads of people I knew would descend on the venue come fight night, all shouting and screaming their support for me. I figured with all the people I knew, friends, family, business associates and a bit of hype surrounding my rather novel entrée into pro boxing, I could shift 200, maybe 300, tickets. The traditional deal between small-hall promoters and fighters was that in addition to the paltry purse you earned, you got a 10 per cent cut of the tickets you sold.

'Howard and I have discussed this and we think it's better for you not to concern yourself with selling loads of tickets,' said Lorna, handing me another cup of tea. 'You're under enough pressure as it is, love. You only need to invite a few of your closest friends.'

'But what about all that lovely lolly I can earn from the tickets?'

'Just concentrate on the fight. Waj Khan from the gym had no support at his debut apart from his brother.'

Great fighters don't just have a gifted ability to fight. They also have an immense capacity to publicise their ability to fight. How would the world know, in vivid colour, that I was the real deal unless hordes of people were there to witness it?

Two days later I travelled to the Claremont Hospital in a leafy suburb of Sheffield for my MRI and MRA brain scans. The purpose of the scans was to detect any neurological abnormalities. A negative brain scan would almost certainly bar me from obtaining a licence. When I reached the hospital I filled out a few forms and was whisked immediately into the scanning area.

The scanner was an impressive piece of kit that looked like one of those cryogenic pods you see in sci-fi movies. The nurse gave me some earplugs and suggested I wear them as things would 'soon get a little noisy'. She laid a paper sheet down on what looked like a sunbed and I laid on top of this, resting my head on a firm plastic support. She placed a guard similar to those worn by hockey players over my face and disappeared from the scanning room, reappearing in a control room behind a large glass partition. I craned my head forward and made out the nurse in front of a control panel of sorts and some PCs. She twiddled a few knobs and I felt myself lower by about six inches, then I slowly glided into the claustrophobic atmosphere of the scanner's main housing.

A loud steady banging started, slowly at first, then the tempo changed and for the next few minutes I was subjected to around 200bpm of what sounded like techno bass. I could hear the muffled sound of the nurse telling me to keep still. I glided out of the scanner and she came back into the scanning room.

'You haven't got a metal plate in your head, have you?' she asked.

'No,' I replied. 'Just a few gold teeth.'

'OK,' she said and returned to her control room. I glided back into the scanner.

For the second wave of the MRI scan, the beat was faster, higher pitched and more resonant than before. I felt like a battery inside a giant vibrator as the scanner hummed and whirred. In total the scan must have lasted around ten minutes or so. Then came the MRA.

'This'll take a little bit longer,' the nurse warbled. 'Keep exactly still now.'

The beat was hard, loud but thankfully pacified by the earplugs. It thumped, it boomed, alternating in tone and pitch. Through all this I zoned out, kept my eyes shut and escaped in my thoughts. I visualised the fight, having sex, discovering I had a brain tumour . . . After about fifteen minutes it was all over.

'What was all that about a metal plate?' I asked the nurse.

'Hmm . . . yes, that was strange. Oh, it's probably nothing.'

'There weren't any complications, were there?'

'No. Not from what I could see. You should be all right. I'll send the results to the Board today.'

The fee for the brain scans was £150 although this was not immediately payable as the Board ran a scheme that allowed a fighter to pay it off in instalments from his first three fights. As I was only having the one fight I would have to settle the balance with them straight out of my pocket at some stage. The procedure was that the hospital gave the results to the Board not to the licence applicant. Obviously, if there were any problems they'd let me know. I'd soon find out if thirteen years of using a mobile phone had taken its toll.

From the Claremont I raced across town to Meadowhall shopping mall for my eye test. I told the receptionist I had an appointment for a test for a boxing licence application. She seemed impressed.

'We get a lot of boxers in here,' she cooed. 'Oh yes, we get them all. Prince Naseem Hamed comes here for his eye test, oh yes. Very nice man. Not like he is on TV.' After a ten-minute wait I was led into a small consulting room and saw a young, balding, bespectacled optician who gave me a thorough ophthalmic examination.

'You've got a slight prescription, but it'd be a sin to give you glasses,' he said, adding that my vision was basically 20/20. He produced a small torch from his shirt pocket and told me he had one last test to perform, an examination of my retinas. He asked me to look up, down, and side to side as he shone the intense light into both eyes. He seemed to be labouring with this particular test.

'Hmm . . . ,' he said, frowning. 'I'm a bit concerned about your left retina.'

'What's the problem?' I could feel a wave of anxiety coming on.

'Well, your left retina has some fading. It's thinner, lighter than your right retina. As I have never examined you before I don't know whether it's simply an anomaly unique to you or something that has occurred over time. Because of the nature of what you do, it gives me some cause for concern. I think I'm going to have to get a second opinion on this. Hang on.'

Shit. I had an eye problem. Jesus. Was I going blind? The optician seemed really concerned. Having already filled out part of my licence application form, if he didn't countersign it I'd be stuck, unless I got another form, had another doctor's examination and sweet-talked another optician into giving me the nod. He returned.

'I've spoken to my colleague and she agrees with me. I think you should see a specialist. We don't have the facilities here to give you a proper diagnosis. I can recommend a consultant who can do it for you. It's a simple test, only takes a minute.'

I had to play this carefully. I sensed the optician wanted to do the right thing by me, but I could also see he had a lot of integrity. He told me that there was a slim chance that the retina could become detached. A more thorough examination would determine if I needed an operation to prevent this happening. I needed him to sign that form, but I didn't want to appear too anxious and frighten him. I wondered how many young men with 'anomalies' had been waved through or given the nod on various medical examinations only to encounter a major problem while boxing. Had the thinning come from boxing? My left eye was of course my lead eye, the one that had taken the most battering over the months. And what about that knockdown? It had certainly temporarily impaired my vision. Even if I convinced the optician to pass me, what level of risk would I be taking with a thinning retina? My eyes were my life. I couldn't afford to wind up like Harry Greb. (Out of 299 professional fights, Greb fought 92 bouts while blind in one eye. Despite his impediment, he beat Johnny Wilson for the world middleweight title in 1923.)

'As it is, the retina is not detached. If there was an immediate problem with it you wouldn't have passed some of the other eye tests. If it became detached while you were boxing, well, your vision would become blurred. You'd have to stop and get it sorted out.'

I smiled cherubically, willing him to take pity on me. Fuck it. It was my health, I'd take the risk.

'I tell you what. I'll sign your form. But I'm going to write a referral for you to give to your GP so you can get that eye checked out. OK?'

I thanked him, took the referral, paid the £17.50 and got the hell out of there before he changed his mind.

chapter 34

In the space of two years, I had shed 42lb. I could now move from 12 stone 12lb to 12 stone 7lb in a matter of hours. From morning to evening, I could lose or gain five pounds. I had weight loss down to a tee.

I received a 'care package' from Canada courtesy of Sass Brown, something to cheer me up as the days plodded on. There was B compound, vitamin C and vials of ginseng and royal jelly, Rubin 'Hurricane' Carter's autobiography, *The Sixteenth Round*, and a video nasty of no-rules martial arts called 'The Ultimate Fighting Championship: Judgement Day'. Sass really knew how to look after a guy.

To have a competitive edge I couldn't rely on just the usual workout and a big breakfast, so the extra vitamins and supplements were a help. My diet was basically based on eating the best that we could afford in the house. Sometimes this meant salmon steaks, vegetables Julienne and a Caesar salad. Often it was pie and mash. The key to dieting was not only eating foods with a high nutritional value but also things with a high feel-good value. A little bit of comfort food was necessary to deal with life's stresses and as self-reward. I just had to remember not to overdo it. My comfort foods were chocolate, Coca-Cola, rice pudding, bowls of cereal, peanut butter on toast and, most of all, apple pie and custard. At times I got hung up about food, memorising the fat, protein and carbohydrate content of different food stuffs. For instance, I knew that per 100g, a Snickers bar had 17.6g of fat, a Flyte 6.7g, and a Tesco prosciutto pizza had 36.8g of carbohydrates per 100g (of which 7.8g were sugars). Whenever Lorna and Howard got heavy about my eating habits I'd keep a supply of goodies including chocolate bars, biscuits and Ambrosia creamed rice stashed under my bed. Low-fat creamed rice contains 0.8g of fat per 100g by the way.

I've always had a sweet tooth and for the first few months I lived with the Raineys I tried to adapt to using the artificial sweetener Howard took because of his diabetes. Ironically, however, I found that I lost more weight when I reverted to my beloved sugar in tea and on cereal and ate chocolate regularly. I was fortunate in that I had a metabolism that could cope with high doses of sugar. Now that my fitness level was high I found that, aside from the obvious daily sports diet requirement of plenty of carbohydrates, fresh fruit and vegetables and several litres of water, diet was subjective and very individual.

One of my latest sparring partners, a super-middleweight called Jon Penn, survived on a daily diet of a malt loaf, a bowl of cereal, a banana, a salad and a jacket potato with baked beans so he could maintain a weight of 12 stone. I could eat that for breakfast and still feel peckish. Howard reckoned that a human being could survive quite comfortably on a diet of wholemeal bread, bananas and orange juice for his entire life. I think he'd been watching too much Discovery Channel lately.

As I wrapped up another day's training, I heard Howard mention something to Scott about Kelly Oliver fighting in four weeks' time at a show in Peterborough. He looked at me pensively.

'Nah, too soon,' he said. He walked over to the doorway between the gym and the changing rooms, his favourite spot for a cigarette, and lit up a Sovereign. 'D'you reckon he'll be ready in eight weeks?' he said to Scott, nodding in my direction. Scott pursed his lips and nodded back enthusiastically.

'Oh yeah, for sure, Howard.'

Howard pulled me to one side and said he was going to talk to John Ashton, about getting me a fight. He said he wanted me to go with someone who had a connection with the gym. Dennis Hobson was an obvious choice but Howard felt he was not the right person to do business with. Dave Lewis was a possibility. He was on the level but Howard felt he didn't have a large enough pool of fighters to get me a 'decent' opponent. Frank Maloney was a waste of time because Lennox Lewis was now taking so much of his attention. That left Ashton and, all things considered, I had no problem with him.

The shark-infested waters of boxing offer little salvation for those who fall overboard. In many respects, skulduggery is par for the course in a business where some of the leading players perfected their negotiating skills in the penitentiaries of America's deep south or while hedging their bets on illicit, bare-knuckle fights in disused warehouses in Essex. What do people expect? Men who pit other men against each other in a contest of violence are hardly role models for students of ethical business. The 'fuck merchants', as one journeyman once described them to me, are in the business of ripping people off. Shifty business is a central tenet of professional boxing. But for all the talk of fighters being in the business for money, most had little or no comprehension of what they earned, how they earned it and where the pounds they fought for went.

The popular view is that managers and promoters rip fighters off. They take advantage of simple men who lack the foresight and education to keep tabs on financial details such as earnings, expenses and tax. The suits who control boxing would argue that 30 per cent of something is a whole lot better than 100 per cent of nothing. Fighters could take it or leave it.

I once heard an allegory somewhere that sums up what promoters are like: a traveller was walking through the desert when he came across a rattlesnake in distress. The rattlesnake looked up at the traveller and said, 'Please help me. I've got a thorn in my side and it's killing me.' The traveller took pity on the snake and pulled out the thorn. Suddenly, the snake bit the traveller, releasing a deadly venom. 'Why did you do that? I just saved your life!' cried the traveller. 'What did you expect?' replied the slippery serpent. 'I'm a rattlesnake for God's sake.'

After months of waiting, frustration, despair and desperation, the end was finally in sight. The feelers were out. I sensed the end was near.

I had become surly and angry, and ill-at-ease with myself. I was agitated and on edge. Things were out of my hands. There were whispers, late-night telephone calls, trips to boxing shows to which I was not invited. Names of possible opponents were bandied around within earshot but I was being kept in the dark. I became quiet and withdrawn. Introspective and economical with what I said and to whom I said it, as though I felt the need to conserve as much energy, as much of my *chi*, as possible. I hated a lot of people right then.

There had been a lot of tension in the gym in recent weeks. Its future was still in the balance and attendance for the amateur club and the kick-boxing classes kept undulating which added to the atmosphere of uncertainty. Carl Greaves had given up training with Howard citing the daily hundred-mile round trip between Newark and Sheffield as insufferable. Shaun Stokes finally made his comeback only to retire again after losing to a journeyman. Topping the same bill, Clinton made another successful defence of his European title in front of a home crowd against the exotically named Spanish champion

King Dongo, which led to the announcement that he would fight former three-time world champion Michael Nunn in a world title eliminator. The prize for the victor was a showdown with Roy Jones Jr, the WBA, WBC and IBF undisputed light-heavyweight champion of the world. For Clinton Woods to step into the ring with Roy Jones was like the man in the street stepping on to the surface of the moon. When I first met Clinton a year ago, when he first won his triple crown, he had just signed off the dole and caught the bus to the gym. Now he was a matter of months away from fighting the pound-for-pound best fighter on the planet and earning a six-figure sum for his retirement fund.

I was curious about what strategy Howard would have Clinton adopt if he met the formidable Roy Jones. Here was a man who had had over forty professional fights and a near-perfect record but for a dubious disqualification. He once played a professional basketball match one afternoon, boxed later that evening and won at a canter.

'If Clinton fought Roy Jones,' said Howard, 'I'd tell him to treat it like a three-round fight. He'd have three rounds to try to knock him out and then after that I'd pull him out the moment he got into trouble.'

This was real *Rocky* stuff. In a matter of months Clinton had gone from zero to hero. It was dreams of success like this that fired the imagination of every hungry young fighter who wanted to make it. But what about me, what about my dreams? I'd played the fight out a thousand times in my mind, ten thousand, a hundred thousand. I fantasised about the glory at the end of the fight, stepping out of the ring and being embraced, celebrated, lionised. I'd wallow in the deluge of praise, accolades and recognition of my accomplishment. My ego would truly have landed. I would finally have the unconditional respect of my peers. I would be the thing, that crazy, hard, dangerous thing I set out to become – a professional fighter.

Behind every fantasy, every dream, however, is the nightmare. I played the nightmare out a thousand times, ten thousand times, a hundred thousand times. I'd be a liar to say the thought of losing never crossed my mind. In the nightmare I'm helped out of the ring. I'm unsteady on my feet having been knocked out. I got one, maybe two, rounds into the fight and got caught with a big, I mean *big* right hand over the top. CRASH! I'm out cold. I come round in a daze. I don't know how many seconds have passed. I'm *helped* out of the ring and I'm embraced, commiserated with, consoled. My bubble has burst. I drown in a cesspool of self-pity. My peers confirm what they always thought would happen and lose their respect for me. I would be the thing, that crazy, pathetic, embarrassing thing I hoped I'd never become – a professional loser.

For the past year my life had been a dream and occasionally a nightmare but that was all about to change. On 21 February I called Howard at the gym to double-check on the time he wanted me in for sparring.

'I want you in the gym straightaway,' said Howard sternly. 'I might have a date for you – 9 April in Alfreton. It's a Sunday afternoon show. D'you reckon you can do tickets for that?'

'Sure,' I said. 'Where the bloody hell is Alfreton?'

'Near Derby.'

'Sure, no problem.' I put the phone down. So now I had a date. Sunday, 9 April 2000. D-day.

The news brought both relief and frustration in equal measure. The relief came from finally having a fight date and knowing that a conclusion was probably near. The frustration came from knowing that the next seven weeks, the next forty-nine days, or 1,176 hours, or 70,560 minutes, or 4,233,600 seconds, would seem like an eternity.

Mark Krence, a cruiserweight prospect who had been training at the gym for a couple of months, was also due to make his pro debut on the same show. That was where the similarities between Mark and me ended. He was a twenty-three-year-old in the prime of life, six foot five and a former ABA champion. I, as you have gathered, was none of these. Mark and I had done a lot of sparring together and in a way it was fitting that we should both be making our debuts on the same show. Howard didn't seem to think so. 'Two fucking pro debuts on the same show. I'm on a right earner, aren't I?'

chapter 35

Hilton Hotel, Huddersfield, Sunday, 27 February 2000. I had awaited the meeting with the Central Area Council of the British Boxing Board of Control with a great sense of anxiety. According to Lorna, technically, I could be denied a licence only on medical grounds. I'd passed all the necessary tests, paid the fee, and trained with one of the best coaches in the country, so I had a highly respected and qualified man to vouch for me. Howard was also a friend of the chairman of the Board, so what could go wrong? Everything now hinged on me getting that licence. If my application failed that was it. More than two years of research and a year of training would be down the tubes. When it came to the fight, I could handle winning or losing, but not to get the opportunity would be crushing.

The meeting was to be held in the ground floor conference room of the hotel. The appointment was for 3.45 p.m. I arrived with Howard and Lorna at 3.43 p.m. Three other guys were waiting ahead of me. One I recognised as Geoff 'The Bounty' Hunter, the heavyweight journeyman whom Scott had beaten at Dennis's Christmas show. Hunter had lost eight fights on the bounce and now the Board were getting a little concerned about his poor performances. The second fella in the queue was also on a losing streak and facing suspension, and the other chap was applying for a second's licence. Fighter number two had red blotches all over his face and down his neck. I had to ask. 'I suffer from nerves,' he said. 'It's a nervous rash.' If he was like this for a routine meeting, what was he like when he . . . 'When I fight, though, I'm all right. I just can't stand owt like this.' Fear. There it was again.

I'd had to overcome so many hurdles to get to this stage. Test after test had followed doubt after frustration after false start. I had to get that licence. But if I didn't get it I had a contingency plan. I'd quick step it across the Irish channel and get myself the necessary paperwork in County Kilkenny or some place like that where they didn't give a stuff about trifling details like brain tumours and detached retinas. Alternatively, I'd head for some banana republic where they operated chequebook bureaucracy. I'd bung the appropriate official eight billion pesos (equivalent to £17.50 sterling) and bribe my way into the professional ranks.

The three men ahead of me were summoned one by one. Each disappeared through the large teak double doors into the conference room while the rest of us waited anxiously, and similarly they reappeared outside to await the verdict of the Council. Hunter got his result first: upon condition of getting himself a manager and providing his next couple of fights were four-rounders, he would keep his licence. Similar conditions applied to the second fighter. The third man met all the requirements of the Board and was granted a second's licence. Now it was my turn.

A head poked round the door. 'David Matthews, please.' I walked into the conference room with Howard in tow for moral support. Once inside I was taken aback by the number of people present. I was expecting around half a dozen. There were at least twenty. They were seated around a U-shaped configuration of desks. I looked round and noticed some familiar faces – Johnny Nelson the WBO cruiserweight king; his trainer Brendan Ingle and his wife; Junior 'The Hitter' Witter, another one of Brendan's boys. In fact, half the Council seemed to comprise Brendan Ingle acolytes.

'You don't mind if I sit in, do ya?' said Howard humbly.

'No, no,' said the Chairman, Trevor Callighan. 'Take a seat please, Mr Matthews.' I sat down directly opposite the Chairman, about twenty feet away. I could see now why the others had been so nervy. It was an intimidating environment. All eyes were on me. These people had the power, the authority to say 'yea' or 'nay'. I wanted to look confident but not arrogant. I focused on the Chairman, sat upright but not too rigid in my seat and tried to adopt the attitude my attire suggested – smart but casual.

The Chairman prattled on about the nature of boxing and asked me if I sought to make a career of boxing. I said, 'Yes,' then he asked me some basic questions about my contract. Did I understand it? Did I have a manager? What was the maximum length of a contract between a manager and a boxer? What percentage of my purse was my manager entitled to? I gave my responses and then the Chairman invited the Board to ask their own questions.

'Why do you want to become a professional boxer?' asked Johnny Nelson. I gave him some fanny about wanting to realise an ambition that I'd always had etc. etc. Howard went to make a comment and the Chairman cut him down in his tracks.

'Howard. Do you mind? We'd like to hear what the boxer has to say for himself.'

'Right oh. I was going to . . .'

'Never mind, Howard,' said the Chairman. I thought these guys were buddies.

A chubby fella who looked like an accountant asked, 'Why have you decided to do this aged thirty-two?' I waffled on about work and education getting in the way of an ambition I've always had etc. etc. The Chairman asked if there were any more questions. There were none.

'If we are to grant you a boxer's licence,' said the Chairman with greater authority, 'and it's still if at this stage, because you have no amateur record to speak of, we would need to see proof of your competence as a boxer. Do you understand?'

'Yes, I understand,' I said.

'Right. Well, to do this we may require you to undergo a trial bout in front of the Board, so we can see that you're able to protect yourself and won't embarrass yourself in the ring. Are you with me?'

'Yes.'

'Right. Could you please wait outside while we discuss the matter.'

'Yes. Thank you.' I nodded and bowed out of the room.

'How did it go, how did it go?' asked Lorna.

'It's looking a bit dicey,' I said. 'They're not going to give it to me. I knew it. I fucking knew it.'

The minutes ticked away as I waited for the decision, waited to see if I would become, as Tyrone had put it months earlier, 'licensed to kill'. The idea seemed reprehensible. Somehow I could, potentially, walk in off the street as a professional fighter and within minutes kill a man with my bare hands. I shuddered to think that, at this moment, someone somewhere may have that idea in mind for me, an unknown competitor who, while maybe a genial sort of fellow at heart, reserved a nugget of bad intent in his soul, just enough hatred to keep him motivated.

One of the most nerve-racking moments had to be going for that licence. I've never been a great fan of tests, perhaps because I've never been particularly enamoured of criticism. Scott Welch's conditioner, Ian Allcock, once tried to steal my thunder by going through every worst-case scenario of my licence application. 'You do know you've got a load of tests to go through, mate?' he said, trying to sound as dour as possible. 'What if you fail your medical? I mean, what if they find a shadow on your brain? Or there's a problem with your eyes? Suppose you fail the AIDS test, what are you going to do then? All that work . . . it's down the drain then, ain't it?'

I tried to explain that not making it to the ring would probably be the least of my worries if I discovered I had a brain tumour or had AIDS but the irony was lost on Ian somehow. Despite his skewed logic, Ian did have a point. I'd come this far, what if I fell at the last hurdle? Where would I go from here? A head poked round the door again.

'Mr Matthews.' I walked in and sat down expecting bad news.

'We've decided to grant you a licence on this one condition,' said the Chairman, raising his index finger like a headmaster, 'that you undertake a trial bout so we can see that you can handle yourself. As long as everything goes well you'll get your licence. If it doesn't, you'll have to come back. Are you all right with that?'

'Yeah, sure. I'm happy to do that,' I said. I'd made it. Just.

'Where and when do you want to do this?' asked Howard.

'Anywhere that suits you,' said the Chairman. 'Give me a call and we'll sort it out.'

We said our thank yous and bid the council farewell.

With hindsight, I could have handled the application slightly differently. For one I wouldn't have allowed Dr Singh to have put 'journalist' on my medical form under 'occupation'. Journalist is the kiss of death. I may as well have put 'spy', 'grass' or 'estate agent' such is the general opinion of us hacks. In the event, I had to blank out the offending word with Tipp-Ex and write 'unemployed' in its place. (OK, unemployment isn't strictly an 'occupation' but when you've freelanced for as long as I have, the two often mean one and the same thing.)

My attitude has always been this regarding my position as journalist on this assignment: I've always been open about what I was up to and never hid my professional credentials or my motivations for becoming a fighter from anyone in or outside boxing. In fact, I always came clean as soon as a stranger asked the inevitable 'how long have you been boxing?' or 'how many fights have you had? or 'when's your next fight?' question.

'There's that many people know who you are now, mate,' said Howard after the meeting, 'that I think they're on to you.'

Yes, I sensed the Council was on to me the moment I walked through the door. They knew the script. When I met Brendan in the dressing room after the Mark Prince fight in Germany I had given him the spiel about the book. Surely he remembered me? Then there was his boy Johnny Nelson, he knew what I was up to; and there were at least a couple of other faces I had seen along the way at the fights or in gyms whom I had spoken to and knew my background. If any of them had asked me what I did for a living, I would have told them straight. I never set out to write an exposé on the 'murky world of professional boxing' (I value my front teeth too much for that). If anything, by giving me a licence they were doing themselves a massive favour. I'd be an ambassador for the sport. I'd shed light where there was previously only darkness. I'd give the Board and the sport of boxing something to be proud of, a written testament to the manly art of self-defence, an ode to the sweet science of boxing, a eulogy to the . . .

Jesus, all I wanted was the bloody licence. The Board was broke anyway. They needed all the dough they could get. In pre-war Britain there were between three and four thousand registered professional fighters. Today there were scarcely three or four hundred. By giving them £35 I was doing them a favour. Yes, the Board needed all the dough they could get. Back in September the High Court ruled that the Board had a duty of care towards Michael Watson, who in 1991 at White Hart Lane collapsed in the eleventh round of a world super-middleweight title fight against Chris Eubank. Watson was left with brain damage. Now the Board were looking at a payout of up to £1 million in damages and facing bankruptcy.

As we sat in the bar mulling over the afternoon's events, a young fighter emerged from the conference room shaking his head and cursing. I'd once seen him at the gym. He was a talented fighter, a former protégé of Brendan Ingle, and had visited Howard with a view to convincing him to take him on. Howard had heard that the kid was difficult and politely declined to work with him.

'They're fucking out of order, man,' said the fighter. 'All I want to do is change me name and they won't let me do it.' The fighter implied that there was something racist about their decision to prohibit him from changing the name that he fought under. It seemed petty that they should not grant his wish but I put it down to personal politics rather than a right-wing conspiracy.

Racism is endemic in British society. So are bad teeth, queuing and, if the media is to be believed, child molesting. Some fighters certainly had a racist element, primarily among their supporters. But considering the racial dynamics of the sport there existed a curious alliance between blacks and whites. The ideal was that fighters were fighters regardless of colour and for the most part this was my experience. I wouldn't be so naïve as to think that boxing was a paragon of racial harmony but whatever racist views fighters held they kept them to themselves or at least within a tight circle of like-minded people. The brand of racism inherent in boxing is largely the consequence of class and economics. In Britain, white promoters exploit black fighters simply because there are an overwhelming number of white promoters in relation to black fighters. Don King watchers could argue that in the US promoters run an equal opportunities policy when it comes to exploitation.

Back in the bad old days of 1929 when the British Boxing Board of Control was formed, regulation 24, paragraph 27 of the Board's constitution was modified so that the qualifying criterion for fighters contesting a British title was 'of white parents' instead of 'of British nationality'. The amendment was made with the apparent approval of the Earl of Lonsdale, the man who gives his name to British boxing's highest accolade. It seems strange that boxing was one of the last sports in this country to disband the colour bar considering the racial mix of it today. Without a doubt, though, there still exists a pecking order, and its simplicity makes the power and economic divisions of the sport all the clearer and more brutal. White men in suits run boxing – period. But then white men in suits run everything. So what's new?

chapter 36

It was 2 March 2000. Howard had been stalling about the details of the Alfreton show for days. With less than six weeks to go to the fight, I still didn't have an opponent. I knew deep down Howard wanted more time to work with me. I suspected he felt pressured, not just by me, but also by Lorna, who had been lobbying for months on my behalf to get the issue straightened out. Getting any sense out of Howard when it came to business was a waste of time, so in her capacity as my (unlicensed) agent Lorna started dealing with Ashton.

This was the deal: I'd get £500 for the fight (£100 over the going rate for a debuting fighter) plus a 10 per cent commission on whatever tickets I sold. It wasn't a fortune but better than nothing; better than what some fighters in Indonesia earned, which was the equivalent of £2 a round and a bonus for winning. The tickets would come in denominations of £20, £30 and £50 ringside 'with VIP buffet'. Ashton warned Lorna that at the very least I had to cover my opponent's and my wages, otherwise the fight was off. I therefore had to sell £1,000 worth of tickets to break even. I immediately set about contacting friends and acquaintances by telephone and email, getting them to spread the word, and started drawing up a list of potential ticket sales.

I got on to my old mate Ned to see if he could shift a wedge of tickets. He had called on a number of occasions trying to talk me out of fighting in Alfreton and, much to my disappointment, was not very forthcoming. He said he had a promoter in London who could put me on in front of a sell-out crowd. He suggested (accurately) that many of my so-called friends and supporters would not be prepared to travel north for the fight. The convenience of a London venue meant more supporters, i.e. more ticket sales, i.e. more money. In theory, all this talk of increased ticket sales, champagne flowing and wads of £50 notes was fine, but I had a bird in the hand. I sensed that Howard was slowly coming around to Ned's way of thinking, and that was dangerous. One of the few criticisms I could make of Howard was that I felt he often procrastinated too much. For a man who used to gamble on cliff faces as a rock climber, he had mellowed into someone who found it difficult to take risks, even when the brunt of those risks were shouldered by another. I reiterated to Howard that for the sake of a few hundred pounds and appeasing the interests of Ned and a bunch of people about whom I really couldn't give a toss, I would carry on as planned and fight on the ninth.

There were so many tiny details to consider. What was I going to wear for the fight? What about a nickname? Terry had come up with a nickname of sorts for me. He had a nickname for everybody. Hagler he called me after 'Marvelous' Marvin on account of my shaved head. I shaved my head regularly, down to the scalp. That dreaded bald patch was getting so big, I looked like a Benedictine monk if I let it grow for too long.

Creating a punchy epithet was a serious business. Howard had dubbed Terry the 'Vauxhall Cavalier' by virtue of his hometown of Vauxhall, south London and being, well, cavalier. Howard said as Terry never got a free car from General Motors, the owners of Vauxhall, the name never stuck. Old Man Dennis had come up with 'The President' for Clinton, but that never stuck, either. Then we had 'Cool' Carl Greaves, Mark 'The Butcher' Krench (in deference to his day job) and my personal favourite, Jon 'Mightier Than The Sword' Penn. I played around with some names myself and bounced a few ideas off friends in London but they still couldn't get their heads round me boxing and came up with ridiculous suggestions such as 'Crusher' or 'Rocky'.

The Americans had the right idea when it came to nicknames. They were nasty like John 'The Beast' Mugabe; macabre like Thomas 'The Hitman' Hearns or Bernard 'The Executioner' Hopkins; proclamatory like Evander 'The Real Deal' Holyfield; or fancy Dan like 'Sugar' Ray Leonard or Mark 'Too Sharp' Johnson.

I couldn't decide whether I wanted to do the satin gown routine or the towel with a hole over the head routine, à la Mike Tyson. These were important details to be considered. I also had to think about the music I wanted to enter the arena to.

'I always wanted Terry to come out to "Well I'm the king of the swingers, the jungle VIP . . . " ' Howard gave a poor rendition of the tune and then lit up a cigarette. I gave it some thought but discounted it on the grounds that it was just too plain stupid. One of Howard's former fighters, Paul 'Scrap Iron' Ryan, used to come out to a recording of the rag and bone song 'Any old iron, any old iron, any, any, any old iron . . .'

'You'll just come out to any old piece of crap, mate,' said Lorna, bringing in the tea. 'You're just another fighter. They're not going to give you your own music.'

'They fucking will,' I said. 'I'll make sure of it.'

We bickered over the issue for a good ten or fifteen minutes. I was adamant I would have my own music. Lorna and I bickered a lot, like brother and sister, good-hearted banter, taking the piss and all that. We were of the same generation and were on a wave length that Howard sometimes couldn't comprehend. Lorna would make an assinine comment and I'd get the joke straightaway, whereas Howard would simply mumble 'bollocks' and go back to channel surfing.

Music, shorts, boots . . . these were serious issues. Fighters are superstitious people given to rituals, good-luck charms and the like. I'd heard of one boxer who fought with a blade of grass from his mother's grave in his glove, believing that it would hold her close to him. I'd once seen a Latino fighter with pictures of his children sewn into his shorts. Lots of guys had tributes written on their shorts; James Toney used to have a Star of David on his in honour of his Jewish manager Jackie Kallen.

It all added to the gladiatorial aesthetic. I had to have a piece of this, so I decided that I would have a love token from Sass. She sent me a gold crucifix inlaid with eleven sapphires for me to sew into the waistband of my shorts. She had wanted to fly over from Canada for the fight but I told her not to bother. I could do without the added pressure of having my muse crying at ringside while I was slowly beaten to a pulp. When the fight came I didn't want to be responsible for anyone's feelings other than my own. The crucifix was a compromise.

I turned up at the gym one afternoon to find Trevor Callighan and Howard standing on opposite sides of the gym, looking serious.

'You're late. Get ready,' said Howard abruptly. Clinton and a moody-looking stranger climbed into the ring and started loosening up in readiness for sparring. Surely I wasn't to do the trial bout now, with no warning?

I got changed and began shadow boxing in the adjacent ring. The buzzer had deteriorated over the months from a proper buzz to a sort of strained hum and it droned on. Clinton and the stranger – a 6ft 4in cruiserweight with a ginger GI hairdo and a youthful but rugged face – stalked each other for a few seconds and then started tentatively exchanging blows. The stranger, using his height, weight and reach advantage, capitalised on his physique initially and caught Clinton with some good shots in the opening round. Early on he looked very tasty but by the end of four rounds the stranger was no match for Clinton's superior experience, fitness and technique. The champion had thrown a series of largely unanswered combinations at will, most of which the stranger accepted reluctantly about the head. When Howard called time his temples were palpably relieved.

According to Howard, the stranger was a former ABA champion and England boxing team captain who had recently turned pro – an ideal match then for a thirty-two-year-old journalist undergoing a trial bout. Howard strapped on my head guard, fastened my gloves and smeared a few blobs of Vaseline across my face.

'Right, get in,' said Howard gesturing towards the ring where the sweat-soaked stranger was pacing up and down, catching his breath.

'How do I handle this geezer?' I asked. 'I mean, what do you want me to do?'

'Just do your thing,' said Howard. 'Jab and move. Slip to the side and let them right hands go.'

I climbed into the ring. The stranger looked not so much at me, more through me. I threw a few air punches – just for effect – but he didn't seem impressed. If looks could kill I was dead meat. The buzzer groaned, we touched gloves, and then went about trying to punch holes in each other. For the first round I stayed out of his reach, throwing lots of speculative jabs, staying on the back foot and making sure not to make any silly mistakes. My muscles still felt cold and I needed at least a round to get going. The stranger had the advantage of being warmed up already – well, not so much warmed up as hot. After taking a licking from Clinton for the better part of four rounds I figured he wouldn't mind wreaking revenge on my sorry ass. That was how it worked in the fight game. Even if you had to take a beating once in a while, there was always some toerag out there you could beat up on. Win, lose or draw, in boxing, everybody takes a beating.

I felt mildly intimidated by my opponent. Unlike 90 per cent of the guys I had sparred with, he was a completely unknown quantity to me. From my familiarity with the boys in the gym, either through direct experience or constant observation, I knew that no one in boxing owed me a favour. This guy didn't know me from Adam's aunt. He was bigger than me, fitter than me, younger than me, better than me – at least as a fighter. He could smash me if he really wanted to. I knew I was out of my depth. But I'd been out of my depth ever since I got into boxing. My eventual opponent would be a complete stranger too, and more experienced than me. I had to deal with the stranger, deal with the fear of the unfamiliar. So I got brave. In the second round, rather than stay on the back foot and box, I tried cutting the ring off, closing my opponent into corners so I could work his body and head at close range. Damn, I would intimidate *his* ass. Dean had told me and so had Bomber Graham. It was one of boxing's best kept secrets. A 6ft 2in black man with a shaved head was an intimidating sight to a white guy reared on the mythology of exotic 'negro' sexual potency and super-human strength. I had an untapped physical and psychological advantage – white people are shit scared of black people. I rushed the stranger, glaring menacingly at him. I was a lion, a tiger, a cannibal. He feared me. All along he was thinking I could whip his ass, throw him in a pot and serve him up for supper and I was worried about *him*. I felt empowered – for about thirty seconds until BOOM! In an instant I was reacquainting myself with the canvas.

'What the fuck happened?' I said, looking round the gym apologetically. Déjà vu. I had wound up on my backside in exactly the same position as the last time I had wound up on my backside. I vaguely remember a looping right hand crashing into my jaw followed by a jolting sensation at the base of the spine. I sat for a moment dumbfounded, pathetic. I managed to force a half-smile. This was, after all, a self-inflicted tragedy. This was my hurt, my pain, my embarrassment. Why, I'd savour every minute of it. Getting decked was an occupational hazard. It was time to stop agonising over such things. Better to experience it in the gym than on the day of the fight. I hadn't been knocked out, only knocked down. Nobody had to carry me out of the ring. I was still standing – sitting. I was still conscious. I was still the man. I got up, dusted myself down and continued sparring, reverting to the original strategy of jabbing and moving, just like Howard had told me to.

'Sorry about that,' said the stranger in a thick Geordie accent, tapping me on the shoulder at the end of the sparring session. 'I weren't even looking for the shot.'

'Don't worry about it,' I said, trying to laugh it off. 'These things happen. My name's Dave by the way.' I offered him my gloved hand. I had no hard feelings.

'I'm Mick,' he said. So the stranger had a name.

'Pleasure doing business with you, Mick.'

Mick grinned and headed off to the changing room. He seemed mildly embarrassed. I continued to train. A few minutes later Mick emerged from the changing room donning a woolly hat and bomber jacket. He looked like a canvasser for the BNP. Callighan gestured towards the exit. Apart from exchanging a handful of pleasantries, he had hardly said a word to me all afternoon.

'I'll be in touch,' he said to Howard, looking gravely at me as I pounded away at the heavy bag. He nodded in my direction and then disappeared with Mick.

I was convinced that being up-ended in front of Trevor Callighan would prove my death knell. He'd had my card marked since the hearing in Huddersfield and now he didn't look too impressed with me in the gym. Howard tried to reassure me that, given the class of opposition I'd been tested against, I'd done well. But even though I accepted the knockdown as 'one of those things', I still beat myself up over what I felt was a mediocre performance. Then on 7 March 2000, the verdict arrived. I got a letter from the British Boxing Board of Control – enclosing my licence. I was now a professional fighter.

The licence came in the form of a brown, cotton-bound ID card which included a suitably menacing photograph of myself with an unrecognisable official stamp across it. It said inside, 'This Licence does not entitle the holder to enter any boxing promotion free of charge.' Damn. Still, I always had my press pass. After more than two years' work and a year of solid training, I'd overcome practically every hurdle put in front of me. Lorna had once told me that she had viewed boxing as 'two men fighting for the right to fight'. I had earned that right the hard way, like everybody else. I had joined the fraternity, the inner sanctum, the firm. By having a professional boxer's licence I had become a citizen of the nation state of the ring, a territory that had its own boundaries, laws and customs.

My licence number was 122701. I wondered what fate held for numbers 122700 and 122702, my contemporaries. I also felt slightly perturbed by the fact that the sum of 122701 was 13. Would this be lucky or unlucky?

Accompanying my licence was a copy of my manager's agreement; an exhaustive set of British Boxing Board of Control rules and regulations; advice to boxers on training, diet, drugs, general health and medical rules and regulations; more advice on drugs; information about HIV and AIDS; and a flyer on personal accident insurance endorsed by Lennox Lewis with the words 'a very important benefit'. Like most fighters, it never occurred to me to take out accident insurance. If you believed you were never going to get seriously injured, why bother with insurance? Insurance complicated things by reminding you that you were worth only fifty grand if you snuffed it in the ring. There was also information provided by the International Olympic Committee Medical Commission on 'prohibited classes of substances and prohibited methods'. I was disappointed to discover that caffeine was a banned substance. So much for my early morning cappuccino.

That licence was now the centrepiece of my rather modest collection of boxing ephemera, which included a ticket stub from Holyfield v. Lewis at Madison Square Garden; an unused Lennox Lewis v. Frank Bruno ticket dated Friday 1 October 1993; a picture of Lennox Lewis and me shaking hands at the opening of an envelope; and a picture of my baby Luca signed by, would you believe it, Lennox Lewis.

I felt increasingly agitated and aggressive in the weeks leading up to the fight. I wouldn't call myself a control freak but not knowing who my opponent was made me restless and edgy. Sparring became much harder. I was punching with more power, more accuracy, assertiveness and malicious intent but so were my sparring partners. The top pros in the gym beat me with impunity because they knew I had become something of a handful in my own way. I was seemingly getting very few favours from my fellow pros in the gym but by piling on the pressure with what Terry referred to as 'bitch licks', they were doing me a tremendous service. For one, becoming accustomed to a higher intensity of fighting benefited me in terms of fitness and defensive and offensive skills; and knowing I could stand up to what the heavier hitters such as Clinton, Terry and Scott had to offer gave me a psychological boost. There was no way my opponent was going to be of their calibre. If I could handle them, I could handle anybody. It was difficult to tell how hard I hit or what level of pain I inflicted on sparring partners. I couldn't speak for their pain, only my own. There were times when I had visibly shaken guys in the ring and this feeling of power, of authority, was satisfying. But the trade-off, of course, meant taking an occasional hiding.

I knew that it was a mark of how far I had come that Howard let me spar with these guys on an almost equal footing. These days when Terry said to me in the ring, 'You hit like a girl, you hit like a fucking bitch,' the provocation was taken for what it was – provocation. Six months earlier these sentiments may have had some foundation in fact. Now at the very least and all things being equal, I could give as good as I got. I could even take my beating like the egotistical macho man that I was.

With three weeks to go before 9 April, I had one of my most tortuous sparring sessions to date. After four progressively hard rounds of sparring with Terry we ended the session with what he liked to call 'a good old-fashioned tear-up'.

We stood toe-to-toe in the centre of the ring. With a minute of the round left I went to the ropes, partly for respite but also because I had been practising defending myself while up against the ropes and in the corners. No sooner had I cushioned myself against the middle rope than Terry fired a blitzkrieg of punches to my head and body. I covered up with my arms and gloves to protect as much of my head and body as possible. Out of the corner of my eye I could see figures in the gym gawping at me, almost amazed by the beating I was taking. I felt paralysed and unable to flee from the ropes, but I refused to yield to the pressure. I felt Terry back off. Had he punched himself out?

'Is that it?' I said, bugging my eyes at him in defiance. He rushed me again, catching me with a looping right hand over the top of my guard. I felt stunned. Suddenly the sounds of the gym became an echo, then muffled, as though I were 10 feet under water.

'Ah, have I hurt your pride?' said Terry, stepping back to admire his handiwork. 'Is little Dave hurt?' He was trying his ritual humiliation tactics. I'd learnt to let such comments go. We finished sparring. I told Howard I could hear hissing in my left ear.

'I think my eardrum's perforated.'

'You'll be all right in a couple of days,' said Howard nonchalantly.

'Did I really perforate your eardrum?' Terry asked later in the changing room. He seemed genuinely concerned. He said he thought I was joking when I mentioned it to Howard and gave me some advice on how to treat the ear. 'Frank Bruno did it to me a couple of times,' he said. 'Get some cotton wool and stick it in your ear. The wax'll run down and after two or three days it'll heal up.' The following day I took a rest from sparring.

I arranged to meet John Ashton that Saturday to pick up my allocation of tickets and posters, which after a two-week delay were finally ready. I had to rendezvous with him at the gym at 1.00 p.m., but when I got there at 12.30 he had already come and gone. I ran into

Mark Krench and his sidekick Victor 'The Pain Inflicter' outside the gym and they gave me my allocation, which Ashton had left with them to pass on to me. I looked at the poster. Ashton had billed the show as 'The Moment of Truth'. How apt, I thought. There in thick black letters was my name and a Godawful picture of me that looked like it had come from a photo booth. They handed over a wedge of yellow, orange and blue cardboard tickets with a note attached indicating how many of each price ticket there was. In total there were 140 tickets. Ashton had left me 140 tickets! With only three weeks to go to the fight, there was no way I was going to shift that many tickets, especially as most of my supporters would be coming from London.

As the gym was closed I went back to the house to pack for my coach trip to London that evening. I took a nice hot shower and as I wiped the mist away from the bathroom mirror so I could take a shave I was shocked and repulsed by what I saw. My right ear had ballooned into a hideous lump! I had a fucking cauliflower ear! I went into a panic. I couldn't believe it. Jesus, this was permanent damage. I was scarred for life. My God, what was I going to do? I stared and stared in the mirror, prodding and poking my ear, hoping it would go away or that it was a figment of my imagination, but it was there, larger than life. It hadn't been there that morning when I'd looked in the mirror. It just appeared.

'Oh dear,' said Lorna when I showed her the ear.

'Is that all you can say?' I fumed. 'Oh fucking dear!'

'Well, sorry, love. There's nothing I can do about it. Wait till Howard gets in. See what he thinks.' Howard was less than sympathetic.

'Ah, it's nothing,' said Howard with customary indifference. 'All my life I've wanted one o' them and you go and get one just like that. Tsch. I don't know what you're worrying about. It'll make a nice souvenir for ya.'

A souvenir! I stormed out of the house and headed to the coach station. When I reached London I went straight to St Mary's hospital in Paddington. After a four-hour wait, I was seen by a doctor who had no idea what to do with the ear. He stuck a needle in it, drew some pus out, bandaged it, gave me some antibiotic cream and sent me on my way. First thing Monday morning I visited Dr Singh.

'You can't muck about with these things,' he said, gung-ho style. 'You got to attack them head-on.' The good doctor produced a small scalpel from a packet. 'This might hurt a bit,' he said, lunging at the ear. A stream of pus and blood shot out over him, me and the surgery floor.

'That should sort the bugger out.' He stuck some cotton wool on the wound, prescribed some antibiotic pills and sent me on my way.

I had brought the problem on myself. For the past fortnight I had sparred without using my head guard because I had broken the buckle on it and couldn't be bothered to get it repaired. I took a break from head sparring for a couple of days and the ear went down. I got the head guard repaired and tentatively resumed sparring. The ear went up again. I squeezed it and pus came out. It went down. 'Stop fiddling with that, will you,' Lorna kept nagging. I had to face facts. With the fight looming I had to put vanity to one side and soldier on. I had a cauliflower ear and that was that. I couldn't quit now because of it. On the bright side, the fear of winding up with an ear like an allotment took my mind off the fight, which was now just a fortnight away.

chapter 37

In preparation for the fight, I did two sessions of hypnotherapy over two days with Paul. Boy did I need it. We worked on 'shrinking' my opponent, making me visualise him as small and insignificant, and on a four-step process that encapsulated all the most important elements I needed for the fight – power, stamina, skill/technique and composure. All these elements were finally wrapped up into one – POWER. This was my buzzword. Paul said I was calm, focused and well prepared for the fight. He sounded a lot more confident than I was.

I still had no idea of my opponent's identity; neither had Howard.

'So where's the weigh-in then, Howard?' I asked.

'Oh, Alfreton Leisure Centre, or Chesterfield, or the Don Valley Sports Academy,' he grinned conspiratorially. I laughed. John Ashton had told Howard I needed to weigh in at a maximum of 12 stone 8lb. I presently weighed 12 stone 9lb. I was bang on target.

With twelve days to go, I was at the pinnacle of madness, feeling horny and having bizarre thoughts about lewd sex acts and blood. I busted the nose of one of my sparring partners and felt titillated by the sight of his blood. I gave him the look. I wanted to break him up, to destroy him. I could see fear in his eyes. He went on the defensive. His shots were ineffectual, designed to buy time, to see me off. I was the hunter. I wanted to smash him. I smashed my right hand into his face and his nose exploded like a firecracker. 'Time. Time. Fucking time!' yelled Howard. I was still pounding at him when the old boy called a halt. I felt a contained rage, a seething malevolence festering inside but I did not feel anger or hate. I understood that boxing was fighting without anger. I could control all that pent-up aggression and channel it into someone's face with the detachment of a contract killer blowing a mark's head off. My violence was strictly business, nothing personal.

Nine days to go.

'Whatever you do, Dave,' said Justin with what seemed like a genuine hint of concern, 'don't fall for the hype and think after you've won the fight – and I've got every faith in you that you will win – don't think, "Oh, I'll have another go at this," then another, then another. Have your one fight, mate, and get out. Take it from me, boxing's a mug's game, a fucking mug's game.'

All the way to Northern General, Justin had laid down the cynicism hard on me. We had sparred that afternoon and even though I had worn my head guard, the ear, like Richard E. Grant's boil in *How To Get Ahead In Advertising*, decided to get uppity with me and inflame. When we got to the hospital, the triage nurse suggested that if I wasn't in a desperate hurry (the waiting time was three hours) perhaps I should wait till the morning and see my GP or the local emergency doctor.

My right ear was totally swollen. It was so sore I knew I was set for permanent damage. Howard didn't seem to give a damn. He just gave me that trophy-souvenir bullshit. Yeah, yeah, yeah. Lorna kept saying the ear looked fine and I was being too vain. I knew she was humouring me. In the run-up to my day of reckoning, Howard and Lorna were trying to deflect all 'negative influences' as far away from me as possible. They had put me on 'lock down' and ordered me to stop writing and start going to bed early. I was being treated like a child. Lorna even wanted to confiscate my mobile phone, my link with the outside world, to avoid me taking any unnecessary calls and they tried to talk me out of going to London fearing Lara would unsettle my nerves. As if.

I had to go back to London one last time to see Luca and flog a few more tickets. I'd only shifted three dozen and needed to pull my finger out. On the Saturday morning before I caught the coach, I saw the emergency doctor in Sheffield. He did a sixty-second examination, prescribed some more antibiotics (28 x 500mg of Erythromycin) and suggested I visit the hospital when I got to London that afternoon.

I did a bit of running around, shifting tickets and marshalling support during the day and went to Middlesex Hospital A&E that evening. After twenty minutes I saw the triage nurse. There was a five-hour wait so I decided to take in Oliver Stone's latest offering, *Any Given Sunday*, which was on at the Odeon in Panton Street. When I returned, I waited another twenty minutes and was seen by a nurse. She peered at my ear with disapproval.

'I hope you didn't get that boxing or playing rugby,' she said.

'Boxing actually,' I said.

'You must be out of your mind to box. Anyone who boxes needs their head testing,' she snapped back, which was kind of ironic considering the brain scans you need to get a licence. I got another lancing, more antibiotics and more bandages, and split.

The following day I went to see Luca, hoping it wasn't for the last time. When I arrived at Lara's place, she noticed I had a black eye in addition to the cauliflower ear (which she had found highly amusing).

'Aw. You look busted up,' she said.

'No more than I deserve.'

Luca was staring at my black eye and cauliflower ear. She'd developed a morbid fascination with it. Lara was always critical of me talking about or demonstrating anything to do with boxing in front of Luca. She was worried she'd turn out like Layla Ali or George Foreman's daughter, I suppose, so I told Luca that the following Sunday I'd be in a 'special contest for big boys'.

I visited my parents that evening. I had totally forgotten it was Mother's Day. My father gave me some advice on how to box, like I needed it from him.

'Set him up with the jab then knock him out. Don't get hit too much.' Thanks for the advice, Dad. 'Try and win, son,' he added.

'I won't just try, I will win,' I said. Then he went into one.

'Frank Bruno wanted to get killed for his country. Fuck that. Now Lennox Lewis . . .' Ever since I'd shown my father a photograph of Lennox and me shaking hands at a charity do he'd been a fan. He said he was going to make a copy of it and show it off at the bookies'.

My mum was dismissive as usual. With just a week to go before the fight she was still poo-pooing the idea.

'Why do you want to do this boxing thing?' she said, giving me a concerned look. 'I hope you're not going to make a full-time job of it.'

'Save the lecture, Ma,' I said. I felt restless and decided to go.

'How about a peck for luck,' said my mother, as I got to the door.

'Sure.' I went to kiss her on the mouth. She offered me her cheek. I kissed it and left.

My parents had been going through a rough patch for the past few months, well, thirty-eight years actually. The house was on the market, they would be selling up and going their separate ways again. My parents had worried me for some time. The once a man twice a child thing – they were becoming increasingly weak and vulnerable. Hypertension, arthritis, depression were all taking their toll on both of them. A couple of months earlier I had had a conversation on the telephone with my mother. We had moved on to the subject of my crazy brother and I'd never heard her so low.

Six days to go.

I had become obsessed with my ear. Today I squeezed it and excreted a fair amount of pus and blood. I think I'm winning the war now. As a result I told Howard I would only body spar as I didn't want to exacerbate the problem with full contact sparring. He agreed, for a day.

Five days to go and I finally find out who my opponent is.

'I was on the phone to Claude Abrams from *Boxing News* today,' said Ashton, chuckling. 'He thinks it's a right crack. So you've never had any amateur fights before?'

'No, nothing,' I said.

'Christ . . . nothing?'

'That's right.'

'This is going to be something else.'

John Ashton. What a guy. His attitude seemed to be why do something today in comfort when you can wait till the very last minute and panic.

'Don't take this the wrong way, Dave, but if you lose on points you've done really well. And if you win . . . well, that'll be just great for you.'

'Yeah,' I said. Thanks for the vote of confidence, John.

'Right, the kid I've got for you is Matt Scriven. He's a short, stocky kid, lost his last four or five fights. He lost to Matt Mowatt last Monday. He's busy, not a puncher, a bit ropey.'

So I had a name – Matt Scriven. I looked him up immediately in the *British Boxing Yearbook*. He was twenty-six and had won four and lost four although the book was out of date and he'd had at least another half dozen fights since publication. As a bonus, his picture leapt off the page. He was a dead ringer for Vinnie Jones! So now I had a name and a face to focus on.

In the days leading up to the day of the fight my moods ebbed and flowed by the minute. One moment I'd feel cool, calm and collected, the next I felt like I was going to internally combust. My nerves were red hot. Nobody noticed it except Howard. Before my penultimate sparring session, as he went through the ritual of applying Vaseline to my face, he said, 'You all right?'

'Yeah,' I said, even though I wasn't. He gave me a paternal pat on the head.

My short-term memory had been reduced to a pulp. I tried not to blame this on having my brains bashed in for the past fourteen months and instead put it down to my endless thinking and preoccupation with a) the fight b) my ear c) getting laid d) food e) my overall health and fitness f) my rapidly increasing nervousness.

I had some strange dreams during that week. I was never able to recall most of the details, only snapshots. One night I dreamed I spilled a pint of Guinness and smashed a glass; another I had visions of courgettes! I think my dreams must have been connected to my preoccupation with food. I daydreamed about eating a big fat juicy steak, trifles, apple pie and custard and hot-dogs, and drinking malted chocolate milkshakes.

By the Thursday before the fight I had managed to drop to 12½ stone, shedding two of the excess three pounds I'd had at the beginning of the week. Training had been marginally lighter this week than in previous weeks. I did a bit of track work and light sparring, just to stay sharp and keep my timing and rhythm up to speed. I had rationed myself to two slices of toast, a small bowl of cereal and a cup of coffee for breakfast and whatever Lorna shoved under my nose for dinner. I did sneakily consume a Cadbury's Ripple, Hazelnut Galaxy and a Galaxy Fruit and Nut over two days in my bedroom.

Two days to go.

'I was talking to Glynn Rhodes last night at that awards dinner about this fella you're boxing,' said Howard as we headed to the track. 'He don't think you'll have any problems with him. He says Mowatt's not a puncher and he stopped him, and Clinton reckons you'd do Mowatt.'

'So in other words, if I can beat the man who beat the man, I can beat the man.'

'Precisely,' said Howard.

'So what do I do? Go out there and knock his head off?'

'No, no. You go out there and keep him out here,' said Howard, jabbing for effect.

'He's apparently busy. Does that mean I let him do all the work?'

Howard peered at me over his glasses scornfully. 'Him do all the work? No, no.'

'What I mean is . . . What do I mean? I suppose I mean I pick my shots and pick him off.'

'Correct,' said Howard.

'I haven't ever really opened up in sparring, Howard. I mean, well, you know how I feel about most of the guys in the gym. I like the guys

I spar with. I still feel funny about hurting them. But this guy Scriven, I don't know him from Adam. I don't owe him anything. As far as I'm concerned, he stands in the way of me achieving what I've worked over two years for. I'm going to go in there and lace that bastard with licks.'

'Well, if you've got more to come than what you've shown in the gym, we're in for an interesting time come Sunday.'

During the course of my training I'd had a problem with hurting people. Yes, I'd inflicted pain on the guys in the gym as they had on me. I'd split the lips, busted the noses and blackened the eyes – I liked to think that I gave as good as I got – but some inexplicable force always stopped me from pushing myself that bit further. From the outset, I harboured a bizarre notion that I had to resist the urge to hurt *with vicious intent*. I actually thought that if I applied myself, I was capable of inflicting greater damage on my sparring partners than they could on me, even though they were way more experienced than I was. As a professional fighter I had flirted with sadism, but I could not come to terms with the thought of inflicting pain on someone, bringing them to their knees, making them submit. An idealist might say that inflicting pain was not the point of boxing, but a consequence of it. Willie Pep, a featherweight champion of the 1940s, once famously won a round of boxing without actually throwing a punch. But punters don't pay to see elusive defence. They pay to see people get hurt and the more graphic that hurt the better. Perhaps nothing had changed since school, in terms of my attitude towards sport. Perhaps I lacked the killer instinct. Perhaps I just wasn't born to be a fighter after all.

My last sparring session was a disaster. My legs were like lead from the morning's session on the track and I felt apprehensive and nervous about moving around with Clinton, Danny and Mark Krence whom I swore were all set to bash the living daylights out of me. I was so preoccupied with my right hand, which I had sprained a week earlier doing pads with Victor 'The Pain Inflicter', that I hardly threw a decent shot for fear of busting it up again, and I was still worried about my ear turning into a freaking floret of broccoli if I took a decent left hook.

The ear hurt, not agonisingly, but with a stinging irritation. The real pain was psychological – my ego was suffering from concussion, my vanity from a slap in the face. I had become so fixated with my ear that I found myself preoccupied with other people's ears. I had been looking at ears in the gym, on the bus, in the street. I furtively examined the ears of complete strangers, checking for abnormalities. If every fourth or fifth person had had a cauliflower ear, I wouldn't have minded so much. Maybe there was a God and as a downpayment for my sins he had given me a cauliflower ear. Christ. To add to my manic depression, paranoia, delusions of grandeur, I was now developing an obsessive-compulsive neurosis.

To take my mind off my ear, Lorna's friend Jay, a lanky student from the Shetlands who had come down to Sheffield specially to see me fight, took me to see *The Hurricane* starring Denzil Washington. The movie told the story of Rubin 'Hurricane' Carter, a middleweight world title contender who was wrongfully imprisoned in 1967 for the triple-murder of three white people in a New Jersey bar. Nineteen years he languished in jail protesting his innocence before a jury acquitted him on appeal. I felt humbled by Carter's story. The movie brought tears to my eyes and reminded me of some home truths. A cauliflower ear was a small price to pay in this world's maelstrom of suffering.

The day before the fight there was a sudden change in plan. Ashton informed Howard that the weigh-in would take place at the venue and not the day before as was normally the case. Section 3.2.2 of the Board's *Rules and Regulations 2000* regarding weigh-ins states, 'All Boxers must weigh in not less than 24 hours or more than 36 hours before the commencement of a tournament. Permission may be granted by the Board for Boxers to weigh in on the day of a tournament provided that no Boxer reduces weight following the weigh-in.' Fighters commonly weighed in the day before a fight several pounds lighter than their eventual fighting weight. Yesterday I had weighed 12 stone 5lb at the gym, so I was three pounds within the limit Ashton had prescribed. I felt comfortable that I could maintain the weight for the next twenty-four hours.

After eating a dinner of poached cod, rice and sweet corn I tried to watch a video of *Fear and Loathing in Las Vegas* with Johnny Depp, but found the movie incomprehensible without the aid of mind-bending drugs. The book was equally indecipherable even with the aid of drugs.

With less than twenty-four hours to go before the fight, the sense of pressure was immense, but it was too late not to handle it. Even during those moments when I'd thrown a tantrum, looking for attention or pity, and threatened to drop it all and return to London, I could never really have given up. I had convinced myself that this moment was my destiny. Not only was I making my professional debut aged thirty-two without any experience of competitive boxing, but I was doing it under a mountain of personal and professional strain. I had, I believed, up to this point accurately authenticated the life of a workaday professional fighter. It was a life of struggle, insecurity and soul-searching. I went to bed early and slept soundly until the small hours when I entered a twilight world of semi-consciousness. Hours passed like weeks and my mind juggled a billion thoughts until daybreak. I awoke the following morning feeling as though I had never fallen asleep. It was time. All that was left was to write the last chapter.

chapter 38

Around 8.30 a.m., 9 April 2000. Lorna cooked me breakfast – scrambled eggs on two slices of toast with baked beans, the condemned man's final meal. I drank a couple of litres of mineral water to keep myself well hydrated and began to focus on the task at hand. The weigh-in would be only an hour or two before the fight so I had to get my eating and drinking out of the way early, to give me time to digest my food and burn off the extra calories.

The house was silent but for idle conversation. No one spoke of the fight. My mouth felt dry and I was in no mood for talking. The boys' presence was irritating me. Lorna had promised that Simon would be staying with his friend over the road for the weekend. Instead, he was still around. At one point, Scott got in my way in the living room and I barged past him. 'MOVE!' I scowled. 'Anyone or anything that gets in my way today is gonna get flattened.'

I tried to calm down. I felt myself sinking deeper and deeper into a state of withdrawal. My palms were sweating, with anticipation more than nerves. I reminded myself that in a few hours' time my baptism of fire would finally bring the months of waiting, frustration and pain to an end. This realisation gave me succour. Given that this day of reckoning had weighed heavy on my shoulders for several weeks, I had anticipated more nerves, more fear. I felt relaxed though, confident and self-assured, more so than I had done in months.

Big Dave, Ben Coward, Paul Wellings and a recent defector from Brendan Ingle's gym called 'Young' John arrived at the house around 10.30. Waj Khan, the flyweight and mini-cab driver, was due soon. Waj was game as old boots. His claim to fame was starring in an action-packed video called *100 Best Knockouts*. Unfortunately, he was one of the hundred fellas who got knocked out. Anyway, he was set to drive Howard, Big Dave, John and myself to Alfreton, which was about an hour's ride away, while Lorna, Ben and Jay were going in Paul's car.

'Lorna, could you sort this out for me, please?' I asked, thrusting my black Everlast trunks and Sass Brown's crucifix at her. She hadn't sewn it into the waistband and I'd convinced myself that this was my talisman.

'Don't worry, I'll take care of it.'

Lorna took the trunks and crucifix and got to work as I quietly packed my bag for the journey – black Lonsdale boots, spare pair of Calvin Klein briefs, white Nike socks, black Everlast T-shirt, track pants, towel, shower gel, groin protector . . . groin protector? I couldn't find my groin protector.

'Fucking hell,' sighed Howard. 'There's always bloody something.'

'I must've left it at the gym,' I said.

'Oh for God's sake. Come on then.'

Howard and I jumped in Titanic and took off for the gym. After a brief search we found the groin protector and ten minutes later, we were back at the house by which time Waj had arrived. The doors opened at the Alfreton Leisure Centre at 2 p.m. and the boxing started at three so we had to get there for 1.30 just to be on the safe side.

I sat in the front seat and spent most of the hour's drive to Alfreton staring out of the windscreen daydreaming. In sixty minutes, I thought about everything and nothing. By the time we reached the Alfreton Leisure Centre, I had no real recollection of the journey. Waj pulled into the car park and I was first out, keen to stretch my legs. I felt the sun catch the back of my neck. It was a great day for a fight.

The car park was around 75 per cent full. Cars and coaches were pulling in as people milled around. With the others close in around me like bodyguards, I made my way across the car park to the venue. In a hall next door, people were showing guinea pigs in competition. I felt conscious of people staring at me. Was it the black eye, cauliflower ear and my solemnity that attracted so much attention? Or were all these people wondering is he the one? There had been a report by Claude Abrams in *Boxing News* two days earlier entitled 'Matthews punchline', which had revealed my motives to a wider audience. Now the cat was truly out of the bag:

Fellow journalist (though I don't know him) David Matthews makes his professional debut on John Ashton's afternoon show at Alfreton Leisure Centre on Sunday [9 April]. Matthews, I am told, started working out with Howard Rainey and, with one chapter to go on a book he is writing, decided to get in the ring for a once-and-only fight. He received a licence from the Central Area Council and is matched against Matt Scriven who is on a losing run and ranked No. 49 of 66 in our British ratings. Ashton says Matthews, 32, should have a slight weight advantage to make up for his inexperience, but 'I hope he gets through all right and lasts the distance.' Matthews has never boxed before, not even as an amateur . . .

Like a lot of stuff you read in the press, the story wasn't entirely accurate. I had made the decision to 'get in the ring for a once-and-only fight' long before I met Howard or started writing this book. The tone of the report seemed snide and designed to undermine my efforts but it only hardened my resolve.

I walked slowly towards the entrance, pausing briefly to take in the Alfreton Leisure Centre in all its splendour. It looked like an old people's home from the outside, with its redbrick façade, big windows and sloping roof. This is what I had come to. This was my arena; home of the small-hall gladiator, odeon of the odious business of boxing, coliseum of the poor drunken fight fan.

Lorna was standing outside the entrance awaiting our arrival. She was wearing an all-black trouser suit – dressed for a funeral. 'Hi, hon,' she said and gave me a hug. She looked anguished. They all did. I made a comment about my entourage being more worried than I was, which drew a few false laughs. Originally, Lorna didn't even want to be at the fight. I had pestered her for months about going but she had vehemently refused to do so. She had a silly policy of not attending or watching live on TV any fight that involved one of Howard's 'boys'. She always feared the worst for the guys at the gym and preferred to watch their fights at home on videotape safe in the knowledge that, forewarned of the result, she knew they had survived relatively unscathed. What nonsense! The excitement of sport, for the spectator at least, was the unpredictability of the here and now, the nerve-racking expectation of the unexpected. Watching recorded sport was a bore, like having sex after ten pints of lager; nine times out of ten you knew the result – dull, predictable, with no climax.

Apart from being very stubborn, Lorna could be pessimistic beyond the point of reason. When the total eclipse came for instance, she urged everyone to stay indoors, drew all the curtains and hid behind the sofa. I had used everything from emotional blackmail to, well, just blackmail to get her to the fight. I wanted her to be there because I valued her support and this was a once in a lifetime opportunity. Unlike with the other 'boys', she'd never get another chance to see me box. In the end, it became a battle of wills.

'I always get my own way, especially with women,' I told Lorna. 'You will come to the fight.'

'Oh, really,' she said dismissing me. 'I don't think so.'

I heard my name called out, turned round and saw a group of friends who had come along to support me.

'Hi,' I said vacantly. More hugs. I didn't say much. I was disappearing into 'the zone'. I was in a daze. People I knew were coming up to me and I barely noticed them. Inside the foyer people were coming and going, idly taking up space or panicking like headless chickens. I remained oblivious to the confusion. Mark Krence and Victor 'The Pain Inflicter' appeared followed by my friend Phil Fisk, a photographer. Other members of the camp arrived including Dennis Hobson who, along with Victor, would work my corner with Howard.

Someone directed our eight-strong group towards the dressing rooms and we set off further into the leisure centre past a lower floor gymnasium where a karate tournament was in progress, and through a small bar that stank of sweat and rubber, cigarettes and alcohol. We passed through a doorway into a dark corridor with faded paintwork and cheap brown carpet, down a short flight of stairs, along another corridor with garish yellows and greens, where the sun broke through double-glazed windows, through another doorway and down a pale blue corridor. A notice on the first door on the right read ORDER BLUE, with a list of seven names beneath. My name was second. This was the blue-corner dressing room.

Dressing rooms in reality were never like those in the movies. In the movies, a fighter always had a dressing room to himself. There was always a massage table, no windows and a single fluorescent light fitting or bulb, and the walls were always bottle green. My dressing room was a dishevelled squash court, pockmarked by a fusillade of a billion rubber balls. I walked in to find two fighters with their trainers milling around inside. The fighters were in stark contrast to each other. One was a hideous caricature of the washed-up journeyman. He had a stretch-marked, poorly conditioned body, acne-riddled skin, a crushed nose the width of his mouth, a bulging forehead, deep-set eyes and ears the size of fists. The conglomeration of his features formed what may best be described as a cauliflower face. The other guy was the antithesis of a fighter. He was so bland he was practically beyond description. He was about as threatening as a Christmas edition of *Reader's Digest*. There were some plastic chairs littered around and a small communal table. We claimed three chairs and set up shop along one side of the court.

Howard settled himself at the table and opened his little blue box. Inside was all the required equipment for the corner – white towels; white petroleum jelly; cotton wool; sterile gauze; swab sticks; adrenaline made into a 1–1000 aqueous solution; a pair of blunt-edged scissors; an ice bag; a roll of one-inch adhesive bandage; several rolls of two-inch soft bandage (maximum length 18 feet); and an N-swell or eye iron.

I started pacing up and down the court, lightly shadow boxing to loosen up. I still had my street clothes on and a leather jacket to keep warm. People were coming and going from the dressing room. It had now gone two o'clock. A few friends popped in but I wasn't in the frame of mind for their idle chitter chatter. They were staring at me, trying to get inside my head, trying to get a feel of what I was thinking, what I was going through. They looked concerned, scared for me even. I didn't mind them being around. It wasn't like I wanted to be alone or anything. I was just in my own little world doing my own little thing. The benefit of hypnosis was kicking in. As the minutes crawled by, I was going deeper and deeper into the zone.

Howard started preparing the bandages for my hands. He took the roll of adhesive tape and started ripping off six-inch strips which he stuck on the wall until he had several strips lined up. He took a roll of soft bandage and slowly unravelled it, continually doubling it over every four inches or so until he had several layers of bandage in a rectangular pad. He repeated this until he had four pads.

I stopped pacing and sat down. A burly Board official dressed in a blue blazer and an old school tie came into the dressing room. He was holding a clipboard.

'Are you David Matthews?' he asked, looking at a list.

'Yeah,' I replied, coolly.

'What colour shorts you wearing?'

'Black,' I said and he wrote this on his clipboard.

'Hang on a minute, son, we want to weigh you in.'

No sooner had he left than the doctor came in and examined me, checking my blood pressure, respiration and eyes. Everything was OK. A few minutes later the burly official returned with a stocky colleague holding a black case and another clipboard. He opened the case and produced a set of electronic scales.

'Right hop on there, son.' I stripped down to my briefs and stood on the scales. The LCD numbers scrambled to find their place. 'Hmm . . . twelve stone ten and a half pounds,' said the second official, tut tutting.

The extra weight surprised me. The officials asked me what I had expected to weigh. I told them the last time I checked I was 12 stone 5lb and I thought I would just make the 12–8 limit. I explained that I had drunk a lot of water that morning and it would probably soon pass out of my system and reduce the weight. They weren't buying that excuse.

'See the problem is,' said the first official, 'that the promoter informed us that you would be weighing in at twelve stone. Your opponent,' he added, pointing to his colleague's clipboard, 'weighed in yesterday at eleven stone nine. Now, you've got over a stone advantage. I think the other corner might want to think about going ahead with the fight.'

How could John Ashton tell the Board I was coming in at 12 stone? The last time I weighed 12 stone Gary Glitter had hair. How could Matt Scriven have weighed in at 11–9? This was supposed to be a light-heavyweight contest. The officials said they would inform the other corner of the situation and let them decide if they wanted to go ahead with the fight. This was looking bad, very bad.

'I don't believe it,' I said, putting my clothes on.

'Fucking hell,' said Howard, shaking his head. In the dressing room faces were dropping like autumn leaves.

'They have to take the fight. Howard, we have to sort this out.' Howard asked why my weight was so high. I told him I had behaved myself. The scales at the gym must have been wrong. 'I'm going for a piss,' I said.

'That's a good idea,' said Howard.

For the first time that day, panic was starting to set in. I faced a potential nightmare. If Scriven didn't take the fight I was ruined. I had over sixty people in the crowd to whom I'd sold tickets. If I didn't box I'd be a laughing stock. Those people wouldn't buy tickets a second time. How long would it be before I got another opponent? Howard went in search of John Ashton. I hadn't seen him all afternoon. He reappeared minutes later with Ashton, still bulging out of that suit I'd seen him in four months ago.

'All right, Dave,' said Ashton with an embarrassed grin. 'We've got a bit of a problem.'

'I fucking know that, John,' I said.

'Scriven's lot don't want to take the fight because of the weight difference.' I fucking knew it! 'Now I'm gonna go and try to sort this out. Just bear with me.' Ashton disappeared.

The nightmare was beginning. Over two years of research down the toilet, fourteen months of training wasted.

'They're playing games with you, man,' said Young John. 'I've seen it all before. They're playing mind games with you. They're trying to unsettle you. Don't worry about them. Just stay cool.'

John was right. This was mind games. I'd stay cool. How could I? I wasn't in a position to call Scriven's bluff. I couldn't say, 'Bollocks. If you don't want the fight, go to hell.' I needed this fight desperately. The first fight on the card was already under way. There was no way I'd be second on the bill. Five minutes later, Ashton returned with Dennis.

'Howard, can I have a word?' said Ashton, pulling him to one side.

'Fucking hell. What a palaver, eh?' said Dennis.

'It's a fucking joke,' I said.

Ashton, Howard and Dennis left the dressing room. Minutes later the hideous fighter reappeared, battered and bruised.

'How d'you get on?' someone asked.

'Lost on points,' said the fighter.

I walked out into the corridor and found Ashton, Howard, a Board official and Scriven's trainer having a confab. Ashton had his head in his hands and was sweating profusely. This was bullshit. I went back to the dressing room cussing.

'Don't listen to a word they're saying,' said Young John. 'They're trying to get to ya. I know all the tricks. They're trying a hustle, they want more money out of the promoter.' Howard walked into the dressing room.

'What's happening, H?' I asked.

'I don't fucking know. Ashton's sorting it out.' What a manager, what a promoter, what a fucking mess! 'Come on,' said Howard. 'You might as well get your kit on, just in case.' I stripped off, got into my boxing gear, and put on a T-shirt. Howard told me to warm up so I started shadow boxing. As I moved around popping out jabs and throwing hooks, I visualised Matt Scriven in front of me.

'Whatever happens in that ring, you'll come out a winner because it takes brass balls to get in there in the first place,' said Vic as I shadow boxed. Dennis too was giving me words of encouragement. The second fight had come and gone, another loser for the blue corner. I sat down and Howard bandaged my hands. I put on a pair of tatty red 10oz gloves. Vic laced them and I warmed up on the pads with him.

'What are we?' growled Vic.

'A winner,' I said.

'What are we gonna do?'

'Go out there and knock his fucking head off.'

'That's it, son.'

I'd gone through this many times in the gym with Vic. He was a good motivator. A bit of a nutter, but a good man nonetheless. I took a break from the pads and Ashton walked into the dressing room.

'It's not looking good,' he said, frowning. 'They don't want to know.'

'I don't fucking believe this.'

'Come out here and let's have a look at you,' said Ashton. 'Let me see you move around a bit.'

Now let me get something straight. Ashton had never seen me spar before. He'd never even so much as seen me do a press-up before. Apart from what Howard would have told him, he had no idea of my boxing ability. I started shadow boxing, feebly.

'Come on, do it properly,' said Ashton. I shadow boxed with my usual sharpness. 'Fucking hell,' he said. 'We got Tommy bloody Hearns here. Jesus Christ! All right, all right, that'll do. I'll be back in a minute.' I watched Ashton disappear next door, into Scriven's dressing room.

A third fight was now under way. Top of the bill was Gregg Scott-Briggs versus Tony Booth for the British Masters light-heavyweight title. I was currently nowhere. Ashton returned. He called Howard, Dennis and me into a huddle.

'They're not happy,' he said, smirking. 'They don't want to take the fight, but they'll take it on one condition and that's this.' Ashton snuggled up to me, conspiratorially. 'If you knock the kid out, you've got to pay him your wages.' I'd heard it all now.

'What you've got to do,' continued Ashton, 'is go out there and box this fella. Don't go mad and put him over.' I couldn't believe this. I was a novice, Scriven was a seasoned pro. Scriven, a serving soldier in Her Majesty's armed forces, had evidently read George Bernard Shaw. It was just as Sergius had said in *Arms and the Man*: 'That is the whole secret of successful fighting. Get your enemy at a disadvantage; and never, on any account, fight him on equal terms.'

For the sake of getting the fight on, Howard and I agreed to Scriven's ridiculous demands. Ashton left the dressing room to close the deal.

'Look, don't think about the five hundred quid,' said Howard. 'As soon as the opportunity arises, you bang this fella out, d'you hear me?' said Howard.

'Yeah, yeah,' I nodded.

'Forget about the money. After all, you don't need it anyway, do you?'

'Right, yeah,' I was drifting back into the zone.

I did need the money – I was thousands of pounds in debt – but that was beside the point. My mandate from the beginning was to become a professional fighter, to fight for money. I had trained to do a job where the intention was to knock the other guy out and get paid for it. Now I was caught between two stools. I had come all this way, sacrificed so much, for what? To blow it away at the last minute? I wanted my money. A true pro kept his eyes on the prize. As Jack Dempsey once put it, 'When you're fighting, you're fighting for one thing: money.'

Scriven was not a contender nor a prospect. He was nobody, just like me, another desperate guy looking for a fight, looking to put a monkey in his pocket and add some credibility to his flagging career. If I knocked him out he'd be suspended from boxing for a minimum of twenty-eight days and be ordered to visit a neurologist and undergo a brain scan. That's why he had introduced the proviso, so he could still make money. He'd also look like a fucking idiot if a writer, a guy who'd never boxed before, knocked him out. I thought I had something to prove. I was in Scriven's way and he was in mine. We were made for each other.

I paced round the dressing room, cussing Scriven and Ashton under my breath. My thoughts became twisted, venal. I focused on Scriven. He was a soldier. What kind of men did we have defending our country if they weren't prepared to fight like men? What was Scriven, a man or a pussy? Yeah, fuck you and your money. I'll go in there and batter this son of a bitch black and blue. I paced up and down, cussing louder, cussing Scriven, Ashton and all those punks who doubted under my breath. They tried to nobble me, eh? I'll smash that little bastard to pieces. Scriven, you little prick – you better get ready for double time in the shithouse, boy, 'cos I'm gonna rip you a new arsehole. I'll shove that monkey so far down your throat, you'll be wiping your arse with five-pound notes.

Ashton returned. The fight was on.

'Right, you're on next.' I started shadow boxing once again. This was the moment. First it was a dream, then it became a nightmare, now it was reality. A weasel of a man in a tuxedo stepped into the dressing room. I stared blankly at him.

'OK, we're ready to go,' he said.

Howard smeared some Vaseline on my face. The entourage pulled out of the dressing room. I felt my heart race then slow down. I took a few deep breaths and felt instantly relaxed. I thought POWER, my hypnotic buzzword. I bounced through the labyrinthine corridors of the leisure centre sandwiched between Howard and Dennis in front, Vic immediately behind me, and the rest of the crew bringing up the rear.

I approached the entrance to the arena. What a shithole. Dennis raised his arm in front of me to stop me from moving any further before my cue.

'Hold on a minute, wait for the music,' he said.

The momentary wait gave me a few seconds to absorb the atmosphere. I focused squarely on the ring but made out images on the periphery. I glanced to my left and saw Bill Mitchell, drawn to him by his cries of, 'Come on, Dave.' I felt the crowd simmering with anticipation. There were hundreds of people out there. Heads turned. The crowd was stirring. The ceiling was low, adding to the clammy, claustrophobic atmosphere. The air felt tight, constricted by cigarette smoke, sweat and heat, presumably from the lights. My music started, a garage anthem by Armand Van Helden called, 'You Don't Know Me'. I chose it not so much for the music, but more for the lyrics, which were simple but had a profoundly personal meaning to me.

I strode through the arena, the main hall of the sports centre. A roar of approval went up. I felt a heightened sense of purpose. I focused harder on the ring – my ring – illuminated, yet dark, familiar yet unknown. I could see the MC holding a mike and a piece of paper. I walked through the crowd, making out snapshots of familiar faces. 'Go on, Dave,' a voice hollered. I reached the steps to the ring and noticed an old friend sitting ringside. In a split second I looked at her as an ape would its own reflection in a mirror, with startled curiosity. Then I looked through her and she disappeared. I walked up three, maybe four, white wooden steps on to the ring apron. I'm in another world. Dennis pulled the ropes apart. The music was still pounding over the PA, battling with applause and shouts for recognition. *You don't even know me but you say that I'm not living right. You don't understand me, so why do you judge my life?* I slipped through the ropes and emerged in the ring. The sensation is mind blowing. The MC made an announcement but all I caught was my name. A chorus of applause rang out. Instinctively, I raised my arms aloft and the crowd responded with a clamour of appreciation. 'Go on, Davey boy.' I recognised the voice, that distinctive

Scouse accent. It was my friend Mike Leigh. I did a couple of circuits slow jogging round the ring, lapping up the applause. I felt as though I had already risen to the occasion.

'Get a feel for the ropes,' said Dennis as Scriven's music – a cheesy dance track – started to play. I bounced off each length of the ring, testing the tension of the ropes. They were taut and felt hard against my skin. Dennis beckoned me over, removed my T-shirt and put my gumshield in. Scriven entered the ring wearing black and white striped trunks and a black hooded cloak. I glanced over at him but he made no eye contact. He looked smaller than I imagined. His music stopped. The crowd settled down, rumbling. I heard raucous laughter, shouts, whistling, a spew of noise. The MC made the pre-fight announcements. 'Introducing in the blue corner, fighting out of Sheffield and weighing in at twelve stone ten and a half pounds, making his professional debut, David Matthews.' I kissed my gloves and hoisted them into the air.

The referee called Scriven and me to the centre of the ring. We're eyeball to eyeball for the first time. I look deep into Scriven's eyes penetrating through to the back of his head. He disappears and all I see are the lights above the ring and the MC reflected in emerald, hazel-brown eyes. I stared him down and tried to remember what Paul Dorking had told me about shrinking my opponent. This was hard because he was around four inches shorter than I was. I kept the stare on him. He stared back in earnest and leaned forward so our foreheads clashed.

'When I say break I want you to break and obey my instructions at all times,' said the referee, a diminutive chap with a GI Joe haircut. 'Now let's have a good, clean fight.' We touched gloves and Scriven flinched.

We went back to our respective corners. I could feel the crowd pulsating. My heart quickened slightly and for a brief moment I slipped out of the zone and looked out into a sea of faces. I saw Justin and Bill in the distance and my friend Tosca at ringside. What a trip! This was so fucking surreal. Howard whispered something in my ear. I had no idea what he said but nodded agreement. Mary Mother of Jesus. I looked over at Scriven who looked straight back at me. I was chomping at the bit. Scriven, I want you. The MC made one last announcement: 'Six, two-minute rounds. Seconds out, round one.' The bell went.

I was drawn to Scriven like a magnet. I lead off aggressively with three jabs which all hit his gloves. He held his guard high, throwing nervous punches in a peek-a-boo style. I throw a fourth jab and he counters with a straight right and a double jab followed by a right hook. The crowd, the referee and the arena have faded into a blur. I block and slip but he catches me with a straight right. I jab again, trying to get my range so I can gain more purchase on my shots, which don't seem to be connecting with enough venom. I feel heavy on my feet. I jab again and he counters with a left-right combination, which I feel. This little punk can pack a punch. I go on the back foot and he throws a right and misses. My hands drop momentarily and he throws another wild left and misses. My feet are too wide, but as if under the influence of a juju, I feel unable to move them closer together. He slips my jab, then he connects with a lunging left hook but I don't feel the blow. I throw a right hand . . . bingo! Falling, falling, falling . . .

Forty-five seconds into the first round of my professional debut that left hook from nowhere connected sweetly. Oh the joy! This was boxing. Here I was right in the thick of battle, consumed by a maddening vortex of punches, grunts, groans, sweat, saliva, screams and obscenity. An inferno of violence engulfed the ring and BOOM! Such a sweet, lucky punch! What an opening gambit. A mere forty-five seconds into the fight. This was perfection. The crowd couldn't have asked for a better curtain-raiser to this bizarre confrontation of men. Falling, falling, falling . . . One punch and there I was seconds from the moment of truth. This was the most exquisite knockdown I had encountered in my brief but colourful career as a professional fighter. Even for a nobody, Matt Scriven hit hard and he hit fast. Fighting for a living was like fighting for your life. As Scott Welch had warned, this was not like sparring. Every round I had boxed before this had been mere foreplay. This was pure, unadulterated orgasm. The adrenaline rush flowing through every vein, every artery, every organ provided an anodyne to Scriven's blows, and an amphetamine to my own. Although they felt harder than sparring punches, they hurt less.

I cascaded towards the canvas. The world around me was caught in suspended animation. My concept of time and space had been relegated to my imagination. Jesus Christ, what had happened? I thought I had just had Scriven over, yet I was the one on the canvas, on the seat of my immaculately ironed satin shorts. I was caught in a bonfire of contradictions. The sensation of slowly dropping was incredible. It was a delicious experience to be put over. How could I enjoy that? I was punch drunk. What in God's name had happened? God? What did he have to do with this? Oh Christ redeem me, forgive me for I have sinned. Now I knew why so many fighters believed in God. When you've been upended by a left hook, you start praying you're going to get up. Getting to your feet requires a leap of faith.

I heard the referee count 'two'; the one slipped by somehow. Yes! He'd reached 'two' only, I was still in the fight. I got to my feet quickly and glanced at the row of Board suits on the opposite side of the ring adjacent to my corner. They looked concerned. 'Well, that's that, then,' they'd be saying to themselves, smug in the knowledge that the journalist, the spoiler who thought he'd come on to our patch and bring the noble art of self-defence into disrepute with his fancy idea of being a fighter, had fucked up. It would be just as George Plimpton had discovered; professional athletes truly were cut from another cloth to that of ordinary men.

'Are you OK?' asked the referee, staring intently at me.

'Yeah, I'm cool,' I said, nodding. Those two knockdowns in sparring ironically had done me a favour. At least getting put over wasn't that much of a shock. But the element of surprise stunned me. I hadn't seen the shot coming and was startled to find myself on the deck, especially so bloody early into the fight. I could see Scriven over the referee's shoulder pacing around the neutral corner waiting for his cue to come back into the fray. Now I could empathise with a fox or a rabbit. I was the hunted. The knockdown would surely boost Scriven's confidence. I steeled myself and determined that I would stay on the front foot and attack him, but with a more measured approach. If I was going out I'd go out fighting, on my shield like a true gladiator. When the ref called us to box, I was surprised by Scriven's reticence in coming forward. Go on, try and finish me, you little punk, I thought to myself. Come at me with that lucky lunge so I can take your fucking head off. No, he was too canny to play that game. Maybe he was shocked that he'd had me over. Having lost his last four fights, maybe he had become unaccustomed to being on top. The bell signalled the end of round one. A huge applause goes up as I traipse back to my corner. Thanks to the knockdown, he wins the round 10–8.

'That's what happens when you don't concentrate,' said Howard. Dennis pulled out my gumshield.

'I know, I know. He just caught me . . . I didn't see it. Shit.'

'You OK?' asked Howard.

'Yeah, I'm all right. I can't believe it. I could've sworn I had him over.'

Howard gives me some instructions. He tells me to keep my hands up and focus. The rest is a blur. The bell goes. Here we go again. I decide on a change of tack. I'm going to rough Mr Scriven up a bit. We get tangled up, turning each other in a twisted ballet and wind up having an exchange of blows against the ropes. The round finishes even.

'When you throw that jab out, fucking mean it,' said Howard during the break. 'Focus.'

Round three, we tangle in the centre of the ring and as I grab his arms and lean on him, I feel my head dipping to his shoulder. I start to open my mouth . . . What the hell am I doing? The devil had got inside me and urged me to bite him. Have I gone mad? Fortunately, the ref didn't see this attempted transgression. Nevertheless, he calls a time out and warns us to clean it up. Scriven has a little flurry of punches most of which I block as the bell goes. His round. Scriven goes on the back foot in the fourth as I start to pile on the pressure. I've warmed up now and am finding my range. He's tiring. This is my round.

'Any problems?' asks Howard.

'No.'

'Right, lovely.' I drink some water and swallow.

'Keep your fucking hands up . . . hands. Focus on what you're doing. Look at what you're doing.' He puts my gumshield back in.

'Have a deep breath.' I take a couple of long hard deep breaths. 'Any problems?' repeats Howard.

'No.'

'Good.' More Vaseline is smeared on my face. 'OK. You'll be all right.'

Dennis pats me on the back and rubs my neck. I take another swig of water and spit into the bucket. I stand up, Vic whips away the stool.

'Seconds out, round five.'

Scriven's gone walkabout again. He's proving very elusive. He's fading. In the weakness of your opponent you find your strength. He keeps coming in low with his head and lunging, looking for that sucker punch again. I swing and miss – can't seem to connect with a decent shot. This is a tiring, unwieldy, fairly even round. I traipse back to the corner, relieved that there's only one more round to go.

I become aware of the crowd stirring again as they anticipate the last round. By my reckoning, I'm still two points behind thanks to that first-round knockdown. My brain is scrambled. I feel exhausted but I know Scriven is tireder than I am. I think about the money. I think about losing. I want to win.

'Seconds out for the sixth and last round.'

We touch gloves. Fuck the monkey. I gonna try to knock him out. The bell goes. I go to him – left, left, right. He goes on the back foot, I chase him into my corner. He throws a right hand over the top of my guard glancing my cheek. We get in a clinch and I slip in an accidental head butt. We go into a clinch and I start rubbing my shaven head over his eye. He grimaces and throws a left hook that just clips me. He drops his hands and goes backpeddling. I get him with a straight left that stuns him. I see blood trickling from his nostril. I try cutting down the ring but he slips out of my reach. He's blowing – he's patently tired. I can hear Mike Leigh's Scouse voice cry, 'Jab him. Fucking jab him up, Dave.' He grabs hold of me and throws a left to my body. I shake him off and he strikes a pose. I throw a right uppercut through his guard that connects with his chin. How much longer can there be? I throw a right hand over the top, a right uppercut and a left hook which catches flush in the face. The bell goes. Surely I've won the round. Scriven goes to shake my hand, I ignore him and offer it to the ref hoping I've got the decision, but he raises Scriven's arm.

A chorus of disapproval rang out as a number of people started booing. I felt a split second of disappointment at not being the winner but the first-round knockdown had sealed my fate. I knew I had lost. I knew the long journey was over. In a sense the relief that the end had come was reward in itself.

Dennis was the first into the ring. He slapped me round the face and gave me a hug. I shook hands with Scriven's corner and we two gladiators embraced, bonded by our shared experience. I felt no animosity towards Scriven. The better man had won. I crossed the ring and leant over the ropes and looked out into the crowd.

'After six absorbing rounds of boxing, let's have a big round of applause for both boxers,' said the MC. Scriven and I touched gloves again. 'Your referee Lee Cook has scored the contest as follows: for Matthews 57 points, for Scriven 59 points. The winner: Matt Scriven. And a round of applause for a very brave boxer, David Matthews.' I received another round of tumultuous applause. Before I left the ring, the MC made another announcement. He told the audience that I was a journalist and I was writing a book and this had been a one-off professional performance, 'although he might change his mind' he added. For this I received yet more applause. I must say, I had never had as much public acclaim in my entire life.

The fight was an intense moment of self-actualisation. It was as if all I had ever lived for was that moment. I had been at the centre of the universe and discovered the attention, the adulation and the respect that men crave. It had taken me fifteen minutes to discover what I had been searching for these last two years. In fifteen minutes I understood why men fought in the prize ring. How could you shovel cement on a building site, drive a forklift truck or write two-bit features for second-rate rags when there was this, this life that was consumed with so much raging passion, pain, love, death, glory, romance. The end did truly justify the means. I would never have known, never have believed what boxing truly was had I not stepped into that ring. It was a moment of self-discovery. My opponent hadn't been Matt Scriven. It had been me all along. Through boxing I had faced up to the enemy within – my fears, my anxieties and my self-doubt.

I had no more reason to question my resolve, my intellectual, spiritual or physical abilities. I reached my goal. I did the job. I met some great people along the way. I had the fight against the odds. I had that enviable sense of feeling that now anything was possible. After this day, I would never be the same person again.

I stepped out of the ring and trudged back through the crowd to more applause. Strangers patted me on the back and said 'well done'. I wound my way back through the corridor towards the dressing room.

'We did it. We fucking did it,' I said. I must've been the world's best loser. I was on such a high for just lasting the distance.

'If we'd had just another month or so, it might've been different,' said Howard, unlacing my gloves. As he cut the bandages away, I could see the disappointment mixed with relief mixed with pride written across his face. I hadn't wanted to let him down. He had put his reputation on the line for me. He took a risk with me and I respected him for that.

One of the trainers in the dressing room came up to me and shook my hand. I recognised him from somewhere but by this point I was so zoned out I could hardly tell if I was coming or going.

'I've been in this game a long time, son. I was Chris Eubank's trainer for ten years so I've seen it all. But I got to say from what I saw out there, you did well, son.' I later found out his name was Ronnie Davies. Ken Morton, an old reporter from *Boxing News*, congratulated me on my debut also.

'Well, you've experienced boxing from the sharp end now,' he said in his lilting Scottish accent. 'Do you think you'll have another go?' I reassured him that a comeback was not on the agenda.

Numerous people came into the dressing room with praise, commiseration, comments, backslaps and handshakes. I started cooling down, so I grabbed my bag and headed down the corridor for the shower. I looked in the mirror. I'd come off fairly unscathed; apart from one or two red marks, I was as handsome as ever. The changing room where the showers were was empty. It was strange but a relief to find this oasis of calm when outside mayhem was reigning.

I stood in the shower, naked, literally and emotionally. 'I did it, I fucking did it,' I said over and over again. More than two years of heartache and frustration culminated in a flood of tears, not tears of sadness or of pain but of joy and relief. I had experienced the insanity and beauty of boxing not as an observer or as metaphor, but as the thing itself. I cried and was baptised by my tears. I laughed. I had lost the fight but yet I had found something pure, something real, something more important than victory. In a boxing ring, in a makeshift theatre of dreams I was complete. I did it. I had finally found myself.

I tried to track down Ashton to get my dough. I felt like a speed freak, I was that 'up'. Finally, I cornered him.

'John, any chance of getting my wages, mate?' I said.

'Yeah, Dave, er, bear with me a second will yer.' He seemed flustered, on the back foot. His mobile was going off, he had a pile of tickets in one hand and an attaché case in the other. He was sweating like a pig. I thought for a split second he was going to do a runner with my purse. A few minutes later I cornered him again, in the bar.

'Right, yes, Dave. Let me sort you out. Where are the tickets you didn't sell?' Lorna had been tailing me and stepped up to give Ashton a wedge of tickets. Without counting them he slung the pile on the bar and pulled out a wad of cash from his inside pocket. 'How much was it again?' Lorna reminded him of the £500 purse we'd agreed and the £1,390 I'd sold in tickets, from which I was due a 10 per cent commission.

'Right, here's four hundred quid.'

'Four hundred?' I looked at Ashton and then at Lorna with that same dumbstruck expression I'd seen countless times before on the faces of fighters who'd felt stitched up.

'Four hundred, mate. Fifty quid's for the Board, for your scan like, and . . .' Ashton leant into me, lowering his voice, 'I had to buy that kid Scriven a drink like, you know for taking the fight. You know how it goes.' He gave a jolly laugh to smooth over the fact that he'd just had me for a paltry chicken-shit fifty quid. I was too high to argue with him. Now I had learnt first-hand what scumbags promoters are. Pat Putnam, a former boxing writer with *Sports Illustrated* once summed up the

303

business side of boxing when he said, 'Take away the larceny and it's just two guys beating the crap out of each other.'

Lorna gave Ashton the £1,390 ticket money she'd been safeguarding and he handed me £140 to go with the £400.

'Let me see if I've got a pound coin in change,' I said sarcastically. Ashton didn't get the joke and said, 'Nah, don't worry about it, kid,' as though he were doing me a massive favour. Promoters. Wankers.

I met Matt Scriven in the bar after the fight. We shook hands yet again.

'Thanks for the fight,' he said humbly. 'It's not like you fought a mug or anything. I've been in with a lot of good kids.' Scriven reeled off the names of a few fighters, some I'd heard of, some I hadn't. He seemed to be justifying himself to me. Why? He didn't have anything to prove, not to me anyway. He had won fair and square. I could see that winning was important to him. Maybe it was more important to him than it was to me. Maybe I did lack the killer instinct. Did I have opportunities during the fight to subjugate him and fail to take them? Maybe subconsciously I embraced defeat to protect myself from myself. If I had won, would the temptation to carry on have been overwhelming? Would winning have only led to a greater loss further down the line? I suppose I was better off losing in the long run. I was still noble in defeat, a gladiator to the end. I had achieved what I had set out to achieve. I had experienced the pain and frustration, hope and glory that is a professional fighter's life.

My short-lived boxing career was over. I was going to take the money and run. In the two years and two months that it took me to become a prizefighter, I had grossed the princely sum of £640 from boxing – the equivalent of £5.57 a week. I didn't earn a fortune from the ring but I earned enough to know that, in the words of Don King, 'when you can count your money, you ain't got none'. And there was me thinking that boxing was a way out of the ghetto.

Epilogue

I couldn't help but laugh as the rain lashed down on Dennis Hobson's big top – a 40ft x 180ft marquee the like of which I hadn't seen since the Chipperfields came to town. Oh, it was great to be a civilian again. Saturday nights like this weren't all right for fighting, regardless of what Elton John said. It was too cold, too wet and too miserable to be boxing in the great outdoors. I'd been to fights in town halls, leisure centres, hotels, motels and Madison Square Garden, but never a show in a circus tent before.

I pulled Scott Lansdowne's Escort into a muddy parking bay between the marquee and a small clubhouse which backed on to a large man-made lake, the centrepiece of the Leicester Jet Ski Centre. I'd taken the wheel from Sheffield to Stoney Stanton on the outskirts of Leicester so Scott could relax in the passenger seat and save his energy for Gary Williams, an opponent he had already defeated on his pro debut and was about to fight again for the – wait for it – WBF Pan European super-cruiserweight title. Scott sat motionless as I switched off the ignition and stared at the dark expanse of water ahead of us.

'You ready to go to work?' I said, my gaze still fixed on the rippling water.

'Yeah, let's rock'n'roll, Dave.'

It had been seven weeks since Alfreton and my baptism of fire, and in those weeks I had gained as many pounds. Without the discipline of the daily grind, without the prospect of a fight, slowly I began reverting to type – stereotype, in fact. I could feel myself metamorphosing back into that beer-swilling hack, that self-indulgent, dope-smoking writer, the foodie, the faddist, the guy who regarded a body simply as a vehicle for ferrying the mind about its business. People asked me if I would keep up the routine of training once I stopped boxing. Initially I bragged that I would, but how could I? Without the end product of a fight, what would I be training for – fitness, vanity, ego?

Before the passage of time had had a chance to put a safe distance between me and that April afternoon of bloodletting, the euphoria that followed the immediate aftermath of the fight was soon corrupted by a bout of melancholy. The high had been high, but the low had been pitifully low. It was momentary, lasting two or three days in the extreme and gradually subsiding after a few weeks. Why was I depressed? Because I was a no-good loser, that's why. Once the reality of defeat sank in, losing really bothered me. I felt inadequate and unable to resist beating myself up. I had a video of the fight, which allowed me to indulge myself in endless self-torment. I watched it twenty, thirty, forty times. I saw every mistake I made, every little lost opportunity to take out Matt Scriven. My feet were too wide, I didn't double the jab, I didn't use the right hand enough. How could I have lost to Matt Scriven? He was not a worthy victor. Oh for Christ's sake, why did I let that little punk off the hook? I couldn't understand myself. Why had I blown it?

Every time I watched that video, with its eerie vision of me cascading slowly to the canvas, I would get a lump in my throat. My palms would sweat and embarrassment would turn to anger. I could've beaten that guy. In fact, I did beat that guy. I was robbed! I was never going to get the decision in front of that guy's crowd. Oh cliché of clichés! No matter how many times I watch the fight, no matter the angle, black and white or colour, with or without sound, the result is the same – I lose. But hey, at least I made history. I now have an entry in the *British Boxing Board of Control Yearbook 2001* and I'm even in the *Boxing News* ratings for light-heavyweights – at the bottom.

A few days after the fight I left the Rainey household. I needed a change of scenery. I needed to stop hearing how well I'd done because I didn't feel as though I'd done well at all. I had become a professional fighter and my mandate was to fight to win. I lost. Was I supposed to feel happy about that? Going the distance, having the 'experience' was not good enough. I'd let myself down. I wanted glory in front of my supporters. I wanted to be in the league of winners. 'Charlie, oh Charlie, you don't understand. I coulda had class. I coulda been a contender.' All that work, all that training, for nothing. Nursing a black eye and a bruised ego, I grabbed a couple of bags, left Sheffield for London and then took off for sun, sand, sea and sex in LA, and tried to forget about boxing.

A couple of weeks later, when I returned to the UK, I arranged for the rest of my property to be brought from Sheffield to my new home in London. I knew Lorna would make a fuss if I returned to the north. I didn't want any tearful goodbyes and while I was coming to terms with life outside the gym, I decided to give Sheffield and the Raineys a wide berth, until I straightened myself out.

As I was going through my stuff one evening at home, I noticed a card that had been placed surreptitiously in one of my bags. On the front was a cartoon of a miserable looking sheepdog holding a suitcase and standing in front of a flock of sheep. 'You're off to pastures new' said the card. Inside was printed 'The whole flock will miss you'. Scrawled across the card Lorna had written: 'It's been a hell of a year honey! We wouldn't change a thing. Would you? Be all you are and want to be, Dave! Best of luck for the book. Your loving family – XX The Raineys XX'

Boxing had been a major part of my life for more than two years. Where once there was boxing, now there was a void, a gaping hole in my existence. Even though it was a ball ache, I knew sooner or later I'd miss the gym, the banter, the lads. What would I do without boxing as my obsession? Opportunities are few and far between for the ex-fighter. There is little out there in the real world to match the intensity and the challenge of the fight game. Perhaps I could do the after-dinner speaking circuit like John Conteh, the world light-heavyweight champion of the late 1970s and professional Scouser; or maybe I could get into the movies as a heavyweight extra, just as Scott Welch had done alongside Brad Pitt in *Snatch*; or what about being a B-list celebrity like Bruno or Eubank, or a satellite-TV pundit like Barry McGuigan or Julius Francis? Why, I might even take up wrestling . . .

I knew what awaited many ex-fighters was a life of destitution. The highs of a life in the ring are often punctuated with the lows of retirement. What could realistically match boxing? When the show was over, there was no one left to wait on you hand and foot. Once you put those gloves on you had an entourage, fans, people at your beck and call. Nowhere else but in the context of boxing could grown men massage your back, fan you with a towel, wipe your bloody nose, quench your thirst with water, even tie your boot laces without any question of impropriety. This was so because you wore gloves. They encumbered you outside the ring, but they still gave you power.

I had found that boxing, among other things, was about men seeking the respect and adulation of other men. Perhaps it was the same for other sports. Sons, brothers, fathers, friends, strangers – men boxed and sought recognition among their peers for a host of reasons, a few of which I explored through my own experiences. By the end of my brief career as a fighter, I had realised that I too had sought and found that recognition. Now it was time to move on.

I knew I had no future as a fighter. Short of winning the fight, I had achieved what I had set out to do. I would continue to write and find inspiration outside the ring. I'd dip my toe in the water now and again, do a bit of training when I wasn't hung over, write a few fight reports, but that would be it. To be brutally honest, if I had known back in January 1998 at the Peacock gym what I know now, if I'd known that boxing would cost me so much personally and financially along the way, I probably would never have got into it. But for all that, as Howard once said to me, 'Boxing's about finding yourself. When you get in that ring you truly find out what you're made of.' And I had indeed found out what I was made of. I would never be the same again. Boxing taught me more about myself than about the sport itself.

Time and space eased the bitterness that failure brought. Many fighters never fully recover, psychologically, from a telling defeat. It was a testament to a fighter how well he could bounce back from defeat. In the ring I had demonstrated I could fall from grace, dust myself off, get up and carry on fighting. On reflection, I was able to look at Matt Scriven and, like all the fighters I had met, regardless of character or ability, respect him as a fellow gladiator, a warrior. As the super-featherweight Kevin Kelley once said, 'When you fight a guy, your souls kind of touch.' Even as adversaries, fighters share a bond unknown in any other sport.

As Scott prepared himself for another step along boxing's Yellow Brick Road, Lee Cook, the referee who oversaw my fight, appeared in the dressing room. Cook was to officiate Scott's bout – small world. Before he had a chance to give Scott his pre-fight instructions, Howard and I cornered Cook, in the nicest possible way.

'We thought we deserved a draw,' growled Howard.

'Yeah,' I said, trying to sound more serious than I actually was.

'Well, it was a hard fight to score,' said Cook, trying to be as conciliatory as possible without making any admission of error in judgement. 'After the first round, when you went down, I thought it was all over. But all credit to you. You came back strong. Like I said, it was hard to score.' Referees have to be diplomats.

I took some satisfaction that evening knowing that I'd made Mr

Cook work harder than Scott did. Of course, that's because I had a six-round brawl and Scott knocked out Gary Williams in one round to become the new WBF Pan Euro whatever it is.

'See that,' whispered Howard, 'another three month and that could've been you.' Here we go again. For the past two days all I'd heard were questions about having another fight and 'making a comeback'. Dennis, Scott, Lorna, Howard, even young Simon, everybody had been on my case about it. It had been assumed that, because I had clearly got off on boxing in Alfreton, I would do it again, and again, and again. Howard had been dropping subtle hints about getting back into training and having just one more fight, for the win, just to set the record straight. After Scott flattened Gary Williams we all returned to the clubhouse bar for a drink.

'I bet seeing Scott win makes you wanna get back in there, doesn't it?' said Lorna, slyly.

'Quite the contrary,' I said. If anything, the speed and ruthlessness with which Scott despatched Williams reminded me of just how brutal, just how dangerous boxing is. But yet there was a slight something. I still felt game. I still ached for the fear, the adrenaline rush. No, no, this was the beer talking.

The following morning Howard dropped me at the coach station in Sheffield. He was still going on about me fighting again. 'Give it another three months and you'll win for sure,' he said. 'Gives you a happy ending – everybody likes happy endings.'

I got on the coach and watched the world slip by at 65 m.p.h. on the way back to London. With the beers and the two (free) plates of food I'd consumed at the clubhouse the night before, I was surely over the 13½ stone mark. Jesus, I had to get a grip. I pledged that I'd start running each morning and go to the local boxing gym at least three times a week before I went to pieces. A couple of days later I got a call from Howard.

'How you doing, kid?' he asked.

'Fine thanks,' I replied. We chewed the fat for a while and got on to the subject of Scott's fight.

'He looked a million dollars, Howard. What are you feeding him on up there?' Howard completely ignored the question.

'Three more months and that could've been you, Captain. You know you could still do it. Dennis has got a show coming up later in the year. September, I think. Three months of training and you'd get a win.'

'Three more months, you say?'

'That's right.'

'You're having me on, Howard.'

'Three months and I guarantee you'd get a win.'

'Hmm . . .'

'That'd be a better ending to your book, wouldn't it? Think about it. Everybody loves a winner. Everybody loves a happy ending.' How many times had I heard that line before?

'Well, I'll give it some thought, Howard. See you around, mate.'

'Tara, babe.'

I put the phone down. Three more months of training and a happy ending. No way. I'd be an idiot to have another fight. What would it achieve? What would it prove? If I lost a second time, I'd have no excuses, my failure would be absolute. Then again, what's another three months out of my life? And 'one win and one loss' does look a whole lot better on paper than just 'one loss'. Damn. Decisions, decisions. I picked up the phone and called Howard. Maybe Dennis could talk to Ashton and get me a rematch with Matt Scriven. We had to talk at least, if only to satisfy my curiosity. I mean, what did you expect? Like the man said, 'Everybody loves a happy ending.'